Economic Issues, Problems and Perspectives

nova
science publishers

www.novapublishers.com

Economic Issues, Problems and Perspectives

Economic Crises: A Review and Directions for Research
Tulus T.H. Tambunan, PhD (Editor) – Professor, Economic Science, Universitas Trisakti, Jakarta, Indonesia
Budi Santosa, PhD (Editor)
2022. ISBN: 978-1-68507-613-9 (Hardcover)
2022. ISBN: 978-1-68507-692-4 (eBook)

Advances in Capital Structure Research
Karel Marleau (Editor)
2021. ISBN: 978-1-53619-948-2 (Softcover)
2021. ISBN: 978-1-53619-969-7 (eBook)

Human Capital and Development
Gary I. Lilienthal (Editor)
2021. ISBN: 978-1-53619-714-3 (Hardcover)
2021. ISBN: 978-1-53619-733-4 (eBook)

The Impact of the COVID-19 Pandemic on International Oil Markets
Alexander G. Tvalchrelidze (Author)
2021. ISBN: 978-1-53619-595-8 (Hardcover)
2021. ISBN: 978-1-53619-698-6 (eBook)

Global Challenges of Digital Transformation of Markets
Elena de la Poza, PhD. (Editor)
Sergey E. Barykin, PhD. (Editor)
2021. ISBN: 978-1-53619-754-9 (Hardcover)
2021. ISBN: 978-1-53619-864-5 (eBook)

More information about this series can be found at
https://novapublishers.com/product-category/series/economic-issues-problems-and-perspectives/

Gabibulla Khasaev, Victoria Bolgova, Sergey Bortnikov, Yurii Shul'zenko and Evgenia Medentseva
Editors

Economic and Legal Foundations of Innovative Development in the Digital Age

nova
science publishers
www.novapublishers.com

DOI: https://doi.org/10.52305/EKWM4899

NOTICE TO THE READER

Library of Congress Cataloging-in-Publication Data

ISBN: 978-1-68507-730-3

Published by Nova Science Publishers, Inc. † New York

Contents

Introduction

A Systemic View of Innovative Development in the Digital Age from the Position of Economics and Law

The digital age is a modern stage of the development of society and economy, which started with the wide use of the first digital technologies (Internet, mobile communication) and reached its peak amid the Fourth Industrial Revolution due to the dissemination of smart technologies (the Internet of Things, artificial intelligence). The digital age has the highest rate of technological progress in the entire history of industrial revolutions, which predetermines two specific features of this age.

The first specific feature is as follows: unlike the previous industrial revolutions, when, despite certain companies' transition to new technologies, other companies – due to the traditional thinking of society – preserved the previous technological mode for a long time, the society progressed together with economy. Digital technologies transform not only the processes of production but also the processes of distribution and consumption of products. The growing demand for digital innovations is strong pressure on the market, which does not allow companies to remain aside from the Fourth Industrial Revolution.

The second specific feature is that digitalization takes place in waves – continuously and over and over again. This is the difference between the Fourth Industrial Revolution and the previous revolutions when the technological transition was momentary and single-step. Due to this specific feature, there emerged a hypothesis that the digital age could have not one but several industrial revolutions. Followers of this hypothesis suggest considering technological progress in the macro-scale, distinguishing the pre-digital age, which was the time of the first three industrial revolutions, and the digital age, which was opened by the Fourth Industrial Revolution. Regardless of the level of the view of the digital age, it is obvious that it requires continuous, step-by-step digital innovations.

The above specific features of the digital age predetermine its comprehensive and accelerated innovative development. Though digital innovations are studied in many scientific papers and books, a serious drawback of the existing literature is its one-sided view of digital innovations. The literature on economics notes high demand for digital innovations and their growing offer, but the markets of the digital economy are not balanced due to legal barriers: absence of certification of quality of the innovative digital products, the uncertainty of the issues of cyber security provision, fragmentary character of telecommunication infrastructure, etc.

Literature sources on legal sciences point out the necessity for updating the legal framework of innovative development taking into account the new realities of the digital age, but there is uncertainty as to which norms of law are in demand in the modern economic practice and how to achieve their support in society and entrepreneurship. Due to the lack of consistency of scientific knowledge, there emerged a gap between legal norms and economic practices of innovative development in the digital age.

Acknowledging the necessity for increasing the digital competitiveness of the economy, the government increases financing of digital innovations, but with low effectiveness: the targeted recipients of government subsidies and other financial support receive only a small part of budget assets, which is not enough for implementing private initiatives. The legal field is late in development compared to economic practice, slowing down the implementation and commercialization of digital innovations.

Thus, there's a need for a systemic view of innovative development in the digital age from the positions of economics and law, which is formed in this book. Due to its multidisciplinary character, the book considers the innovative development in the digital economy through the lens of institutions, which allows specifying the fundamental nature of this process and determining the logic and regularities of its course in economic systems.

The institutions considered in this book include the institutions of state and corporate management of innovative development in the digital age. This book shows that state and law are to create favorable conditions – "rules of the game", which are fair, just, and supported by all participants of the market – which create stimuli for implementation and commercialization of digital innovation and allow implementing the corresponding entrepreneurial initiatives in practice.

The tasks of state management of innovative development of the digital economy include also support for social adaptation to constantly changing conditions of the digital age. The criterion of successfulness of this support is equal mastering of new technologies by all groups of the population. Special attention should be paid to the adaptation of senior people, slowdown of ageing of personnel in the markets of the digital economy, and provision of equal access to telecommunication infrastructure, digital knowledge, and technologies to all groups of the population. These issues are considered in the book from the position of the institution of digital inequality and perspectives of its reduction.

The institution of corporate management of innovative development in the digital age is oriented by this book at the realization of the entrepreneurial and creative potential of the economy's human potential, accelerated diffusion of digital innovations, and optimization of investment flows. This book provides a new view of the above institutions, which shows the necessity to replace state financing of the innovative development with private investments.

The book also pays attention to the institution of the regional digital economy. It is noted that a serious problem is the unequal innovative development of regions within a country in the digital age. It is inadmissible to establish the regions' status of underdeveloped regions in terms of the level and rate of innovative development (digital outsiders). For this, the authors offer – on the example of Russia – the applied recommendations to improve the mechanism of budget federalism and the formation of "healthy" competition of regions for reducing their digital inequality.

Another institution that is studied in this book is corruption. As shown in the book, corruption is preserved in the digital age but acquires new forms and manifestations. On the one hand, digital innovations are susceptible to corruption and the shadow economy. On the other hand, digital innovations could be used for the modernization of state bureaucratic machine and the fight against corruption. The authors offer applied recommendations for using new opportunities to overcome corruption in the process of innovative development of the digital age.

The above institutions are reconsidered in the book, and three requirements to them are formulated. The first requirement: sustainability. Innovative development in the digital age should take place according to the adopted goals in the sphere of sustainable development. The second requirement: effectiveness. It is necessary to avoid "institutional traps" – outdated institutions which remain due to traditions. Innovativeness is not just a goal but also a principle of building institutions in the digital age. Institutions of the digital economy must create advantages for innovative development, which exceed the negative consequences for government and law, society, and the economy.

The third requirement: high technology. To conform to the realities of the digital age, the institutions of innovative development must envisage the use of leading technologies. As shown in this book, compliance with these requirements envisages the modernization of state management and legal regulation of the economy based on artificial intelligence. Thus, an institution of smart state and law emerges, which is expressed in automatized taxation and tax administration, systems of e-government, and digital public services.

This book's contribution to the literature on digital innovations is due to offering a new scientific and methodological approach to managing innovative development in the digital age. The main feature of the new approach is active, continuous, and comprehensive interaction between government, society, and entrepreneurship. The advantage of the new approach is the increase of effectiveness of state and corporate management of innovative development, as well as accelerated and well-balanced adaptation of society to the digital age.

This book is aimed primarily at scholars studying digital innovations. For them, the book offers fundamental developments, empirical overview, case studies, and scientific and methodological recommendations in the sphere of innovative development of state and law, society, and economy in the digital age. Due to its multidisciplinary character, the book will also be of interest to the representatives of various humanitarian disciplines: legal, social, and economic.

The book will be also of interest for practicing experts involved with the practice of corporate management and for bodies of public administration of innovative development in the digital age. For them, the book offers various issues of economic and legal regulation of innovative development in the digital age, due to which it could be a theoretical and methodological guide for improving this management. The book materials could be used in the educational process of modern universities for such disciplines as "State and law", "State and corporate management", "State regulation of economy", and "Management of innovations".

Chapter 1

Legal Analysis of the Institutionality of Digital Economies

Sergei P. Bortnikov[1,*] and Gabibulla R. Khasaev[2]
[1]Samara State University of Economics, Samara, Russia
[2]Samara National Research University, Samara, Russia

Abstract

The chapter is devoted to issues of changing the factors of production and economic order with the development of a phenomenon of economic digitalization, artificial intelligence, big databases, and distributed ledgers. The authors pose the question of whether paradigmatic factors of production change, whether qualitatively new changes in the essence of economic order take place under industrial automation. The authors investigate the general principles of legal regulation in the context of the digital economy as well as their fulfillment in particular examples of economic and social life. In particular, the effects of robotizing the production and the social area, as well as related issues of employees' release, are highlighted. Some aspects of qualitative changes in the foundation of a market economic order (competition) are investigated. The article examines the regulation of using digital technologies in the production activity and state governance of economic management. In addition to studying the principles of regulation of the digital economic environment and specific features of legal regulation of individual types of activity in modern conditions, the article draws attention to the threat of market fundamentalism ideology to Russia. This ideology lacks the understanding of patterns of technical and economic development that don't allow pursuing modernization policy for the patterns to be used. The chapter puts forward the thesis on the inevitability of centralization of

* Corresponding Author's Email: serg-bortnikov@yandex.ru.

In: Economic and Legal Foundations of Innovative Development …
Editors: Gabibulla Khasaev, Victoria Bolgova, Sergey Bortnikov et al.
ISBN: 978-1-68507-730-3

information resources and the basics of managing artificial intelligence precisely in the hands of the government and large corporations and estimates the possible consequences.

Keywords: digital economy, artificial intelligence, production factors, a market economy, enforcement

JEL Codes: K10 • K23 • M14

Introduction

Value-Based Foundations of a Market Economy

One of the primary conditions for studying the economy in the digital era is to abandon the politicization of research and not to investigate topics of short-term importance. On the contrary, it is necessary to distinguish the fundamental points of the impact of long-term digitalization processes on economic factors.

The study suggests that we acknowledge the existence of universally recognized fundamental institutions that develop the phenomenon of the economy and economic relations. At the same time, the study should reveal the impact of the new technological paradigm on the development of the economy and maintaining the development in the context of freedom.

On the one hand, the hybrid war unleashed by the USA against Russia requires changing macroeconomic policy to make it exposure-resistant.

On the other hand, pursuing an out-of-date macroeconomic policy and ignoring modern techniques, methods and technologies are mistaken and dangerous. The market fundamentalism ideology threatens Russia because it's devoid of understanding the patterns of technical and economic development that don't allow pursuing the modernization policy for the patterns to be used. If Russia "sleeps through" the next technological revolution based on a system of nano- and bio-engineering technologies like the USSR failed to take advantage of the developments of the previous ICT revolution, then a similar political risk will arise due to inevitable technological lag and impoverishment of working population that is unacceptable for Russian public consciousness.

Modern digitalization of life implies the replacement of the next technological paradigm; over two decades ago, a strategy for the accelerated development of the Russian economy was developed and continuously updated [5].

The self-asserting fight of the West in the name of "supply and demand," "free prices," "free competition," and "free business" has become out-of-date and has been replaced by a combination of the advantages of strategic planning and mechanisms of market competition to increase public welfare, state ownership of infrastructure facilities and private enterprise regulated in the public interests. The Communist Party of China has established a fundamentally new system of production relations that meets the requirements for the development of modern productive forces. The progress of this system is manifested in the high growth rates of production and the living standard of the population. China has been a leader with a 3-fold margin concerning capitalist countries for three decades. Following the PRC and introducing similar institutions of economic management, Indochina countries, India, and Ethiopia catch up with the pace of leaders in the socio-economic development.

Scientists dealing with "long" cycles in human development note the transient nature of the modern era that combines change varying-frequency cycles up to periods of the civilizational millennium [16]. The study of the patterns governing the interaction of these cycles, including the change of technology and world economic paradigms that determine the current global economic crisis, is particularly difficult.

The ongoing change of technological paradigms gives rise to a structural crisis of the leading world economies that are associated with the exhaustion of the growth opportunities of the current technological paradigm and the development of technological growth paths of a new one. In this period of a new technological paradigm to be born, the countries that have managed to be the first in mobilizing resources to master the key industries of the new technological paradigm break through, while former leaders suffer from the depreciation of capital invested in the production of the previous technological paradigm. Exactly this way, the economic miracle was created in post-war Japan and Western Europe, the USA, and Russia gained upper positions in the world. Now China and India spurt similarly.

The struggle for technological leadership in artificial intelligence has already become a ground of global competition. Not only an economic breakthrough in the development and introduction of artificial intelligence but also the necessity to ensure Russia's technological sovereignty in this field is an essential condition for the viability of Russian business and the economy, the quality of population's life, and security.

In 2017, there were only five countries in the world engaged in planning the development of artificial intelligence technologies. To date, their number is over thirty.

Technologies based on artificial intelligence have been already actively used, for example, in the banking sector, communications, transport, public services, commerce, etc.

Methods

The research methods are system analysis, expert evaluation, polling and interviewing, modeling.

At the first stage, the authors analyzed the existing approaches to entrepreneurial values and entrepreneurship as values from the financial, economic, and legal points.

At the second stage, the authors carried out monitoring and diagnostic assessment, developed the model of entrepreneur's readiness to changes, and investigated the system of how the most significant values in the business environment are investigated.

At the third stage, the outcomes of diagnostic assessment were processed and analyzed, objectives for further research were stated.

Results

Proclamation of the Digital Era in the Economy

In the industrialized world after a crisis of 2008, the left-wing economic policy was activated, which is characterized by a combination (various combinations – in particular, situations) of state interference typical for a planned economy (but non-conforming to the planned economy, i.e., non-abolishment or non-violation of the price mechanism performance), with continuous inflationary pressure (full-time job, cheap money policy, planning of indicators of circular flow and balance of payments).

The effectiveness of government interference as a result of the crisis relief is obvious; a group of countries daring to pursue the specified political course gradually rises to the surface within this dominant system. Such a policy is aimed at releasing the economy from the legacy of the financial inflationary method as soon as possible and restoring a logical, most consistent economic order, which entrusts traditional economic categories with the management of the economy within a "neutral" (equally preventing both inflation and deflation) monetary and credit policies. The proclamation of the digital era in the economy has not yet proposed any new economic categories; digital elements more tend towards methods, tools, and the technologization of management.

The essence of economic digitalization is to propose a solution that harmoniously unites all the goals instead of pursuing an out-of-date policy. Rapid technological development and structural changes in the production system do much to destroy past social forms and remind of the need to find a new social harmony.

Replacing a person with a robot, changing the sources of population's income, speeding up operations, etc. poses new challenges: the release of workers reduces their consumer opportunities, the uncompetitiveness of households with robotic low-cost industrial production leads to their ruin and destruction.

Thus, according to the results of the latest studies, in 2022 about 22 percent of new jobs in the global economy will be created thanks to new "digital professions" [2]. The fact that today and shortly, recruiting staff with the required digital skills is recognized by top managers of recruiting companies. Moreover, 73 percent of recently interviewed CEOs already face the trouble of finding such highly skilled specialists [12].

A social market economy is now entering a new phase. If the things done are continued, it will get new specific features with social policy coming to the fore (allowances, subsidies, tax exemptions, etc.).

The Issue of Economic Order and the Digital Market Economy

The prospect of studying a dispute on the impact of artificial intelligence on a market economy makes the researcher raise the issue of an emerging a new economic order with the development of engineering and technology, the place of the price mechanism and competition, the peculiarities of competition development, regulation of capital acquisition and growth as well as employment policy, property issues, etc.

One of the possible tools that makes it possible to come nearer to the solution of the problem posed may be an approach based on the assessment and development of long-term economic cycles concerning the national economic system. According to this approach, as well as relying on the theory by N. D. Kondrat'ev, large cycles are formed due to disturbance or restoration of the economic equilibrium in a long period [7]. The researcher argued that science and technology inventions are developed before the growth phase, and subsequently be transferred to the real sector of the economy, thereby they predetermine a breakthrough in the improvement of productive elements and the economic development of the entire system. Moreover, upturn arises as a result of capital accumulation, which makes it possible to dramatically refit production resources.

In this article we do not intend to discuss socialism or capitalism, a planned economy, or the market, we just try to assess the impact of the new industrial revolution on the economic order. The industrial revolution of the 17th-18th centuries in a system of other factors had a major impact on the transition to a capitalist system; however, all the subsequent technological changes, the advent of computing facilities, and the modernization of fixed assets did not structurally change the economic order.

Nevertheless, the phenomenon of digitalization and its importance in the economy is unanimously assessed by the authors. In 2000, Nobel Laureate Richard Stone analyzed the industries where computers have increased productivity and found that it's only one industry – computer manufacturing.

Computer performance for a period of computer development has grown by 250 billion times. It was one-of-a-kind technology. Computers are introduced, but labor productivity has fallen by 10 times, that is, computers have brought the economy to nothing.

The enunciated fourth industrial revolution [15] implies changing the physical world both in communication with artificial intelligence and in economic matters, where the scientists have long been trying to develop models of future changes.

To date, the prospects and opportunities for the Russian economic system to be in the wake of the fourth industrial revolution notionally called Russia 4.0 gather pace. This type of economic development is based on fundamentally new principles of human development underlying the near-complete absolutization of cooperation of human, biological, and digital technologies. According to estimates of several leading experts and expert agencies, it is expected that by the end of 2035 the number of robotic and automated workplaces will reach about 95 percent, nearly half of the present jobs will fall out of demand [6].

Mechanisms of increased demand for innovative products, including technological, product-based, and process-related innovations, gained impetus in 2006-2012. Regarding that the transition term of projects from the R&D stage to the industrial development is 10-15 years on average, the technological paradigm in Russia will change under the development trend of the indicator under consideration, in the period (2016-2021)-(2022- 2027).

All previous industrial revolutions led to a continuous reduction of jobs (from steam to electrification, and then to the automation of production), but labor remained a significant production factor. In the era of artificial intelligence, the point is not that who owns the means of production, but that how they should be coordinated in the national economy. The integration of large databases and the increasing role of artificial intelligence will lead to the centralization of the systems and their management.

W. Ropke also noted that a market economy in a fully atomized, proletarianized, and massed society is something different from a market economy in a society with widely diffused property, sustainable sources of living, a healthy social framework [14], etc. A robotic economy where there is no place for labor will also have its peculiarities regardless of its capitalist or post-industrial type.

One of the most radical long-term forecasts, for example, states that the global unemployment rate will reach 75 percent by 2100 [10]. As a conservative short-term scenario, let us refer to the assessment made by WEF President Klaus Schwab. In his opinion, robotics and AI technologies eliminate about 5 million jobs in the fifteen largest developed and developing countries of the world by 2020 (which is equivalent to only 1.25 percent of the total number of jobs in these countries [13]).

An important goal has become to coordinate artificial intelligence and large databases, the policy of the corresponding economy (market or other relations) with a policy that creates and maintains these systems.

The release of labor and a vast number of workers and employees in a robotic economy makes the government solve the problem of income distribution either through continuous financial policy and the socialization of consumption, or the use of rents, subventions, etc.

We should note that the Russian economy has a huge capacity not only in terms of synchronization of entry to the fourth industrial revolution drastically absorbing the global economic system but also in terms of proactive movement towards a new type of economic paradigm.

In our opinion, K. Peres [11] rightfully mentioned in his writing that "the concept of a technical and economic paradigm reflects the interaction of the technological paradigm with the socio-economic environment mediating the processes of evolvement, growth, and replacement."

Relying on the works by N. D. Kondrat'ev [7], several authors proposed a predictive mechanism for modeling economic cycles on the simulation and assessment of the expectations of economic agents [9], which depend to some extent on scientific and technical factors such as artificial intelligence, blockchain, big data, digital technology, etc.

There is a need for the development, scientific justification (verification), and testing of economic models developed on the above factors of digital reality that would be high-responsive to changes in the external and internal environment of the economic system.

The study of the importance and effects of the expected digital revolution suggests that these factors should outstrip the reference series – gross domestic product (industrial production index) as the main indicator of the development path of the economic system and also take into account the whole of parameters affecting the adjustment of economic activity of business entities.

Competition as a Mechanism of a Market Economy Performance in the Digital Era

The goal of performance incentives is to establish conditions that would ensure coordination through the price mechanism at the highest quantitative and qualitative level.

It is expected that the entrepreneur immediately responds to any market fluctuations. Offering conditions that ensure the preference of consumers, etc. are based on information, feedback, and the ability to make the right decision in risky terms.

In the modern context of the advancement of science-technology progress and the robotization of many processes in the economy and society suggests that the economic process at all stages is fitted with the most powerful drivers, which nature meets the required functions. However, the introduction of artificial intelligence, the accumulation of data and information, as well as the connection to large databases is quite capital-intensive, which puts the government, transnational corporations, and individual entrepreneurs in a non-competitive position. The objective of the economic order becomes coordination and assistance to the drivers. It is also important for deciding on cultivating fruitful competition within a collectivist order, for example, by developing a synthetic competitive system.

Russia has adopted a digitalization program according to hereto the government recognizes digitalization as a priority for the state and undertakes the management of this process. The concepts of integrated legal regulation of relations arising in connection with the development of the digital economy and arranging the management of changes in the regulation of the digital economy have already been approved. They provide for broader activities within the federal project, also by making the legal regulation of the digital economy more flexible through other branches of legislation. The position of the Russian Federation on issues contributing to the development of the digital economy and the harmonization of approaches in this area at the EAEU level is determined [1].

Developing a unified information system, using a dispersed data system at the macro level, etc., is impossible without a government that will be its owner and beneficiary.

Robotization and artificial intelligence will monitor, predict and manage demand, provide logistics solutions in the consumption, run production, suggest competitive solutions, etc. Owning an intelligent system will provide non-competitive advantages or change the concept itself that will require the content of the market as a phenomenon and economic order to be reconsidered.

As early as 1948 W. Eucken wrote: "Competition can be applied to increase efficiency, but it cannot be used as a mechanism for management of important economic sectors without resignation of central authorities" [4]. But the phenomenon of large databases and the connection of the system of all bodies and organizations to them cannot do without the leading role of the government.

L. Robbins means the same when he speaks about collectivism: "Here, there is a clear trend to adjust rather people to a plan than vice versa."

Of course, one can object that the global network, by the example of cryptocurrency, has shown its viability against the will of most states, however, it is governments that control and authorize the Internet operation on their territory, prohibit, allow or promote the use of digital mechanisms.

Competition as the dominant form of the market cannot exist without compromise and attenuation of postulates; it depends on the historical situation and policy, economic crises and sanctions, the intensity of legal regulation, and the external environment. The advent of artificial intelligence can also be considered as a new phenomenon, a legal phantom of an independent person whose behavior does not always coincide with a preset program or algorithm developed by a programmer.

It is assumed that it is the consumer who determines the volume and composition of goods through the demand in the market economy. "Consumer sovereignty" is predetermined by the price mechanism implicitly obeying the laws of free competition, while any monopolistic restrictions undermine this sovereignty. Even now some programs allow manipulating consumer's behavior, pressing goods and services on them, making a demand for particular goods. All of the above mentioned is affordable for a wealthy corporation, but not for an individual entrepreneur. Digital technologies are capital-intensive, their implementation from the R&D stage to industrial use takes 10-12 years.

Restriction of competition means a violation of the performance principle, which the entire market economy as well as highly efficient and fair, and therefore "social," economic order that comprises entrepreneurial responsibility and risk, depending on.

The Policy of Economic Order in the Digital Era

As noted above, the digitalization of the economy and social life, the use of artificial intelligence, social goals related to the release of human labor, objectives of state protection of exclusive rights to intellectual labor, and its results will entail the database system to be concentrated, secured, used and administered. The use of a distributed database system (blockchain, etc.) does not cancel the system concentration in the hands of the state and its monopolization by the government.

Russia has set its state priorities in the research field, including statutory regulation of the digital environment; information infrastructure; HR for the digital economy; information security; digital technology; digital public administration.

Currently, there is no methodology for raising funds and calculating domestic costs for the development of the digital economy. The federal project "Digital Public Administration" provides the development of a methodology for statistical observations and measuring the parameters of the digital economy, including the effects of the digital transformation of economic and social sectors, until December 31, 2018.

Among the indicators used in statistical accounting, the companies' costs for information and communication technologies (which have increased from 2011 to 2017 by 2.5 times to 1,488 billion rubles (about 23.5 billion dollars)) can be proposed for the evaluation of the costs for the development of the digital economy.

The basic value of the indicator of internal costs for the development of the digital economy at the expense of all sources by the share in the country's

GDP is estimated and calculated as the ratio of companies' ICT costs to GDP. The growth rate ranges from 12 percent in 2018 to 20 percent in 2022 and subsequent periods [1].

Transnational corporations can compete with the state in terms of their financial power and might, dominate at a certain stage in the corresponding historical context, and develop their databases, distributed data systems and introduce artificial intelligence.

The "hyper-liquidity" of artificial intelligence becomes a premise for centralized management. There is a very unusual fact from the standpoint of the traditional approach to information handling that for the growth of the data value it is often enough to change only their scale, rather than update, deepen, or otherwise improve their qualitative characteristics. Unrivaled opportunities provided by modern digital technologies are qualitatively changing the principles of information use, the criteria for the assessment of its value, and, accordingly, the models of potential threats to confidentiality. Data has now become an asset of tremendous due to the so-called alternative value that is used for new purposes and implementation of new ideas [8].

The current economic order and system of central banks [3] mean the regulation of cash and credit flows by the planning government (central bank). This situation implies that both money emission and expansion are managed by the central bank; attempts to use the cryptocurrency as an alternative money or settlement funds that are not related to public ones have failed; it is also exposed to financial factors, speculative influence and has only made the governments themselves to think about the potential use of cryptocurrency for national currencies.

The very role of money, its function, and goals in the digital economy have not got any new features and do not give any expectations of meaningful changes.

Such a significant economic factor as the insufficient amount of savings is also changing in the system of a mass release of physical labor, and its competition with robots. The required social policy of the government has become searching for new forms of capital mobilization. Form this follows the tendency to the fiscal nature of management.

Employment policy is associated with demography, the pace of changes dictated by scientific and technological progress, the shift to intellectual labor. Intellectual labor and its results become an independent factor of production. The subsequent replacement of these intellectual workers with robots, a neural network, and artificial intelligence, even more, will aggravate the issue of employment, savings, and social security.

The function of the entrepreneur is to manage the share of the productive forces of the national economy accrued to the enterprise in a competitive economy (i.e., without monopolistic or interventional support) for the benefit of the community (i.e., for the best and cheapest supply to consumers). In a system based on artificial intelligence, there is no place for the initiative, entrepreneurial attitude, creative endeavor, and risk.

Conclusion

Digital technologies are dramatically changing the traditional forms and methods of economic life around the world. Both businesses of individual companies and entire industries, regions, and states are changing. Digitalization is beginning to extend beyond the changes of the technology itself and even in business; they become a macroeconomic and political factor.

If the above premises for the homogeneity of the future economic robotic order are ignored, then one will have to pay the price. There will be errors and failures in the performance of the corresponding economic order that will be attributed by some experts to the economic order itself but not to foreign elements that cause disbalance. And it can come to a catastrophic reboot. It would be a great mistake to think that the "socialization" of employment relations and the subsidization of human existence can be combined with a market economy without severe and almost irreversible changes. It is the scale of the already discernible trend of production robotization, social life, human digitalization, transfer of the decision-making sovereignty to machines that can become the main cause of severe economic upheavals of the future.

Economic relations should be legalized and regulated. The development of the digital economy in the country requires adjustment of Russian legislation to new types of relations and set of facts (new objects and parties of information legal relations, specific rights, duties, and liability). Legal relations always arise in respect of objects that are represented in the digital economy, as a rule, by data, elements of infrastructure, and activities in these fields.

If the state applies a competent and integrated approach to the legal regulation of information legal relations, it can undertake synchronization, enhancement, and provision of the security of operations effected in the digital economic community that is truly important as the studies carried out within this paper show.

References

[1] Passport of the National Program "Digital Economy of the Russian Federation" (approved by the Presidium of Council for Strategic Development and National Projects under the President of the Russian Federation, protocol No. 16 as of December 24, 2018). URL: https://www.consultant.ru Accessed July 12, 2019.

[2] Accenture. 2015. The Future Needs of the UK Economy for Digital Skills.

[3] Bortnikov, S. P. 2020. The State Sovereignty in Issues of Cryptocurrency. *Digital Age: Chances, Challenges, and Future*. Switzerland AG: Springer Nature.

[4] Eucken, W. 1948. On the Theory of the Centrally Administered Economy: An Analysis of the German Experiment. *Economics,* May 1948, Part I, 79-100.

[5] Glazyev, S. 2010. The Strategy of Advancing the Development of Russia in the Context of Global Crisis. Moscow: Economy. The Report by Scientists of Economic Section of the UN of RAS, 2011. In: S. Glazyev (Ed.). *Competitive Capacity of Russia and Way of Fulfillment to Ensuring National Security*. S. Glazyev's Report at a Meeting of the Security Council of Russia in 2015.

[6] Kalinin, T. 2017. *Russia 4.0: How to Prepare the Country for the Fourth Industrial Revolution.* URL: https://www.rbc.ru/opinions/economics/13/01/2017/5878d2389a79470077130332.

[7] Kondrat'ev, N. D. 1989. *Issues of Economic Dynamics*. Moscow: Ekonomika, 536 P.

[8] Maier-Shenberger, V. 2014. *Big data. Revolution That Will Change the Way of Living, Working, and Thinking*. Moscow: Mann, Ivanov, Ferber. 132 P.

[9] Safiullin, M. R., Elshin, L. A., Prygunova, M. I. 2016. Methodological Approaches to Forecasting the Mid-term Cycles of Economic Systems with the Predominant Type of Administrative-Command Control. *Journal of Economics and Economic Education Research* 17(2):277-287.

[10] Ford, M. 2015. *Rise of the Robots: Technology and the Threat of a Jobless Future.* Oneworld Publications.

[11] Perez, K. 2011. *Technological Revolutions and Financial Capital. Dynamics of Bubbles and Periods of Prosperity*. Moscow: Business.

[12] PWC. 2015. People Strategy for the Digital Age. A New Take on Talent.

[13] Atkinson, R. D. 2017. *In Defense of Robots. National Review*; April 17, 2017. URL: https://www.nationalreview.com/article/446933/robots-jobs-industrial-future.

[14] Ropke, W. 1950. *Mass und Mitte. Erlenbach-Zurich*. See especially Chapters V, VI, and VII.

[15] Schwab, C. 2018. *Technologies of the Fourth Industrial Revolution: translated in English.* In: C. Schwab, N. Devis (Eds.). Moscow: Eksmo. 320 P.

[16] Yakovets, Yu. 2016. *Political Economy of Civilizations*. Moscow: Economy.

Chapter 2

Legal Regulation and Sustainable Innovative Development of Society: Myths and Reality

Victoria V. Bolgova*
Samara National Research University, Samara, Russia

Abstract

The purpose of the study is to define the parameters of evaluating the impact of legal regulation on innovative development of public relations, as well as to describe the state of the system of state-legal regulation of innovation activity in Russia in modern times. Methodology. In the course of the research, we have applied the methods of system analysis, which made it possible to explore the innovation-making in relation to the goals and scope of state policy and assess the impact of individual means of legal regulation on innovation performance. Subject-matter. The legal definition of innovation outlined in Russian legislation is investigated. It is shown that the use of the economic features of innovations for the development of a legal rule is an unsuccessful technique of legal engineering, and the application of the existing legal definition is one of the obstacles to the appropriate development of the state support system for innovation activity. Through examples, we show that uncertainty in the parameters of the state order for innovation is a constraining factor of innovative development. The article studies the performance of the "legal vacuum" to stimulate innovation activity. Findings. The legal definition of innovation and regulatory definition of the parameters of innovation activity is necessary solely for public-law effects, in particular, for developing the system of state support and state order of innovations. Law is an effective means of influence on the

* Corresponding Author's Email: vv1976@mail.ru.

In: Economic and Legal Foundations of Innovative Development ...
Editors: Gabibulla Khasaev, Victoria Bolgova, Sergey Bortnikov et al.
ISBN: 978-1-68507-730-3

corresponding processes only to the extent when it allows establishing parameters for evaluation of the effectiveness and performance of the state support system. The system of state influence not assessed in parametric terms is a constraining factor of innovative development. There is an urgent need to clearly define the areas of innovation support, as well as to legally enshrine the requirements for state innovation support programs concerning the evaluation of their performance not by the amount of funding, but by effect from the sale of a new product, service or technology.

Keywords: innovation, innovative system, legal regulation, public policy, efficiency, venture capital market, legal definitions, legal engineering

Introduction

The relevance of the impact of legal regulation on the innovative development of society is determined by at least two points. Firstly, the modern Russian state in some policy papers and strategic documents states that the only possible development path today is shifting the economy to an innovative socially oriented development model. The state has a purpose to ensure such a transition. In accordance with the Decree of the President of the Russian Federation No. 596 as of May 7, 2012 "On Long-Term State Economic Policy," the goals of the state economic policy are to increase the rate and ensure the sustainability of economic growth, raise real incomes of citizens of the Russian Federation and achieve technological leadership of the Russian economy. An important condition for these goals to be achieved is the implementation of the Strategy for Innovative Development of the Russian Federation until 2020, approved by Decree of the Government of the Russian Federation No. 2227-p as of December 8, 2011, which suggests the turn of the Russian economy towards innovative development by 2020, and the Fundamentals of the Policy of the Russian Federation on the development of science and technology until 2020 and for future, approved by the President of the Russian Federation in 2012. Secondly, the idea that modern technological innovations, in particular in the development of information and communication technologies, create a new space and new reality that requires new means of legal regulation, the transformation of traditional institutions, and even alteration of our notion about law as a method to regulate public relations, is fairly stable in theory and modern political and economic practice

[6]. But unfortunately, some basic, key issues remain unresolved. In particular, the very parameters of the goal set by the state are not defined.

Analysis and Discussion

The very concept of "innovation" has remained rather intuitively comprehensible, but ambiguous for a long time [9]. The situation changed only in 2011 with amendments made to the Federal Law No. 127-FZ as of August 23, 1996 "On Science and the State Science-Technology Policy" (hereinafter referred to as also "Law No. 127-FZ"). Currently, Law No. 127-FZ defines this concept as follows: "Innovation is a new or greatly improved product (commodity, service) or process, a new sales method or a new organizational method in business practice, workplace arrangement or in external relations" (Article 2). Definition provided in the law is not "innovative" and nationally specific, it completely reproduces the definition given in the "Guidelines for Acquisition and Mining of Data on Innovation (Oslo Guidelines)" (joint publication by the Organization for Economic Cooperation and Development and the Statistical Office of the European Union) [3].

Legal experts have repeatedly pointed out that such a literal translation of European experience is pretty unsuccessful [9]. Firstly, Oslo Guidelines is not a statutory act, it is a conventional method of data acquisition for analytical work. Secondly, the definition stated herein and then translated to Law No. 127-FZ is economic, extremely broad, which causes uncertainty in practice.

The lawmaker in Russia associates the public-law effects with the fact that some person is a producer of innovations (a participant in innovation activity) [1]. Thus, for example, according to Art. 67 of the Tax Code of the Russian Federation, carrying out an implementation or innovation activities by the company, including developing new technologies or improving existing ones, manufacturing new types of materials is one of the grounds for an investment tax credit to be granted. Article 284 of the Tax Code of the Russian Federation settles the VAT rate at 0 percent for income from the sale of shares by companies of the high-tech (innovative) sector.

Foundations for support of scientific, science-technology, and innovative activities are established under Law No. 127-FZ and the funds for their establishment is recorded for tax purposes in accordance with Art. 332.1 of the Tax Code of the Russian Federation. According to Art. 16.2 of this Law, the state supports innovation activity in the Russian Federation through the exemption of taxes, fees, customs duties; provision of educational services and information support; consulting and assistance in making up project documentation; generation of demand for innovative products; financial support (including subsidies, grants, credits, loans, guarantees, contributions to the registered capital); implementation of target programs, subprograms and holding activities within the state programs of the Russian Federation; promotion of export; infrastructure provision; other forms that do not contradict the legislation of the Russian Federation. An integrated interpretation of operating legal rules shows that having given an "economic" definition of innovation, the lawmaker had to "narrow" it in situations when it comes to state support. Thus, reproducing the provisions of the Oslo Guidelines, lawmaker classifies four types of innovation: product-based, process-related, marketing, and organizational. Bearing this in mind, he sets out the requirements for statistical tools (Order of Rosstat No. 487 as of August 06, 2018 (as amended on January 14, 2019) "On Approval of Statistical Tools for Arrangement of Federal Statistical Monitoring of Activities in Education, Science, Innovation and Information Technology") used for data acquisition.

Let us note that statutory and regulatory acts of Russia don't contain the terms "product," "process," "marketing," etc.; therefore, for example, special reservations are introduced in the Tax Code of the Russian Federation that companies participating in innovation activity have the right to tax preferences in high-tech production. The definition of "high-tech" production is also not stipulated in the legislation.

Talking about the features of innovation, the lawmaker introduces only one thing, i.e., novelty. In particular, innovations are new products (services), new processes, new sales methods, etc. Etymologically, the term is interpreted correctly. But from the standpoint of applying exactly public measures on support for innovation activity, it is hardly sufficient. Any criteria for determining the novelty of innovative objects are not legally enshrined.

The criteria for assessing activity as innovation one in the Rosstat order mentioned above are revealed more broadly. Statistical tools establish the concept "results of innovation activity," which includes, for example, expanding the range of goods, works, services; maintaining traditional sales markets and developing new ones, increasing the energy efficiency of production, reducing labor costs, improving working conditions and occupational health & safety, increasing yields, etc. The ideology of the statistical report is that the organization independently determines both the fact of engagement in the production of innovations and the impact of this activity on its performance. It should be noted that the results of this subjective assessment are summarized by Rosstat and used to assess the overall innovation activity in the country.

The criteria to assess the efficiency of budget expenditures on support for innovative activities do not clarify the concept of innovation (Resolution of the Government of the Russian Federation No. 392 as of March 31, 2018). The main criterion of efficiency is the achievement of project target indicators, which can be various.

The above said allows us to conclude that defining innovative development as a goal, the state does not set the parameters of this goal since it does not set the criteria for innovation itself. Talking about legal regulation, we should point out that the legal definition of innovation (innovation activity and other related terms) is primarily associated with the public branches of law (administrative and financial one) [1; 4] since the engagement of one or another object into innovation activity is directly related to economic, organizational, financial and legal preferences obtained by some physical entities and companies from the state. For a private-law regulation system, there is no need to define innovation. Producing new objects of civil rights and transferring titles to them from one party to another is exhaustively described in the current civil-law framework [10]. In this regard, it seems obvious that the public law (and primarily administrative) field of using the concept of innovation requires a sufficient certainty that makes it possible to distinguish innovations from non-innovations, and innovations that should be supported by the state or not [2].

The current gap in the legislation is rather painless in relation to innovative activities in the proper sense of the word, which, in our opinion, is a natural companion of any production of goods, works, and services in the duly organized economic system. But it creates conditions for the "erosion" of state funds and undermines state influence on the economy and its effectiveness [5].

One of the solutions to the problem would be to establish a list of areas of activity (production) that can be supported by the state. This technique is applied in the Federal Law of the Russian Federation No. 244-FZ as of September 28, 2010 “On the Skolkovo Innovation Center”[1]. The objectives of the innovation center are as follows:

---

[1] Russian Journal. September 30, 2010. Issue 5299.

1. energy efficiency and energy saving, including the development of innovative energy technologies;
2. nuclear technology;
3. space technology, primarily in telecommunications and navigation systems (including the construction of appropriate surface infrastructure);
4. medical technology in the development of equipment and pharmaceuticals;
5. strategic computer technologies and software (Clause 8, Article 10 of the Federal Law).

In our opinion, the suggestions in the literature on solving the problem of legal regulation of innovation activity by a special regulatory act (some kind of basic law on innovation activity) [7] cannot be supported. It seems that the reliance on the possibilities of law is excessive in this case. Law is an effective tool, but only if it is used for its intended purpose. We suppose that the provision of state support for innovations should be adjusted through a clear statement of the desired results: what product, term, and qualities are needed and what problem (developing a fundamentally new product, replacing a foreign analog, etc.) it is designed to solve. These parameters should be set in the system of state order and state programming. The current legal tools with the adjusted concept of innovation, which can be supported by the state, are sufficient. Accumulation of regulatory framework and commitment to the specialization of innovative legislation will not give the desired effect.

We are also far from agreeing with the point that the system of legal regulation of modern Russia is the only obstacle to innovative development. Since 2010, Russia has experimented establishment of a "legal vacuum." Developing Skolkovo, the lawmaker limited the scope of the national legal regime and established the "Skolkovo jurisdiction" to promote innovation. Following the provisions of Art. 13 of the Federal Law "On the Skolkovo Innovation Center"[2], administration company of Skolkovo independently decides on the application of technical regulations, codes, standards, etc. (not only Russian ones) on the territory of Skolkovo. The Foundation has similar powers in the customs (Article 11), sanitary-epidemiological (Article 14), urban planning (Article 15), and healthcare (Article 17), etc. State bodies authorized in the corresponding areas are only informed of the Foundation's decisions. There are no local self-government bodies, public hearings,

[2] Russian Journal. September 30, 2010. Issue 5299.

environmental assessments. The rules of the Tax Code of the Russian Federation establish tax holidays for Skolkovo residents for up to 10 years. The center has been working for several years. Are there any results from such lawmakers' decisions? Let us remark that any targets were not initially set for Skolkovo. Allocating substantial funds and property on a non-paid basis, the state did not specify what it wants to get finally.

According to the Skolkovo performance report for 2018, 2,027 grants for a total amount of 13.7 billion rubles (in 2012 –3 billion rubles) were allocated, 1809 companies became participants of the startup program in Skolkovo. Annual reports show a growth of the quantitative and volumetric indicators of activity; the innovation infrastructure of several companies is located on the territory of Skolkovo (for example, Sibur, S7, Magnitogorsk Iron, and Steel Works, etc.). There is no information about the "breakthrough" innovations that have become widely known. But if we put off the skepticism and admit that there is progress from Skolkovo, and then we have to recognize that they appeared thanks to, but contrary to the state regulation system, since its elements do not work on the territory of Skolkovo. That is, innovation activity is successful under the absence of state regulation, including standardization, licensing, and taxation. We are not sure. But the Skolkovo example could be used as an indicator of gaps in state regulation for evident restrictions and obstacles to be promptly removed.

International experience shows that innovations are developed if there is a demand for them. A product, technology, processes are in demand if they make or are can make a profit for the manufacturer. Innovations are getting involved in technological processes; manufacturers are investing in scientific research. There is no other way. The growth of research costs in the absence of demand for the results is a dead end. In Russia, there is no systemic domestic demand for innovation.

It is illustrative that the success of an innovation project in Russia is currently being assessed by demand on international markets. In general, this methodology is right and justified, but provided that the copyright holder is in Russian jurisdiction and the technology itself remains in Russia. Unfortunately, now this is not the case.

Cite an example of the above said. Rock Flow Dynamics, a resident of the Skolkovo Foundation, has developed a product for complex oil and gas fields. The software package for hydrodynamic simulation of the formation excited interest and was bought by the American company Pioneer Natural Resources. There was no demand for this product by Russian oil-producing companies.

Product was developed at the expense of the foundation, which obtained ownership of the capital from the Russian Federation.

Another example is RealSpeaker applied for a Skolkovo grant on December 21, 2011. In 2012, 3.8 million rubles were approved and RealSpeaker carried out testing in Silicon Valley. The tests showed that the technology proposed by RealSpeaker improves the performance of the Google Voice Search engine by 20 percent. In December 2012, another 500,000 rubles were awarded as "Zvorykinsky Prize" for the best IT project, and Startobaza acquired a stake in RealSpeaker. Since the beginning of 2011, Osetrov received eight grants, six of them –from bodies fully or partially funded by the state. However, as far back as July 2012, Osetrov established the American RealSpeaker USA Inc., which took a 23.08% stake of "RealSpeaker Lab OOO." Nowadays, the company has been divested the status of the Skolkovo resident and is registered in Ireland.

In 2017, "Bioenergy OOO" received 16 micro-grants under the Skolkovo programs. The foundation cites this as a successful example and the 2018 report shows that the company was transferred to the jurisdiction of the EU and the USA. Also, it signed contracts for the supply of equipment to South Korea, the UK, and Kazakhstan.

The list can be continued. Of course, it is very encouraging that the technologies produced in Russia are in demand in international markets. But is government support effective in this situation? For what purpose had it been carried out? What is the effect on the national economy?

Let us provide some different examples. Projects of "Academic Research and Production Enterprise DIGITAL SOLUTIONS" were supported by Skolkovo and put forward for a competition of the Ministry of Industry and Trade of the Russian Federation. The projects won and the company entered into a contract for 500 million rubles within the state defense order.

The Skolkovo company "Twins Technologies" is the developer of the AIS Dispatcher system, a complex of software and hardware tools for continuous monitoring of industrial equipment in real-time and for predictive analytic assessment to raise equipment efficiency. Based on the results of the acceleration program, a project on equipment of the enterprises of holding "Vertolety Rossii OOO" with the AIS Dispatcher monitoring system was launched, and contracts are being executed with companies of United Aircraft Corporation and Rosatom groups.

Both examples from the 2018 Skolkovo report are shown as positive experiences. That is, a technology was developed at the expense of state funds and was sold to the state. It is hardly cost-effective.

The problem is the lack of clearly defined parameters and conditions for the provision of state support, which should include, in our opinion, requirements for conferring the titles to innovative products manufactured under state support within the jurisdiction of the Russian Federation.

The Ministry of Economic Development of Russia and the Russian Venture Company annually draws up a report on the state of innovation activity in Russia [8]. The report of 2017 in detail describes the dynamics of Russia in various ratings of the innovation system. But it is noted that the country's share in the world export of high-tech goods (global leadership in high-tech markets) and the ratio of gross value added to the average annual number of employees (labor productivity) are low. Russia lags far behind most EU and OECD countries in the short and long term. Since 2014, there has been a decline in labor productivity; the country's indicators on the commercialization of the results of innovation activity are still low.

The report of 2017 is thematic. It is dedicated to the state of venture investment in Russia. Experts involved in making up the report and operating venture capital companies unanimously note that one of the main problems is the non-entry of an innovative product to the domestic market. Successful ideas are more easily and faster implemented in the West since there is a demand for them [8].

And another very interesting point is highlighted in the report of the Ministry of Economic Development. Investors interviewed in making up a report note the disincentive effect of the dominance of state funds in the support of young entrepreneurs in the currently used forms. The success of government activities is measured by the number of funds, the number of supported projects, but not their quality and performance. Profit from the project is no longer the goal of the development reports are made up based on the expenditures. As a result, there is a lack of market for innovative products, the demand for technological innovations, and technological entrepreneurship. When assessing market development barriers, 34% of investors and 34% of tech-entrepreneurs mentioned inflexible measures of state support for innovations as such, and 29%of tech-entrepreneurs and 28% of investors called regulatory restrictions on running and developing a business.

The conclusions were made by the market participants themselves. They should be guidelines for government bodies and companies that are declared as the infrastructural foundations of an innovative economy (for example, the Russian Venture Company). The system for evaluating the development of innovations by the number of expenses without taking into account the return is initially flawed and should be adjusted.

Conclusion

1. The concepts of "innovation" and "innovation activity" in legislation should be legally enshrined exclusively for public-law purposes. The state aims its policy to promotion of innovation that is associated with significant financial costs. Given the need to observe the principles of budget regulation, in particular, the efficient spending of budget funds, appropriate concepts should be stated.
2. The law should fix the parameters for assessing the novelty of a product, service, or technology, which allows obtaining state support.
3. The Law should establish a list of prioritized technological areas and directions. Measures of state support should be taken only in these areas.
4. There is no need to elaborate special legislation on innovation, it is necessary to improve the existing legal tools.
5. Using the "legal vacuum" technique and establishing territories with non-application of the legal regime of the Russian Federation (by analogy with Skolkovo) is unacceptable. Analysis of the performance of the Innovation Center since 2010 shows that legal exemptions granted to the Skolkovo management company are ineffective.
6. It is necessary to introduce clear criteria that should be met in the provision of state support for innovation activity. Besides, assessment of efficient use of an innovative product (profit or cost reduction) and the claim to maintain titles to a product invented under state financial support on the territory of the Russian Federation should be legally enshrined.

References

[1] Burtovoy, M. Yu. 2011. Administrative and Legal Regulation of Innovation activity in the Constituent Entities of the Russian Federation. Ph.D. in Law thesis. Chelyabinsk, 238 P.

[2] Golichenko, O. G. 2011. The Main Factors of Developing National Innovation System: Lessons for Russia. Moscow, 48 P.

[3] Guidelines for Acquisition and Mining of Data on Innovation 2010. Oslo Guidelines, Organization for Economic Co-operation and Development, Joint Publication of the OECD and Statistical Office of the European Communities. Moscow.

[4] Kuz'mina, E. O. 2011. Administrative and Legal Regulation of State Participation in Innovation activity of the Russian Federation. Ph.D. in Law thesis. Saratov, 10 P.

[5] Kuz'mina, E. O. 2011. Administrative and Legal Regulation of State Participation in Innovation activity of the Russian Federation. Ph.D. in Law thesis. Saratov, 2011. 203 P.

[6] Lapaeva V. V. 2004. State Science and Technology Policy: Topical Issues of Legal Framework. Legislation on Science: Current Status and Development Prospects. Editor-in-Chief V. V. Lapaeva. Moscow: Norma. 18 P.

[7] Lapina M. A. 2017. Legal Regulation of the National Innovative System of Russia. Administrative and Municipal Law, No. 2.

[8] National Report on Innovations in Russia 2017. URL: https://www.rvc.ru/upload/iblock/c64/RVK_innovation_2017.pdf.

[9] Sergeev, A. V. 2017. On the Issue of the Concept of Innovations in Russian Legislation. URL: https:otrasli-prava.rf/article/27944.

[10] Volynkina, M. V. 2007. Civil-Law Form of Innovation activity: Doctor of Law thesis. Moscow: RANEPA.

Chapter 3

Development Stages of Legal Regulation in the Digital Era

Elena B. Kalashnikova[*], Elena A. Efremova and Alexei V. Dashin
Samara State University of Economics, Samara, Russia

Abstract

Relevance. The development of the digital economy inevitably leads to the digitalization of the sectors of the Russian economy such as healthcare, education, science, industry, agriculture, retail trade, transport, energy industry, housing and utilities, and the financial services market. The introduction of digital technologies contributes to the development of telemedicine, online learning, unmanned vehicles, smart home systems, and the Internet of Things; it will ensure transparency in business and government administration at all levels. Along with the obvious advantages, the digital economy brings equally obvious challenges and threats that are directly related to its peculiarities and features. Thus, expanding the range and customization of digital services leads to deterioration in the performance of monitoring of digital services and increased opportunities for offenses. Besides, the risks of information leaks become higher, requiring stronger protection and additional investments in information security. In Russia and the whole world, the proportion of social relations associated with the use of global computer networks is increasing, which predetermines the need to ensure their effective legal regulation [13]. At the same time, in domestic legislation and doctrine, there is no universally accepted approach to the principles of legal regulation of such relations.

---

[*] Corresponding Author's Emal: kalashnikova-helen@yandex.ru.

In: Economic and Legal Foundations of Innovative Development …
Editors: Gabibulla Khasaev, Victoria Bolgova, Sergey Bortnikov et al.
ISBN: 978-1-68507-730-3

Purpose and objectives of the research. One of the main objectives of the modern policy of economic transformation in Russia is to upgrade the regulatory functions of the state in the context of taking a new level of socio-economic development, i.e., the information economy of civil society that is typical for developed countries. Studying the development paths of the legal regulation of the digital economy should make theoretical scientists and legal practitioners address this problem. The authors are aimed at studying the impact of the information economy and IT development on Russian law in general and individual industries; investigating the general principles of legal regulation of the digital economy in Russia; and developing the general stages of establishing legal regulation of the digital economy.

Findings. The modern economy has entered a new era called digitalization that transforms both the economy and its principles and the types of its legal regulation. A similar process occurred during the transformation of the economy from agrarian to industrial one in the late 19th – early 20th centuries. Now the economy is shifting to the digital stage of development, therefore there is a need to change the principles of its regulation. The legal regulation of the digital economy is emerging.

Keywords: digital economy, types of legal regulation, law, financial technologies, branches of law

Introduction

The digital economy is a worldwide network of economic activities, as well as commercial transactions and professional cooperation which are provided by information and communication technologies. The development of the digital economy in our world is lightning-fast. Legislative acts are being signed all over the world, projects are being approved, and suggestions on improvement are being considered. And Russia is no exception. For the development of the digital economy in the Russian Federation, the Government of the Russian Federation approved the program "Digital Economy of the Russian Federation" by Decree No. 1632-p as of July 28, 2017. This program develops the main provisions of the Strategy for the Development of the Information Society in the Russian Federation for 2017–2030, which is approved by the Decree of the President of the Russian Federation No. 203 as of May 9, 2017. The digital economy is the future of the economy that has become the present little by little [10]. But no one economic system can fully operate without due legal regulation.

Methodology

Following the goals and objectives of the research, the authors within the systematic approach applied the subject-object, structural-functional, and historical-logical methods from the dialectic-materialist standpoint that should ensure the accuracy and reliability of the results.

Findings

The term "digital economy" appeared in 1995. It was associated primarily with the intensive development of information and communication technologies (ICT). Today, the development of the Internet and mobile communications are the "core technologies of the digital economy." Economic digitalization ultimately has affected all sectors of the economy and areas of social activities, including production, healthcare, education, financial services, transport, etc. Law has not been left without attention. The World Bank defined digital economy (in the broad sense of the word) as a system of economic, social, and cultural relations based on the use of digital ICT. The development of technological infrastructure and utilization of large databases have caused a mass-scale digital transformation of our society. The previous stage of digitalization was distinguished by the expansion of Internet access for millions of consumers, but the new stage is characterized by the integration of a wide range of digital services, products, and systems into the cyber-physical system.

Discussion

Some scholars define the digital economy as an economy, which the inherent feature is the best possible satisfaction of the needs of all the participants through the use of information, including personal ones. This is possible due to the development of information, communication, and financial All the above will provide all participants of economic activity with the opportunity for full-scale cooperation in the hybrid world (actors and objects of manufacturing, distribution, exchange, and consumption of goods and services) [5].

It is necessary to reveal the social patterns of emerging digital relations and ensure their due legalization [14]. The "digitalization" is developing exponentially, thereby stimulating changes and technological innovations that pose legal problems (The New Digital Economy: How It Will Transform Business). For example, these are the security of personal data and the protection of intellectual and constitutional rights [16]. One of the main problems is the type of legal regulation in the law of the digital economy.

The transition to a digital economy is a trend of modern society. For some societies, it is associated with the emergence of a new reality and its essential interpretation in the traditional socio-economic and legal structures, for others – it is a fantasy [9].

The main goal of the legal regulation is to establish a new regulatory environment that provides a favorable legal regime for the emergence and development of modern technologies, as well as for economic activities related to their utilization in the economy [2].

The theory of state and law classifies legal regulation into permitting and generally allowing. The first type means the principle "everything is prohibited, except for explicitly permitted." The second type is based on the principle "everything is allowed except for explicitly prohibited". In legal science and practice, there are no pure forms of legal regulation. In any branch of law, they exist in a combined form.

To determine what type of legal regulation is used in the digital economy, we should analyze the directions of developing the legal framework for the performance of the digital economy.

First, the digital economy can lead to the situation that most of the labor relations will become distant, which means augmentation of the population's labor mobility. Another trend is a growing volume of several jobs combined by the same person. Currently, the legislation does not provide for the opportunity of electronic registration of labor relations.

The proper execution of legally important electronic documents implies the system of digital signatures to be polished up. This is one of the manifestations of the unsolved problem related to the identification of legal participants of a digital society. When using digital information processing tools, there is no "environment of trust" where a physical or legal entity would be clearly identified and legal importance would be correspondingly given to any of their actions.

In accordance with the demands of the digital economy, the transformation of antimonopoly law arises too. It is expected to adopt regulatory acts that will ensure the elimination of legal restrictions in the antimonopoly law and its adjustment to the needs of the digital economy, the complementation and clarification of the nomenclature and basic concepts of competition law concerning the specifics of the digital economy.

The digital environment gives impetus to a reconsideration of approaches to the institution of intellectual property both in Russia and abroad. The new reality is that the "traditional" methods and algorithms for the intellectual property turnover and protection of intellectual property rights cannot be applied in a digital environment. It is important to take into account the new realities of digital space. Content protected by copyright and freed from the material cover acquires additional commercial value due to its possible delivery to any place of the world under minimal costs and with extra consumer properties. This property determined the global-scale use of works and increased the investment value of culture, science, education, business, and entertainment [3]. Presently, traditional property law does not work concerning property existing in the electronic environment [4]. This leads to the situation that users have no protection in the face of numerous restrictions.

Amending the legal framework to introduce and use innovative technologies in the financial market, including improving the mechanisms for the provision of electronic financial services and ensuring their information security are becoming topical [6]. The amendments will be made, for example, to the Civil Code of the Russian Federation, the Federal Laws "On Currency Regulation and Currency Control" and "On Banks and Banking Activity", etc.

It is necessary to establish contemporary favorable legal conditions for the acquisition, storage, and processing of data. This will require systemic changes both in operating regulatory acts, and the adoption of new ones for these conditions to be established. Particular attention should be paid to the use of new technologies that enable the accelerated development of the basic mechanisms of the digital economy and display the specific features of technological communication in digital relations given the protection of the rights and legitimate interests of the actors and data owners [8].

To develop the Internet of Things, it is suggested to amend and supplement the Federal Law "On Information, Information Technologies and Protection of Information" and other legislative acts regarding the consolidation of the rules for the disclosure of data on equipment used within the Internet of Things, quick connection to the Internet and safe operation of network devices. Also, legal conflicts between legislative acts and subordinate acts of the authorities that restrict the use of equipment within the operation of the Internet of Things should be settled.

The new tools to promote the development of the digital economy regarding the turnover of intellectual results should be devised and introduced.

Therefore, the Government should adopt regulatory acts oriented at the introduction of tools to stimulate the development of the digital economy regarding the turnover of the intellectual results, including digitization and digital turnover of the accumulated arrays of intellectual property items, to encourage their application for the needs of innovative development and the digital economy, and to overcome the types of intellectual rights' abuse that hinder the innovative development [7].

For example, for information to be included in the economic turnover the Government should fix it in Art. 128 of the Civil Code of the Russian Federation as an object of civil rights. It is advisable to develop modern rules for the turnover of programs for electronic computing machines that regard the specific features of mobile applications, cloud programs, etc. The digital economy also requires the procedure for the conclusion of licensing agreements and ones on the alienation of exclusive rights to be simplified, maybe a renunciation of the mandatory written form or their digitalization [1].

One should pay particular attention to the development of legislative rules on the regulation of the legal status of digital models, incl. 3D, the application of the patent law regime to intangible objects, such as digital models containing a reserved invention. The status and peculiarities of the performance of Internet television operators should be legislatively stated, the legal opportunities for utilization of broadband Internet access should be broadened [11].

One of the new directions is the establishment of legal conditions for the use of technologies of decentralized ledger maintenance and certification of rights, including a legal experiment in this area. In this regard, shortly, it is expected to conduct a legal experiment and ultimately adopt regulatory acts that provide legal conditions for the introduction and use of decentralized ledger maintenance and certification of rights [15].

According to forecasts of Russian experts, a favorable legal regime for the emergence and development of modern technologies and associated economic activities in the digital economy will be completely established by 2024.

Conclusion / Recommendations

The system of legal regulation of the digital economy cannot develop intermittently. It should go step-by-step. At the first stage, it is necessary to develop and put into practice the concept of priority measures to improve legal regulation for the expedited development of the digital economy. First, a list of key valid legal restrictions that prevent the development of the digital economy should be made up and suggestions on their elimination should be summarized. Then, it is necessary to introduce amendments to the regulatory framework that will concern the principles of legal regulation and will be brought into balance with the technological features of the digital economy performance. At the third stage, the concept of an integrated legal regulation of the digital economy relations should be stated. Ultimately, the regulatory environment should provide a favorable legal regime for the emergence and development of modern technologies and associated economic activities in the digital economy to the full extent. Only regarding the full range of both economic and legal aspects, the national economy will take a rightful place in the global economic system and digital economic system.

References

[1] Corrales, M., Fenwick, M., Forgó, N. 2017. *New Technology, Big Data, and the Law.* Springer Nature Singapore Pte Ltd. 2017. URL: https://doi. org/10.1007/978-981-10-5038-1.

[2] *Digital Economy in Japan and the EU – An assessment of the common challenges and the collaboration potential.* Tokyo, March 2015. URL: https://www.eu-japan.eu/sites/eu-japan.eu/files/DigitalEconomy_final.pdf.

[3] Entin, V. L. 2017. *Copyright in Virtual Reality (New Opportunities and Challenges of the Digital Age).* Moscow: Status.

[4] *Intellectual Property Rights in Today's Digital Economy.* ITU 2011 URL: https://www.itu.int/ITU-D/treg/Events/Seminars/gsr/GSR11/documents/05-Intellectual-property-E.pdf.

[5] Keshelava, A.V., Budanov, V.G., Rumyantsev, V.Yu. 2017. *Introduction to the Digital Economy.* All-Russian Research Institute of Geosystems, 12 P.

[6] Kilpatrick, B., Kobel, P., Këllezi, P. 2018. Antitrust Analysis of Online Sales Platforms & Copyright Limitations and Exceptions. *Springer International Publishing AG, part of Springer Nature*. URL: https://doi.org/10.1007/978-3-319-71419-6.

[7] Lundqvist, B. 2018. *Regulating Competition and Property in the Digital Economy – The Interface between Data, Privacy, Intellectual Property, Fairness, and Competition Law*. Stockholm University, Faculty of Law. January 17, 2018. URL: https://papers.ssrn.com/sol3/papers.cfm? abstract_id=3103870.

[8] *OECD Digital Economy Outlook* 2015. URL: https://doi.org/ 10.1787/9789264232440-en.

[9] Serova, O. A. 2018. Robots as Participants in the Digital Economy: Issues of Establishing the Legal Nature. *Civil Law* 3: 22 - 24. http:doi.org/10.18572/2070-2140-2018-3-22-24.

[10] Sukhova, V. A. 2018. Digital Economy: Opportunities for Countries and Methods of its Regulation. *Young Scientist* 21: 303-306. URL https://moluch.ru/archive/207/50579/ Accessed October 09, 2018.

[11] Terroir, P. 2014. Rebalancing the Patent Economy. *Intellectual Asset Management* March/April 2014(71).

[12] The New Digital Economy: How It Will Transform Business. A research paper produced in collaboration with AT&T, Cisco, Citi, PwC & SAP. URL: https://www.pwc.com/mt/en/publications/assets/the-new-digital-economy.pdf.

[13] Trofimenko, A.V., Eliseeva, S.N., Korobeinikova, I.S. 2017. Digital Economy: Enhancing the Efficiency of Entrepreneurs' Rights in Cyberspace to Be Ensured. *Bulletin of the Saratov State Socio-Economic University* 4 (68). URL: https://cyberleninka.ru/article/n/tsifrovaya-ekonomika-problemy-povysheniya-effektivnosti-obespecheniya-prav-predprinimateley-v-kiberprostranstve.

[14] Vaipan, V. A. 2017. *Theory of Justice: Law and Economics*. Monograph. Moscow: Yustitsinform, 127 P.

[15] Yankovsky, R. M. 2017. Organizational and Legal Forms of Venture Investment (Part 2): Venture Capital Funds in the Form of Partnerships. *Law and Economics* 7: 58 - 65.

[16] Zakharov, A. L., Sidorova, A. V. 2016. Information Inequality: History and Modernity. *Issues of Economics and Law* 10: 17.

Chapter 4

Social Inequality in Technological Transformation of Society and Economy

Anna V. Guryanova[1,*], Nikolai Yu. Guryanov[2] and Elmira R. Khafiyatullina[3]

[1] Samara State University of Economics, Samara, Russia
[2] Medical University "Reaviz", Samara, Russia
[3] Samara State Technical University, Samara, Russia

Abstract

The purpose of the paper is an in-depth exploration of the problem of social inequality in modern society, which is associated with the widespread diffusion of information and communication technologies (ICT). The concepts of "IT development" and "digitalization", "social inequality" and "economic inequality", "digital inequality" and "digital divide" are defined. The premises and peculiarities of the transformation of social inequality into digital one are investigated; technological, social, and economic indicators that determine this process are revealed. Digital information inequality is qualified as a natural effect of IT development and the digitalization of modern society. It underlies the inherent system of socio-economic relations, escalates further stratification of society where occurs a gap between "information poor" and "informationally rich" social groups. Thanks to the digital divide, the introduction of ICT in the management and production as well as economic development is slowing down, people's life quality and living standards are being restrained. Regarding the snowball of the negative consequences of digital inequality, we proposed recommendations on overcoming it. This is the provision of the technological opportunity to

* Corresponding Author's Email: annaguryanov@yandex.ru.

In: Economic and Legal Foundations of Innovative Development …
Editors: Gabibulla Khasaev, Victoria Bolgova, Sergey Bortnikov et al.
ISBN: 978-1-68507-730-3

use ICT services; motivate to use them; target training aimed at socially unprotected, "informationally poor" social groups; bringing ICT cost in balance with the level of real incomes of the population; state planning of digital projects and monitoring of their implementation; establishment of the required research background for digitalization that determines the contemporary socio-economic development.

Keywords: social inequality, digital information inequality, digital gap, IT development, digitalization, information and communication technologies (ICT), the fourth industrial revolution

Introduction

Today, an increasing number of people around the world cannot imagine their lives without ICT, which has an impact on all areas of human life, including society and economy, healthcare, education, and science, and predetermine the development trends. Thanks to the introduction of ICT, labor productivity is increasing, the quality of manufactured goods is improving, the performance of state authorities is growing, and their communication with society is facilitated. Under the influence of ICT, the role of information and knowledge in the life of society keeps on growing, a global information space is being developed, the level of cultural and professional education is being raised, and new approaches are being applied in technology, economy, and science.

In the course of ICT development, all areas of modern socio-economic life are dramatically transformed, temporal and spatial limitations are reduced, and the quality of human life is improved. Moreover, nowadays IT development seems to be involved in an even broader context of digitalization, which is a complicated level of ICT development. And more precisely, IT development can be interpreted as an integral part or even as a condition for digitalization, since the digital skills and competencies are obtained today through the use of information technologies, which start to be regarded as digital ones.

The impact of digital technology on society is a subject matter of hot discussions. Indeed, in modern conditions production, as well as culture, and even human consciousness become digital, personal life and work of millions of people are transferred to virtual reality. Live communication is displaced with social networks, paper media are replaced with e-books, and cyberculture is associated in the minds of young people with the cultural heritage of mankind in general. What, then, this digitalization that is gathering pace finally leads to? There is no certain answer to this question today. But in the context of the changes occurring in modern society, it can be surely stated that digitalization is an impersonal and inevitable process, which cannot be stopped (therefore, it doesn't matter positive or negative consequences it will bring).

In an era of increasing demand for scientific and technological innovations, the ICT that underlies digitalization help to manage information flows and form a special information system based on them. This assists to ensure the desired transparency, quality, and effectiveness of information, a higher rate of diffusion and reproduction [6]. But it's quite obvious that the above problem of modern ICTs cannot be tackled without assistance. Their resolution is directly related to the elimination of information and digital social inequality. In this situation, it is suggested the classification of people who master modern ICT and have access to digital information and ones who haven't this kind of opportunity and skills. In this regard, the issue of social inequality getting dramatically transformed in the technological transformation of modern society and economy is of particular importance and relevance.

Methodology

We have used the following methods to study the issue of social inequality in the technological transformation of society and the economy:

1. The descriptive method is used for the description of the specific features and common features of society and the economy in the digital era.
2. The information method is used for selection and investigation of necessary papers on IT development and digitalization, for example, records and reports on this issue, such as the reports of World Bank [12] and the US Department of Commerce and the National Telecommunications and Information Administration (NTIA) [4, 5].
3. The comparative method is applicable for carrying out a comparative analysis of social, economic, and information-digital inequality.

4. The dialectical method is used for exploring the phenomena of industrial revolutions and technological changes in society and the economy in their historical development, interrelation, and interdependence.
5. The predictive method is applied to develop and summarize the necessary recommendations for mitigation and, under a perfect scenario, removal of digital inequality from the system of future socio-economic life.

Results

Technological Changes in Society and the Economy as the "Fourth Industrial Revolution"

Modern society has entered an era of global-scale changes. Presently, all the main areas of social life, such as economy and law, management and production, science and security, take a new form and get new content. The man is also drastically changing [8], which inevitably entails the transformation of the entire system of social relations. Digital technologies will penetrate deeper into social life that, most likely, will become one of the main specific features of the future world. Its image will depend to a large extent on the progress in information technology, telecommunications, and microelectronics, as well as digitalization, which involves the translation of all types of information (including textual and audiovisual) into digital form.

Since 1982, the Internet has started its operation. We can assume that a special virtual world originates dates back to this time. Since then, the virtual environment has been actively developing and incorporating new components, such as forums, social networks, online computer games, etc. Every single block is both a structural element of the virtual world and a link uniting it with the real world. These two worlds are interrelated and their merger is in full swing, and it cannot be stopped [9].

The changes occurring in modern society are often called the "Fourth Industrial Revolution". Klaus Schwab, a well-known economist, founder, and executive director of the World Economic Forum in Davos was a herald of a new revolution [10].

In his opinion, mankind has already undergone three industrial revolutions and now faces the fourth one. In his famous book "The Fourth Industrial

Revolution," C. Schwab writes that the first revolution fell in the 1760-1840s and was associated with the invention of the steam engine. The second revolution is dated by him in the late 19th – early 20th century. The advent of an incandescent lamp, the spread of electricity, and assembly-line production technology dates back to this time. The third industrial revolution occurred in the 1960s when semiconductors were adopted by mankind.

Today, the industry around the world is again undergoing a revolutionary breakthrough. Moreover, by dynamics, complex nature, and scale of occurring changes, this revolution is much different from the previous revolutionary overthrows. It dramatically transforms our way of life and social structure. Modern man is a witness of impressive technological breakthroughs in a wide range of areas. This is artificial intelligence and robotic application, 3D Printing and Big Data, Cloud and Cognitive Technologies, Virtual and Augmented Reality, the Internet of Things and the Industrial Internet of Things, Nano and Biotechnologies, and so forth. According to K. Schwab's opinion, the first three industrial revolutions were caused exclusively by the emergence of new technologies, but the fourth one is distinguished by the rapid diffusion of technologies and their full-fledged application.

As characterized by M. Castells, the Internet at the present stage of development is equally important as electricity in the industrialization era [2].

Consequently, digital ICTs lie at the heart of a new technological model of socio-economic development. These new digital technologies possess enormous development capacity, but there are also high risks associated with them. After all, the fourth industrial revolution will most likely be lightning fast. And the speed of decision-making, as well as the developmental level of individual participants in digital relations (countries, companies, social groups, individuals) is markedly different. Therefore, many of them couldn't be able to keep up with quickening innovations. This situation foregrounds the issue of social inequality in its new information-digital dimension.

Transformation of Social Inequality in the Context of Digitalization of Modern Society and the Economy

Social inequality in modern society is transformed due to the combination of the contradictions rooted. On the one hand, the development of ICT significantly broadens the opportunities of the man, and on the other hand, it leads to a digital divide in society resulting in a combination of economic and social restrictions for the citizens who cannot be involved in information-digital communications for some reasons. Due to the intensive development of a market economy, social stratification is growing [7]. In this context, access to digital information and opportunities and resources provided becomes the most important factor in social inequality.

The structure of information-digital- inequality is based on the difference in the level of ICT development between and within different states, between their constituent institutions and institutions. But, it's even more important that information-digital inequality causes a divide associated with the very access to information between different social groups (rich and poor, urban and rural residents, people of different ages, sexes, professions, etc.). First of all, it's about unequal access to ICT where we see two opposite groups, the so-called "informationally rich" and "informationally poor".

According to the World Bank, in 2014 only 31% of the population of developing countries had Internet access, while in high-income countries this figure was 80% [12]. The level of literacy and civic engagement is steadily declining among the categories of the population that do not have access to ICT or the opportunity of using them. The language and inter-generation divide are widening, which leads to a hierarchical classification of its members into the "informationally poor" and "informationally rich". Leisure and entertainment are dramatically changed since the "informationally poor" groups of the population just do not have the opportunity to join. Labor resources are mostly linked to ICT, which is expressed in recruitment issues increasingly becoming automated.

Currently, information technologies are rapidly developing and generating advanced evolutionary shifts in many areas of social life, which allow confirming its qualitative improvement. But along with this positive trend, the level of information-digital inequality is soaring. A significant number of people are either limited access or do not have access to digital information services falling into a group of social outcasts and mediocre people. In this regard, an analogy can be drawn between information-digital and economic inequality, which, as a rule, is deteriorating over time [7]. The matters with information-digital inequality are nearly the same.

In light of the key role played by the market economy and information, ICTs are designed mainly for people who have the opportunity to pay for their acquisition and use. "The gap in the affordability of digital technologies and the scale of their use persists... Only 15 percent of the world's inhabitants can afford to pay for broadband Internet access... and about 60 percent of the world's population does not have access to the Internet... The digital divide within the country may be as deep as the divide between different countries... The likelihood of using digital technologies or digital devices by women is lower than by men. The divide is even deeper between young people (20%) and people over 45 years old (8 percent)" [12].

The Concept of the "Digital Gap" and Its Role in the Interpretation of Social Inequality

Digitalization is always unfolding within a certain social environment, being initially targeted by the latter and having a significant impact on it in the future. An important role here belongs to the level of scientific and technological progress, the combination of socio-economic and political conditions of a particular society [11]. They largely determine the content of the digitalization, as well as its rate and effectiveness. The difference in the level of economic development of countries, incomes of the population, and state of human capital caused the emergence of a fundamentally new type of social inequality, i.e., digital inequality, in modern society.

Today, the "digital inequality" or is often called the "digital divide" is a global-scale phenomenon with its peculiarities in countries with different levels of economic, scientific, and technological development. Modern ICTs act as a fundamental factor that determines the specifics of the organization and performance of a society. Social practices and institutions are transformed, labor activity, mentality, and people's lifestyle are changed under their direct influence. But, along with this, the "information-digital gap" is widening.

The issues of the digital divide were first addressed in a report of 1995 "Falling Through the Net: A Study of the "Poor in Rural and Urban America" by the US Department of Commerce and the National Telecommunications and Information Administration (NTIA) [4].

The experts who made up a report analyzed traditional US race differences, and at the same time introduced a new indicator of social stratification related to access to information resources and digital technologies. At that time, it was important to state the fact that race differences in the modern world are replaced by differences in income and information. In the 1999 report "Falling Through the Net: Defining the Digital Divide" [5], the digital divide was clearly defined as the divide between those who have access to new ICT and respectively those who don't due to the race, economic, demographic and other differences in the society.

Subsequently, as ICT develops, digital inequality has evinced in many countries around the world and has become a fundamental form of modern social inequality. The digital inequality in society is a significant obstacle to its potential development, and the fragmented coverage of ICT by the population is a barrier to the full-fledged display of digitalization advantages.

Digital Inequality as the Basis of Modern Socio-Economic Relations

The digitalization of modern society belongs to a particular social environment and directly depends on it. The science-technology basis of this society, created a social climate, established system of socio-economic and political relations determines the course of the digitalization, its rate, and scope, the manifestation of various components and performance. Moreover, the development of a digital society includes the bundle of previous social contradictions and, at the same time, generates fundamentally new ones.

As noted above, differences in the economic development of regions, population incomes, and human capital have led to the emergence of a new type of social inequality, i.e., digital inequality. But the economic inequality of past times, the classes of the rich and the poor not only did not disappear but also get qualitatively transformed in the face of opposition between the real and virtual environments: the real financial situation of people largely determines their preferences, needs, and opportunities in the virtual space.

The prevailing system of economic and political relations determines the emergence and combination of "informationally rich" and "informationally poor" groups of the population.

As a result, the fundamental cause for the modern information-digital inequality in all its forms and manifestations (interstate, interregional, inter-social, anthroposocial) is, ultimately, the traditional economic gap between rich and poor that comes to a new round of his evolutionary development. In a perfect scenario, "the greatest effect of IT development is achieved if the entire population is involved in the information space" [3]. If access to ICTs is limited or unavailable, this diminishes the individual's opportunity for full-fledged use of the necessary information and slows down social development in general.

The social inequality interpreted in this way is further aggravated in the context of the opportunities provided to the individual by the latest means of digital communication. Continuously updated and increasingly sophisticated ICT provide their users with ever-increasing opportunities for geolocation, monitoring the physical state of the body, managing the human environment ("smart environment", "smart home", "smart city", etc.). "Digital communication eliminates the difference between a location in one place and movement. The emergence of new channels of movement (virtual travel) gives rise to new spatial inequalities since they simultaneously increase the opportunities of those who can introduce them and reduce the opportunities of others" [1].

Thus, in the context of technological changes in society and the economy, ICT accessibility is becoming an integral part of the life maintenance system, an essential element of social infrastructure, and getting especially important. However, access to ICTs is still related to the monetary threshold to a large extent. It is due to the difference in the level of income of the population (economic inequality); the number of population in different countries, their geographical and territorial features, cultural and psychological attitudes, the mentality of residents, the level of technological development, involvement of people in globalization; the predominant age composition of the population in one or another society, the level of digital literacy typical for this population, etc.

Conclusion

Technological changes unfolding in modern society and the economy entail some positive consequences of social nature, for example, the availability of any information regardless of a person's specific location. The opportunity for prompt communication between different societies, their state, and institutional bodies, as well as between individuals. As a result, previous geopolitical and geographical factors that were extremely important are "erased". They lose their primary importance and give place to other forms of social communication based mainly on ICT. Therefore, education, education, creativity, work, leisure, entertainment, etc. are dramatically transformed.

However, there are negative consequences. It is a further escalation of social inequality and its transition to a new round of information-digital development in particular. Digital inequality slows down economic development, prevents the improvement of the quality of life, deepens socioeconomic stratification, and hinders the introduction of ICT in the system of administration and public services.

In this situation, it is necessary to provide for the technological opportunity of using ICT services, motivate their use and carry out targeted training aimed primarily at socially unprotected categories of citizens. It is also important to equalize, or at least bring ICT costs in balance with the level of real incomes of the population; plan digital projects at the governmental level and monitor their implementation; establish the required research background for digitalization that determines the contemporary socio-economic development.

References

[1] Bestuzheva, O.Y., Vershinskaya, O.N., Makhrova, A.N. 2014. The Development of the Society of Digital Mobility. *Population*, 4: 115-125.

[2] Castells, M. 2000. Information Age. Economics, Society and Culture. Moscow: Publishing House of State University "Higher School of Economics."

[3] Dronov, V.N., Makhrova, O.N. 2015. Digital Inequality of Ryazan Region. St. Petersburg: Publishing House of St. Petersburg University of Management and Economics.

[4] Falling Through the Net: A Survey of the "Have Nots" in rural and urban America. 1995. National Telecommunications & Information Administration, U.S. Department of Commerce, Washington, D.C. URL: https://www.ntia.doc.gov/ntiahome/fallingthru.html.

[5] Falling Through the Net: Defining the Digital Divide. 1999. National Telecommunications & Information Administration, U.S. Department of Commerce, Washington, D.C. URL: http://www.ntia.doc.gov/report/1999/falling-through-net-defining-digital-divide.

[6] Guryanova, A. Astafeva, N. Filatova, N. Khafiyatullina, E. Guryanov, N. 2019. Philosophical Problems of Information and Communication Technology in the Process of Modern Socio-Economic Development. In: E. G. Popkova and V.N. Ostrovskaya (Eds). Prospects for the Use of New Information and Communication Technology (ICT) in the Modern Economy. *Advances in Intelligent Systems and Computing*, Vol. 726. Springer International Publishing AG, Springer, Cham, pp. 1033-1040.

[7] Guryanova, A., Guryanov, N., Frolov, V., Tokmakov, M., Belozerova, O. 2017. Main Categories of Economics as an Object of Philosophical Analysis. In: E.G. Popkova (Ed). Russia and the European Union: Development and Prospects.

Contributions to Economics. Springer International Publishing AG, Cham, Switzerland, pp. 221-228.

[8] Guryanova, A., Khafiyatullina, E., Kolibanov, A., Makhovikov, A., Frolov, V. 2018 Philosophical View on Human Existence in the World of Technic and Information. In: E. G. Popkova (Ed). The Impact of Information on Modern Humans. *Advances in Intelligent Systems and Computing*, Vol. 622. Springer International Publishing AG, Springer, Cham, pp. 97-104.

[9] Keshelava, A.V. 2017. Introduction to Digital economy. Moscow: Vniigeosystems.

[10] Schwab, K. 2017. The Fourth Industrial Revolution. Moscow: Eksmo.

[11] Shestakov, A., Noskov, E., Tikhonov, V., Astaf'eva, N. 2017. Economic Behavior and the Issue of Rationality. In: E.G. Popkova (Ed). Russia and the European Union: Development and Prospects. Contributions to Economics. Springer International Publishing AG, Cham, Switzerland, pp. 327-332.

[12] World Development Report. 2016. "Digital Dividends". World Bank, Washington, D.C. URL: https://openknowledge.worldbank.org/bitstream/handle/10986/23347/21067.

Chapter 5

Legal Policy in the Field of Digital Economy

Aleksei V. Azarkhin*, Aleksandra P. Korobova, Anna G. Bordakova and Dmitrii A. Karev
Samara State University of Economics, Samara, Russia

Abstract

Relevance. Information technology is penetrating our lives much deeper and increasingly encompassing new areas of public life. Ten years ago, the term "digital economy" was a novelty, but now the issues of legal regulation of the digital economy have become one of the most important areas of government activity. Therefore, we can say that forging a competent legal policy in this area means keeping pace with time.

The purpose of the study is to develop the concept of legal policy in the digital economy, reveal its specific nature as one of the varieties of state policy, determine its priorities, outline the range of goals and objectives, and describe the main directions at the current stage of development of Russian society.

The methodological background of the study is general scientific methods such as analysis and synthesis, logical and system-structural one. The formal-law method, one of the private legal research methods, is also widely used. In particular, a definition of legal policy in the field of the digital economy has been developed with the help of the above method.

Findings and their value. In the course of the study, the statutory and regulatory acts mediating activities in this area have been analyzed, the main strategic objectives in the development of the digital economy have been revealed, priorities and main directions of legal policy have been

* Corresponding Author's Email: e-mail: aazarhin@mail.ru.

In: Economic and Legal Foundations of Innovative Development …
Editors: Gabibulla Khasaev, Victoria Bolgova, Sergey Bortnikov et al.
ISBN: 978-1-68507-730-3

outlined, and a range of measures to implement these priorities and directions have been determined. It is concluded that now the legal policy of the Russian state concerning the digital economy is being actively developed.

Keywords: law policy, legal policy, legal regulation policy, legal activities, digitalization of law, digital economy

JEL Codes: K10, E66

Introduction

The category of legal policy is referred to a few phenomena of legal reality that were undeveloped in Soviet jurisprudence, except for single studies, and have been recently introduced into daily scientific use (if we talk about legal policy, it's the end of the 90s of the 20th century). And this phenomenon immediately has been studied at all levels of legal science from the theory of state and law to applied sciences.

However, despite the keen interest of scientists in this issue, and perhaps thanks to it, common approaches to the interpretation of this concept have not been developed in the theory of law. So, researchers have different opinions primarily on the scope of this concept. On the one hand, they identify legal policy with legal ideology and understand it as some system of ideas, measures, objectives, goals, programs, principles, and attitudes implemented in the scope of the law and through the law [6]. But ideas themselves are not policy, but rather its core, content, motivational message. The legal policy is an activity anyway. As noted in the literature, this is a scientifically based, systemic political and legal activity of the state with the participation of civil society in the field of legal regulation, which can ensure strategic goals of the state to be achieved [4]. Thus, it would be reasonable to understand legal policy not as a legal ideology, but as an activity on its development.

We dealt with this issue, however, what the essence of this activity is. How broad can we interpret it? For example, there is an opinion that legal policy can be reduced to the development and determination of goals, principles, main directions, forms, and methods of a particular activity [2], i.e., the same ideology, strategy, and tactics. On the other hand, some authors pay attention to the need not only to develop but also to put into practice the strategic legal ideas developed. One cannot but agree that two states of legal policy (two sides - static and dynamic) that are designed to complement each other should be discussed [7]. Thus, legal policy gets shifted from ideas, thoughts, and plans to legal practice to guide and arrange the latter.

The legal policy is also associated with the legal system [5], legal regulation [1] and its mechanism, strategy, and tactics of public administration [8], areas of state activity [3], government activities in the field of legal regulation and other legal phenomena.

Results

Summing up the above, we should note that, on the one hand, the legal policy cannot be imagined without its ideological component, does not exist without or beyond ideology; its essence consists primarily in the development of particular legal ideas of strategically nature. On the other hand, it cannot be limited to this, since any idea needs practical implementation, some kind of life testing. The legal policy is an organic unity of ideological and activity-based components and consists in the development and practical implementation of legal ideas of a particular kind.

Like any activity, the legal policy is constituted by various areas, and the most common criterion is one or another area of legally regulated public relations. This allows distinguishing constitutional-law, criminal-law, administrative-law, civil-law, environmental-law, and other types of policies in the structure of the legal policy. It is easy to notice that such a classification of legal policy follows the system of current branch-based Russian law. Any significant changes within this system entail the development of new areas of legal policy. The aforesaid fully concerns the law of the digital economy, which has become more recently developed.

The legal policy in the field of the digital economy is the development and implementation of strategic legal ideas in the economic activity with digital data as a key production factor, the processing of large data volumes and application of the data analyzed can significantly increase the efficiency of various types of production, technologies, equipment, storage, sale, delivery of goods and services compared with traditional economic forms [10].

The priorities of the legal policy in the field of information technology and the digital economy include in particular:

a) to develop information space with regard to the needs of citizens and society in high-quality and reliable information;
b) to enhance information and communication infrastructure of the Russian Federation;
c) to design and use Russian information and communication technologies, ensure their competitiveness at the international level;
d) to establish a new technological foundation for the development of the economy and the social area;
e) to protect national interests in the field of the digital economy.

National interests in the field of the digital economy are:

a) creating new ICT-based markets and ensuring leadership there through the efficient use of knowledge and development of the Russian ecosystem of the digital economy;
b) cementing the Russian economy, including the sectors developing business through information and communication technologies that will provide competitive advantages to Russian organizations, ensure production efficiency and raise labor productivity;
c) boosting the volume of Russian non-resource exports, foremost goods, and services that are in demand with foreign consumers, using new technologies;
d) enhancing the competitiveness of Russian high-tech organizations in the international market;
e) ensuring technological independence and security of the infrastructure designed to sell goods and provide services to Russian citizens and organizations;
f) protecting citizens from infringing and substandard goods;
g) ensuring the legitimate use of personal data and information provided by industrial, transport, and communication infrastructures, as well as data received from state information systems;
h) protecting the interests of Russian citizens, providing them with jobs (the development of a digital economy should not infringe on the interests of citizens);
i) maintaining technologies and methods for the production of goods and the provision of services in the traditional sectors of the economy;
j) ensuring the protection of interests of Russian organizations selling their goods in traditional (non-electronic) markets;

k) improving antimonopoly legislation, also when providing software, goods and services through the Internet to persons located in the Russian Federation;
l) meeting the requirements of the legislation of the Russian Federation by foreign participants of the Russian market on a par with Russian organizations;
m) forging trade and economic ties with strategic partners of the Russian Federation, including within the Eurasian Economic Union (EAEU).

We should note that nowadays many issues arising in connection with the use of information and telecommunication technologies in different areas of the life of the Russian society have been generally regulated by current legislation, i.e., we can talk about the development of a regulatory framework in this area. However, the lack of the main strategic document that would set goals, objectives, and priorities of the legal policy in the field of the digital economy, could not but lead to gaps in the regulatory acts that prevent the establishment of new institutions of the digital economy, the development of information and telecommunication technologies and related types of economic activity. The first document of this kind has become the "Strategy for the Development of the Information Society in the Russian Federation for 2017 – 2030" approved by the Decree of the President of the Russian Federation. It has appeared only in May 2017, and two months later, the program "Digital Economy of the Russian Federation" was adopted and approved by the Government of the Russian Federation [9]. The latter document particularly notes that the Russian Federation ranks 41st in terms of preparedness to the digital economy with a significant margin from the top ten countries, such as Singapore, Finland, Sweden, Norway, the United States, the Netherlands, Switzerland, Great Britain, Luxembourg, and Japan. And in terms of the economic and innovative results of using digital technologies, the Russian Federation ranks 38th surpassed by the leaders, such as Finland, Switzerland, Sweden, Israel, Singapore, the Netherlands, the United States, Norway, Luxembourg, and Germany.

Insufficient development of the digital economy is explained, on the one hand, by the gaps in the regulatory framework on the digital economy, as we mentioned above, and, on the other hand, by the unfavorable environment for doing business and innovating and, as a result, low application of digital technologies by business entities.

The objectives of the legal policy in the field of the digital economy are as follows:

- developing an ecosystem of the digital economy of the Russian Federation with digital data as a key production factor in all areas of socio-economic activity and effective communication, including cross-border, business, between scientific and educational community, government and citizens;
- forging required and sufficient conditions of an institutional and infrastructural nature, remove obstacles and restrictions for setting up and (or) developing high-tech business and preventing new obstacles and restrictions both in traditional sectors of the economy as well as in new industries and high-tech markets;
- increasing competitiveness in the global market of both individual sectors and the entire economy of the Russian Federation.

Conclusion

Many sources use the expression "legal policy of the state." Thus, it is emphasized that the state is one of the most active participants of the legal policy, but hardly the only one, especially at the stage of practical implementation of the main strategic objectives. The fulfillment of the specified program suggests efficient close cooperation of the state with business and science, since the main result of implementing strategic legal ideas in this area should be setting up nearly a dozen national leading companies, namely high-tech enterprises that develop the so-called "cross-cutting" technologies and manage digital platforms operating on the global market and surrounding themselves with a system of start-ups, research teams and industry-specific enterprises, which provides the development of the digital economy.

Legal policy in a specific public area has a particular vector of development. If we talk about the digital economy, then there are five main vectors:

- statutory regulation;
- HR and education;

- development of research expertise establishment of technical groundwork;
- information infrastructure;
- information security.

Let's consider each of them in detail.

The main goal of statutory regulation is to establish a fundamentally new regulatory environment designed to provide a favorable legal regime for modern technologies to be designed and developed and economic activities that are associated with the use of these technologies (digital economy) to be performed.

The following measures are provided within this vector:

- to set up a continuous mechanism to manage changes and competencies (knowledge) in the regulation of the digital economy;
- to lift key legal restrictions and establish independent legal institutions designed to deal with the priority tasks on the development of the digital economy;
- to fix a comprehensive legal regulation of relations arising in connection with the development of the digital economy;
- to adopt measures aimed at encouraging economic activity related to the use of modern technologies, data acquisition, and use;
- to devise a policy on the development of the digital economy in the Eurasian Economic Union, harmonization of approaches to legal regulation that contribute to the development of the digital economy within the Eurasian Economic Union;
- to establish a methodological background for the development of competencies in the regulation of the digital economy.

The next vector of legal policy in the field of the digital economy is HR and education. The main objectives within this vector are:

- establishing key conditions of HR training for the digital economy;
- improving the education system, which should provide the digital economy with high-skilled staff;
- the labor market that should be based on the requirements of the digital economy;

- elaborating an incentive system for mastering required competencies and participating staff in the development of the digital economy of Russia.

The vector related to the development of research competencies and technological groundwork is mainly intended to devise a research support system in the field of both search and applied digital economy (research infrastructure of digital platforms), which would ensure the technological independence of each direction of world-competitive cross-cutting digital technologies and national security.

This vector involves the following measures:

- establishing an institutional environment for R&D in the field of the digital economy;
- laying the technological groundwork in the field of the digital economy;
- training competencies in the field of the digital economy.

The vector relating to the information structure pursues the following goals:

- to develop communication networks that meet the economic needs for the collection and transfer of data belonging to the state, business, and citizens in accordance with the technical requirements of digital technologies;
- to expand a system of Russian data centers, which provides the state, business, and citizens with accessible, stable, safe, and cost-effective data storage and processing services, and also allows exporting these services;
- to introduce digital data handling platforms to meet the needs of government, business and citizens;
- to establish an effective system for collecting, processing, storing, and providing consumers with spatial data that meets the needs of the state, business, and citizens in up-to-date and reliable information on spatial objects.

And finally, the main goal of information security vector is to achieve a state of security of the person, society, and the state from internal and external information security threats, which ensure the exercise of constitutional rights and freedoms of man and citizen, decent quality and standard of life, sovereignty and sustainable socio-economic development of the Russian Federation in the digital economy. Achieving this goal involves:

- ensuring the unity, stability, and security of the information and telecommunication infrastructure of the Russian Federation at all levels of the information space;
- ensuring organizational and legal protection of the person, business and state interests in communication within the digital economy;
- forging conditions for the leadership of Russia in the export of services and information security technologies, as well as regard to national interests in international documents on information security issues.

It should be noted that the Program under consideration pays attention not only to the development of basic principles of the digital economy but also to their practical implementation. In particular, it is highlighted that "the measures in particular sectors of the economy (fields of activity), primarily healthcare, smart cities and public administration, including control and supervision activity will be implemented based on this Program amended by corresponding sections as well as action plans developed within of Program execution management system. Although it is obvious that implementation issues are out of the scope of this document.

Thus, summing up all of the above said, we can conclude that nowadays legal policy in the field of the digital economy is actively developing. The main strategic objectives and goals in this area have been set, priorities have been outlined, the main directions of legal policy and the range of measures that will be taken to implement each direction within close cooperation between the state, business entities, and representatives of the scientific community have been determined.

References

[1] Babaev, V. K. 1991. *Theory of Modern Law*. Nizhny Novgorod. 12 P.
[2] Ivanov, V. F. 2003. *Penal Policy. Russian Legal Policy: Course of Lectures.* In: N.I. Matuzov and A. V. Mal'ko (Eds). Moscow, 397 P.

[3] Lopashenko, N. A. 2003. Criminal Law Policy. Russian Legal Policy: Course of Lectures. In: N. I. Matuzov and A.V. Mal'ko (Eds). Moscow, 363 P.
[4] Mal'ko, A.V. 2000. *Modern Russian Legal Policy and Legal Life*. Legal *Policy and Legal Life*, 15 P.
[5] Mal'ko, A.V., Afanas'ev, S.F. 2014. Russian Judicial Policy: Peculiarities of Making with Regard to National and International Aspects. *State and Law* 7: 19.
[6] Matuzov, N.I. 1997. Concept and Main Priorities of Russian Legal Policy. *Legal Science* 4: 8.
[7] Matuzov, N. I. 2004. *Legal Policy as the Critical Problem of Russian Legal Science. Legal Policy: from Concept to Reality*. In: N. I. Matuzov and A. V. Mal'ko (Eds). Moscow, pp. 13-14.
[8] Rudkovskii, V. A. 2001. Law Enforcement Policy in the Structure of the Legal Policy of the Russian State. *Legal Policy and Legal Life* 3: 36.
[9] The program "Digital Economy of the Russian Federation" approved by the Resolution of the Government of the Russian Federation No. 1632-p as of July 28, 2017. *Collected Legislation of the Russian Federation*, 2017, No. 32, Article 5138.
[10] The Strategy for the Development of the Information Society in the Russian Federation for 2017-2030 approved by Decree of the President of the Russian Federation No. 203 as of May 9, 2017. *Collected Legislation of the Russian Federation*, 2017, No. 20, Art. 2901.

Chapter 6

Principles of Digital Economy Law

Aleksei V. Azarkhin*, [1], Aleksandra P. Korobova[1], Anna G. Bordakova[1] and Dmitrii A. Karev[1]

[1]Samara State University of Economics, Samara, Russia

Abstract

Relevance At the present stage of the development of the national economy, there is an arising need for its legal regulation within digitalization. The legal regulation of the digital economy will be more effective if it is based on fundamental requirements, i.e., principles of law. The principles of law are governing rules of law that determine the scope and directions of legal regulation.

The purpose of the study is to classify the principles of law that structure legal groundwork for the regulation of relations arising in the digital economy.

The methodological background of the study is the general scientific methods of formal logic and the system-structural method, as well as the specific scientific method (formal-law). The methods of formal logic made it possible to describe, compare, classify, analyze and synthesize the principles of law from the standpoint of their specific regulatory content (regulatory reduction). The system-structural method allowed classifying revealed principles of law and defining their place in the system of legal principles.

Findings and their value. When determining the classification of the principles of law in the field of legal regulation of the digital economy and digitalization of public relations, we understand that it is possible to raise efficiency both in economic and other significant areas of civil

* Corresponding Author's Email: aazarkhin@mail.ru.

In: Economic and Legal Foundations of Innovative Development …
Editors: Gabibulla Khasaev, Victoria Bolgova, Sergey Bortnikov et al.
ISBN: 978-1-68507-730-3

society due to its governing legal scope. However, it is in the production, as well as in the distribution of intangible value the role of the principles mentioned below is of particular high-performance.

Keywords: classification, legal regulation, principles of law, digitalization of law, digital economy

JEL Codes: K10, E66

Introduction

Currently, the most important objective of developing a digital economy in Russia is to establish legal, technical, organizational, and financial conditions.

The development of the digital economy implies corresponding amendments to the understanding of economic processes and ensuring rights.

The present statutory regulation of the digital economy in Russia is based on the regulation of a traditional (non-digital) economy. There is a tremendous array of acts, which provisions can be applied (and being applied) to the digital economy. At the same time, there are several acts specially designed for regulation of the digital economy that convey its specific features.

A social order that has been developed in Russia requires the law-maker to take specific approaches to the legal regulation of social relations, particularly in the legal regulation of the digital economy. This regulation will be more effective if it is based on principles regarding the specific nature of economic relations in modern Russia.

Legal principles are of high attention of domestic and foreign authors-lawyers [10, 11].

Despite the disputes on the concept of the principles of law in the scientific literature, we can say that they are the fundamental requirements that are enshrined in the legal rules, meet the moral, political and economic values of society, and govern law-making and law-enforcement.

The principles of law are expressed in more specific rules and ensure the legal nature of the legislation. We can stability a distinctive feature of the principles of law since it is this help to determine the essence of operating rules, as well as the basis for future statutory and regulatory acts [9].

Legal science classifies *general, inter-industrial, and industrial* principles [6].

When determining the classification of the principles of law in the field of legal regulation of the digital economy and digitalization of public relations, we understand that it is possible to raise efficiency both in economic and other significant areas of civil society due to its governing legal scope. However, it is in the production, as well as in the distribution of intangible value the role of the principles mentioned below is of particular high-performance.

In our opinion, the general legal principles are as follows:

- rule of law. It's the top priority of the state and an important factor that ensures economic growth. This principle predetermines the duty of all participants of the digital economy, i.e., state and municipal authorities, officials, enterprises of all forms of ownership, public organizations, and citizens, to abide by legislative rules;
- the principle of publicity of the digital economy. The provisions of Article 15 of the Constitution of the Russian Federation claim that any statutory acts concerning the rights and freedoms of man and citizen, as well as his duties, must be published. This allows ensuring public control, as well as carrying out an expert assessment of draft laws to avoid possible mistakes until they are legally enshrined. In this connection, when performing economic activities in the Russian Federation, the government must inform the citizens of the content of draft legal acts, reports on the budget execution, audit results, etc.
- the principle of the free exercise of the rights and legitimate interests of the digital economy. Here we can mention the freedom of communication, exchange, dissemination, and consumption of information of the digital economy, equal respect for freedom of expression in the digital and non-digital fields, freedom of e-business, etc.
- Within the rapidly growing pace of development of information technologies, there is an arising need for new models that regulate the processing of personal data, ensure appropriate security, and exercise the principle of free exchange of information, which can be called the primary stage of the effective development of the digital economy. Therefore, the facilitated circulation of information as the subject matter of transactions should be a general trend, and the protection of personal data and privacy should become the scope of state regulation in respect of the part that can be ensured. Corresponding rules should be reasonably limited due to the balance of interests.

- inadmissibility of establishing differences in the course of legal regulation of the digital economy and the application of the law in respect to economic agents;
- recognition, respect, and protection of the rights and freedoms of man and citizen declared the highest value that defines the meaning, scope, and application of laws, the activities of the legislative and executive authorities and local self-government bodies;
- reduction of transaction costs (transaction costs are spent on the search for the necessary information, negotiations, protection of the ownership rights of a company or enterprise. They also include the costs to avoid unreliable counterparties who can refuse from the agreements established between them and the company for their benefit and gain) incurred by state and other business entities in respect of the contract conclusion. Legal regulation should be fitted with a mechanism on the reduction of costs for information, negotiation and supervision, services of third-party market actors (legal services, corporate advertising, etc.).

The essence of the above-mentioned principle is that the state offers public benefits, such as physical protection, defense of human rights, protection from emergencies, the appropriate cultural, moral, and educational level of the population, a high level of development of science, information, transport, and energy infrastructure, etc., through legal instructions [5].

- ensuring the most favored nation principle of the private economic initiative of actors through the development of an appropriate economic strategy of the state.
- an equal combination of formal-law and informal ethical rules in regulating the behavior of the digital economy agents. Therewith, it is necessary to regard the consistency of informal ethical rules in economic relations with progressive legal rules enshrined in statutory and regulatory documents. Besides, these rules should oppose out-of-date legal rules.

Consequently, informal ethical rules in this event will play the role of a specific adjuster of current legal norms, as well as a regulator of economic activity;

- the principle of consistent legal regulation of the digital economy. Its content is that the legal rules should be consistent with the existing social system of the country, the values, and the mentality of legal persons. Besides, the principle of consistency is understood as a criterion of the performance of these rules. There is feedback through which legal persons have an opportunity to inform of the disadvantages of these rules or the reasons preventing its implementation;
- the principle of information exhaustiveness of the digital economy. It should be noted that means the availability of information and its exhaustive regulatory nature. The performance of the legal regulation of the digital economy directly depends on observance of this principle, since information is aimed at filling the gaps, decreasing the probability of chaos and disorder in economic relations, which is achieved by stuffing the legal consciousness of the subjects with the necessary information.
- the principles of arrangement and performance of the digital economy (principles of an open Internet network). The principle provides protective measures on each device and each network that ensure the user access to the full and open Internet to satisfy the need for data of the digital economy without blocking or interrupting competing services (the right to freedom of choice when accessing legitimate Internet content of digital economy; the right to launch any applications and use any services, if this does not contradict the requirements of law enforcement; the right to free connection of any legitimate devices in the event of non-damage to the network; the principle of competition between Internet providers; application and service providers; content providers.
- the principle of state digital sovereignty (on the Internet). State "digital" sovereignty covers, as a rule, the national segment of the Internet, as well as Internet legal relations, including their subjects and objects closely related to a particular state.

The activity of foreign companies processing personal data of clients that are residents of the Russian Federation (Facebook, Google, Twitter, etc.) can be an illustrative example of the issue of ensuring state sovereignty. Based on the explanations of the Ministry of Communications of the Russian Federation, "the provisions of the Federal Law "On Amendments to Particular

Legislative Acts of the Russian Federation Concerning Specification of the Procedure for Processing Personal Data in Information and Telecommunication Networks" [4] do not apply to non-residents of the Russian Federation located and working on the territory of other states.

- equality and non-discrimination in the development of information systems and their operation.

It is inadmissible to legally enshrine unjustified advantages related to the use of information technology. The state must ensure the rights of access to the data of the digital economy (access to the Internet) and govern relations arising in the course of ensuring these rights from the standpoint of the public order and international legal duties (obligations) of the corresponding state.

The constitutional legal status of an individual of the Russian Federation involves freedom of thought and speech (Part 1, Art. 29 of the Constitution of the Russian Federation), including both individual and collective freedom of speech and thought, as well as freedom of information (Part 4, Art. 29 of the Constitution of the Russian Federation). If these principles and rules of international law are interpreted in a system, they cover the entire subjective right of access to the Internet. The specified relationship (in our constitutional system it's Part 3, Art. 29 of the Constitution of the Russian Federation) is recognized by the UN [1].

Thus, the concept of Children's Information Security [8] also declares the principle of state responsibility for ensuring the respect of legitimate interests of children in the information field; the strategic goal of state policy in the field of children's information security is the development of the younger generation under elimination of all the negative factors associated with the establishment of a hyper-information society in Russia.

- ensuring the interests of national security in the development of information systems, their operation and protection of the information contained;
- the principle of privacy. The privacy issues of users of the digital economy in Russian law are governed by general rules on the necessary protection of privacy and personal data [3]. The issue of ensuring information security and protecting privacy is the most urgent concerning big data from the point of information assets. In the digital era, data (or information, computational data, data sets,

information assets) are a key object of emerging legal relations. Russian legislation establishes special legal regimes for information processing that have particular value. Thus, state secret, commercial secret, personal data (any information relating directly or indirectly to a specific or determined individual), insider information, professional secret (tax, banking), etc., are classified as restricted information. But the fact is that the unprecedented opportunities provided by modern digital technologies qualitatively change the principles of using information, the criteria for value assessment, and, respectively, the models of possible privacy threats. Data becomes an asset of tremendous value due to its so-called alternative value, as it is used for new purposes and the implementation of new ideas.

- ensuring state protection of the interests of Russian citizens in the information field [2].

Findings

Thus, we have examined the general theoretical aspects of the principles of law and classified the general, industrial and inter-industrial principles of law.

We have concluded that, on the one hand, the principles of law can be considered as the initial principles of legal regulation, which ensure the consistency and performance of the entire system of legal norms in general, and on the other hand, as a direct regulator of the behavior of all participants of public relations.

Legal measures related to the implementation of national interests in the digital economy claim abidance of antitrust laws, as well as equal tax conditions by national residents and non-residents, and the establishment of rules for non-discriminatory access to goods and services manufactured or sold by Russian companies.

The transition to a digital economy will affect not only current economic models, but will also require a substantial legal framework, which in turn should meet all the requirements of operating legislation. Also, this legal framework will become the basis for the regulation of legal relations in the field of the digital economy.

Conclusion

The foundation of the effective performance and exercise of legal relations in the digital economy is primarily the principles of digital economy law. It is the principles of law that lay the ideological and moral basis for the application of legal rules, set the goals and priorities for the development of the legal framework that governs the digital economy, determine the procedure for performance and practical application of legal rules, and constitute of a single system regulating legal relations in the digital economy.

A key principle of introducing reforms on the development of the digital economy should be the achievement of balance in ensuring the free exchange of information and a higher level of privacy and confidentiality, which is a really difficult task nowadays.

References

[1] Danilenkov, A. 2015. Copyright Fees and the Internet-Law Status of the Individual. *Economy and Law* 7: 83-94.

[2] Efimushkin, V. A., Ledovskikh, T. V., Scherbakova, E.N. 2015. Info communication Technological Space of the Digital Economy. *T-Comm.* 5: 15-20.

[3] Federal Law No. 152-FZ as of July 27, 2006 (as amended on December 31, 2017) "On Personal Data." *Collected Legislation of the Russian Federation*, 2006, No. 31 (Part 1), Art. 3451.

[4] Federal Law No. 242-FZ as of July 21, 2014 (as amended on December 31, 2014) "On Amendments to Particular Legislative Acts of the Russian Federation Concerning Specification of the Procedure for Processing Personal Data in Information and Telecommunication Networks". *Collected Legislation of the Russian Federation*, 2014, No. 30 (Part I), Art. 4243.

[5] Kuz'min, E. A. 2013. Theoretical and Empirical Study of Transaction Costs in the Economy: Transaction-intensity of the Russian Economy. News of Saratov University. New Series.i Economy. *Management. Law* 1: 29-37.

[6] Marchenko, M. N. 1996. *The Concept and Essential Features of Law. Theory of State and Law*. Moscow: Zertsalo, 295 P.

[7] *Principles of Russian Law: General Theoretical and Industrial Dimensions*. 2010. Saratov: Publishing House of Saratov State Academy of Law.

[8] Resolution of the Government of the Russian Federation No. 2471-p as of December 02, 2015 "On Approval of the Concept of Children's Information Security". Collected Legislation of the Russian Federation, 2015, No. 49, Art. 7055.

[9] Sidorkin, A. S. 2009. Principles of Law: Concept and Role in Legal Regulation. *Bulletin of the People's Friendship University of Russia, Series "Legal Sciences"* 4: 5-12.

[10] Skurko, E. V. 2008. *Principles of Law*. Moscow, Os'-89.

[11] Yavich, L. S. 1976. General Theory of Law. Leningrad: Leningrad State University, 384 P.

Chapter 7

Total Digitalization of the Modern Education System

Anna V. Guryanova[1,*], Elmira R. Khafiyatullina[2] and Ivan V. Stepanov[3]

[1] Samara State University of Economics, Samara, Russia
[2] Samara State Technical University, Samara, Russia
[3] Samara State Medical University, Samara, Russia

Abstract

The paper explores the transformation of the education system in the context of omnipresent digitalization with an emphasis on the humanitarian issues, worldview components, and social prospects of this process. The authors pay much attention to the phenomena of digital literacy, digital culture, and the digital educational environment. The latter is considered in the context of the latest educational technologies, namely the practice of online learning and lifelong learning, continuous professional education, individualization of the educational process based on advanced learning technologies. The social and economic implications of educational digitalization, as well as the specific features of arranging the modern educational environment that change the traditional roles of the tutor and student, are investigated. In the modern context, the tutor must be an advanced user of the digital educational environment resources; for students, digitalization means the targeted use of mobile and Internet technologies in the educational process, which significantly broadens the cognitive opportunities. The involvement of students in the independent search and selection of information, and in participation in project activities by the tutor develops their competencies essential for social adjustment and personal self-fulfillment in the 21st century. It is concluded that the modern education system should

In: Economic and Legal Foundations of Innovative Development …
Editors: Gabibulla Khasaev, Victoria Bolgova, Sergey Bortnikov et al.
ISBN: 978-1-68507-730-3

confidently lead society to the digital era committed to the augmentation of labor productivity, new types of labor, and the satisfaction of growing human needs.

Keywords: education, IT development, digitalization, information and communication technologies (ICT), digital educational environment, online course, digital literacy, digital culture

JEL Codes: Z10, Z13, Z19

Introduction

The modern digital revolution is far from the first revolution in human history. It was preceded by no less important revolutionary transformations, which drastically pushed the limits of the information space that was necessary and useful for a man.

According to the classification by C. Schwab, the next revolution unfolding right before our eyes is the fourth in a row [9], and, as many researchers believe, is not the last of this kind. Its key innovations are a mass-scale cheap computer, multimedia, and the Internet. A modern man has a true opportunity to get rid of quite troublesome and time-intensive work related to the collection, storage, processing, transfer, and receipt of information, and making compound computations and calculations. Multimedia has opened up for the first time the opportunity to combine different types of perception of information (for example, verbal and visual), transform it, build a virtual world and act in it. The mass-scale access to the Internet made a "miracle," having eliminated the information disunity of people and having developed a planetary information space.

All the above became possible due to the growth of the technological wave associated with the development and introduction of new technological innovations that are particularly useful for humans along with the information wave. So, for example, at the very beginning of IT development (that is, about a hundred years ago), the power of computers doubled every three years, then (in the middle of the 20th century) – every two years. At the present stage of civilization development, it is doubling annually. The result visible today, i.e., the new global digital revolution changing the world around and the person living in it, had been achieved exactly this way [2].

Innovations are actively being introduced into different areas of human life that, on the one hand, aim people at continuous development, enhancement of their knowledge, skills, competencies, mastery of new activities. On the other hand, routine work is increasingly delegated to machines, various technical devices, and a man should have the qualities, such as creative initiative, flexible thinking, willingness to cooperate with colleagues in the search for new solutions and, that is especially important, the ability to critically evaluate the information received as to the accuracy and possible logical integration into current tasks.

The importance of incorporating these qualities in the structure of modern life fundamentally changes the education system as the structure of the pedagogical process and the requirements to the tutors and students skills. Today, in primary school one should be able not only to read, write and count but also to arrange various data resources, make fruitful cooperation, productively collect information, adequately evaluate, and efficiently use it. Therefore, a competency-based educational approach has become widespread in the modern context.

All of the above stated allows talking about the need of a modern man in a special digital culture as an element of the common culture and an indispensable condition for a convenient life in society.

The targeted development of digital culture is one of the priorities of the modern education system. Successful implementation requires adjustment of the man to the continuously changing demands and conditions of a digitalizing social life. The man is changing to a great extent, being in a dialectical symbiosis with the latest digital technologies, which puts on the agenda the issue of emerging a new anthropological type, the so-called "homo informaticus" gradually turning into "homo digital" [3].

In this situation, omnipresent digitalization of the modern education system should be the subject matter of a targeted analysis with a focus on the humanitarian issues, worldview components, and social prospects for this process. This article is dedicated exactly to this topic.

Methodology

We have used the methods of philosophical, dialectic, historical, and conceptual analysis, as well as modeling, descriptive, comparative, and prognostic methods.

The method of philosophical analysis is traditionally aimed at developing a general idea and an integrated view of the object under study. Using the philosophical method, we have thoroughly studied the modern education system and its transformation in the context of omnipresent digitalization. We have emphasized the humanitarian and worldview components of this process, its social and economic premises, implications, and prospects. In the course of the analysis, we have applied several theoretical concepts that reveal the nature and essence of digitalization, and education transformation models that connect the philosophical method with the prognostic and modeling methods respectively.

We have used dialectical and historical methods that allow considering the object under study, namely the transformation of the educational system in the context of omnipresent digitalization, in its inherent variability, historical evolution, and dynamics. The application of the dialectical method also makes it possible to demonstrate the large-scale changes occurring in the modern education system in their interrelation and interdependence. We are talking, in particular, about the dialectical interaction of ICT and digital infrastructure, life-long-learning practices and online learning, communication between students and tutors in the context of omnipresent digitalization, etc.

The descriptive method is intended to describe the transformation of the education system from IT development to digitalization and to reveal the specific features of these two adjacent periods. It is complemented by a comparative method to compare the stages of IT development and digitalization of society in general and the educational system in particular. Using this method, we concluded that the IT development stage is successfully completed to date, while digitalization, on the contrary, is gathering pace. It s a new stage of education system modernization designed to take society to the digital level of development.

Findings

Transformation of the Modern Educational Environment: From IT Development to Digitalization

Until recent times, researchers mainly discussed the IT development of education [5]. This term is usually understood as a system of measures on the transformation of pedagogical processes by introducing information products, tools, and technologies into training and education. However, IT development today can be deemed completed. Educational institutions of all levels have been equipped with a computer and tutors have completed training and retraining courses on the use of information and communication technologies (ICT) in the learning process. The main areas of ICT application in education are the development of pedagogical software for various purposes, educational websites, methodological and didactic materials, the management of real objects, arranging and conducting computer experiments with virtual models, and the targeted search for information [1].

It should be recognized that all these impressive innovations brought by the era of IT development have already become part of our everyday life. IT development of education has laid the foundation to take a new qualitative level that is aimed at training specialists who have demanded skills on the labor market, easily and freely use mobile and Internet technologies, as well as at continuous self-education and advanced training through e-learning. The modern world has advanced even further, moving to the next round in the development of new technologies.

An intensive IT development was followed by a new era, i.e., omnipresent digitalization or, as it is also called, the era of Big Data and the related technologies.

On the one hand, digital technologies contribute to further growth of production output and efficiency, and on the other hand, they allow applying an individual approach to different areas of human and social life. So, for example, using 3D printing technology makes it possible to develop the most complex devices in a single copy that was unprofitable and impossible within traditional industrial production.

It is well-known that the term "digitalization" itself emerged in relation to the intensive development of ICT. The catalyst for digital transformation itself was the development of semiconductor electronic computing machines in the 60s of the 20th century, personal computers – in the 1970s of the same century, and the Internet – in the 1990s. According to K. Schwab s forecasts, the further development of technologies will move towards the intensification of the Internet omnipresence, technology mobility, miniaturization of technical devices, and the development of artificial intelligence [9]. Most predicted innovations can be already observed in modern reality.

The emergence and quick diffusion of the Internet marked the development of a special virtual world filled with new information and communication networks, such as online games, social networks, etc. Moreover, the real and virtual worlds were found to be interdependent, and their merger led to the formation of another "hybrid" world [4]. In a hybrid world, a person takes necessary actions in the real world using the capacity and resources of the virtual world. An indispensable condition for successful interactions is the efficiency of ICT and the availability of digital infrastructure.

Digitalization as a New Stage of the Education System Modernization

Digital resources widely used today in the everyday life of a man have a significant impact on the educational environment and make it possible to overcome the traditional education barriers. This is expressed in the development pace of educational programs, in the available choice of a tutor, as well as forms and methods of training. The modern education system is designed to confidently lead society to the digital era. Therefore, it should be committed to the augmentation of labor productivity, the introduction of new types of labor, and the satisfaction of growing human needs. It appears that all this will become possible by engaging in the educational process the best possible number (all people under perfect scenario) of the social groups, developing individual "learning paths," managing own learning achievements, and including them in real, virtual, and augmented reality.

It should also be noted that digital technology in the modern world is not only a tool but also a special existential environment that opens up truly unlimited opportunities for a man, namely: training at any time convenient, life-long learning technology, the opportunity of the consumer to be a direct electronic resources developer, etc. In education, digitalization is primarily aimed at ensuring the continuity of the learning process (education throughout life) and continuous professional education [7]. Individualization of education based on advanced-learning technologies is also important. The latter term is not yet established, but usually, it means the use of Big Data in learning particular subjects by every single student and therefore the automatic adaptation of the learning process to a large extent. A full-fledged application of virtualization techniques augmented reality, cloud computing, and many other modern technologies are also expected.

The digital environment arranged this way puts forward completely new demands both to the educational system itself and to its direct creator-tutor.

Nowadays the tutor is expected to have a fundamentally different mentality, up-to-date worldview corresponding to the modern level of ICT development, new approaches, and techniques in communication with students. The tutor thereby becomes not only a bearer of knowledge generally shared with students but also their guide to the digital world. He must be digitally literate, be able to create and apply content through various digital technologies, including computer programming skills, search for information and exchange of it, use of electronic communication resources, etc.

Thus, educational digitalization directly depends on the tutor s proficiency in digital technologies to be efficiently used in educational activities. In this regard, developing the ability to navigate the flow of digital information, efficiently use it, process it, and incorporate it into new technological solutions [6] has become of particular importance. Such changes require the tutor to be an advanced user of the digital educational environment resources. For students, educational digitalization means the use of mobile and Internet technologies that expands the cognitive horizons of knowledge and make them truly endless. The efficient use of digital technologies, the involvement of students in an independent search for information and its selection as well as in participation in project activities develops their competencies essential for social adjustment and personal self-fulfillment in 21st-century society.

Social and Economic Implications of Educational Digitalization

As noted above, IT development at the initial stages was reduced to purely technical measures, such as automation of technologies, the spread of the Internet, mobile communications, social networks, the advent of smartphones, growth of human needs related to the acquisition and use of new technologies, etc. However, digital technologies rapidly became an integral part of the economic, political, and cultural life of society. Today, information and knowledge are the foundation of effective economic progress where traditional concepts and models are almost unacceptable [11]. The most important distinguishing feature of a specialist relevant to the realities of the digital economy is in-depth knowledge of digital technologies, as well as skills of their application in the professional activity [10].

Unlike the electronic form, the digital one promotes a more accurate presentation of information, ensures its free circulation, publication, processing, and use in computer networks. However, today digitalization is not only the direct translation of information into digital form and not even a digital method of communication, recording, and transmission of data via digital devices. Digitalization implies changing the entire paradigm of communication between people and society, which, in turn, have an impact on the infrastructural, managerial, behavioral, and cultural areas of modern society. In this regard, the concepts of "digital ecosystem," "digital environment," "digital community," "digital economy," etc., appear in different areas of social life.

The "digitalization of education" under analysis is no exception. Nowadays, digitalization is an integral part of the educational process that becomes indeed mass-scale in terms of its impact on the education system. A logical implication of educational digitalization is changing in the labor market at the intersection with educational services, precisely in educational standards. It helps to reveal new needs and develop new competencies of the population. In general, digitalization is aimed at the re-arrangement of the educational process and the re-evaluation of the strategy of communicative interaction between the tutor and student.

On the one hand, digitalization undermines the inherited methodological basis of the educational system, and on the other hand, it provides tutors and students with access to the most diverse information (textual, audio, and visual). Accessibility of information requires a continuous search for and selection of relevant, informative, and interesting content, as well as a high processing rate. Thus, the digitalization of education leads to its fundamental qualitative restructuring. All its participants, and first of all, tutors should learn to operate with new technological tools and practice almost unlimited information resources if necessary.

Digital Educational Technologies and Their Role in the Transformation of Education

Digitalization transforms the social paradigm of human life. It opens up the opportunities of acquiring and enhancing knowledge, and broadens the horizons. Virtual reality technologies make it possible to use digital simulators irrespective of the workplace, which automatically expands the scope of their potential consumers.

Technologies of modern mobile learning allow studying anytime and anywhere. Children of different ages adjust the quickest to the digital environment. They invisibly, gradually absorb the initial digital skills and abilities for their subsequent targeted development. The further development of particular competencies happens at different levels of the educational system. But, we should make a point that digital competencies are developing throughout the entire life of the man.

In recent times, open online resources have been actively developed and used in the educational environment, starting from individual tasks and tests to full-scale courses (modules) aimed at cultivating necessary competencies. The dynamics of online learning is rising over time. The online course is developed using software solutions that enable the course to be made up of available information resources in a specialized software medium. The primary goal of the education system in the context of introducing new technological tools and consuming truly unlimited information resources is precisely to learn their efficient use [8].

The first step on this path is the practical implementation of online courses and blended learning, which opens up a pool of unlimited educational opportunities committed to high-quality education of every single person regardless of the place of residence and skills and in accordance with individual interests and abilities. In a perfect scenario, all operating and newly developed online course platforms should be integrated into a system similar to the "single-window." The students will be able to choose courses by priority criteria, such as demand, tutor s rating, and popularity. Students will not have to puzzle brains about the transfer of course credits to another university since all the information will be automated into a single database.

Given the foregoing, a long-term purpose of the modern education system is to raise tutors digital literacy, which is reflected not only in the development of online courses but also in the consistent use of the digital medium in the learning process. Digital literacy is the ability to understand the cultural context of the Internet environment, made up and apply this content through digital technologies, including skills of computer programming, searching for and exchanging information. This is the ability to communicate in online communities and self-develop.

As we can see, the meaning of "digital literacy" is clarified in general to date. But the term will be completely clear if control and communication between man/society and the latest digital technologies are specificated. Competent management of digitalization is feasible provided that unified databases and criteria for the effectiveness of training (in other words, under an integrated approach that clearly defines the goals, framework, and content of the educational process) are developed.

Conclusion

In modern conditions, the education system is designed to confidently lead society to the digital era committed to the augmentation of labor productivity and the introduction of its new types, growing human needs. It is possible through the engagement of all social groups into the educational process, development of individual "learning paths," management of own learning achievements, and targeted use of capacity and resources of virtual and augmented reality. Digitalization of education leads to educational standards to be amended, needs for the development of new competencies of the population to be revealed and the labor market to be transformed respectively.

Omnipresent digitalization is oriented toward re-arrangement of the educational process and re-evaluation of the role of tutors and students. On the one hand, digitalization undermines the inherited methodological basis of the educational system, but on the other hand, it makes information accessible in its diverse forms and manifestations (textual, audio, and visual). Accessibility of information foregrounds the need for continuous search and selection of relevant, cognitively valuable, and interesting content, as well as high speeds processing rate. Thus, the digitalization of education leads to its fundamental qualitative restructuring. The priority of a contemporary tutor is to learn how to use new technological tools and operate with almost unlimited information resources.

Digitalization transforms the very social paradigm of human life, opens up new opportunities for acquiring and enhancing knowledge, broadening the horizons. Digital technologies in the modern world are not only a tool but also a special existential environment with truly unlimited opportunities for a man.

This is training at a convenient time, the opportunity to get life-long learning and continuous advanced training and to master learning material through online courses, etc. Omnipresent digitalization requires the students to use mobile and Internet technologies, thereby broadening the horizons of their cognition. The efficient use of technologies, the involvement of students in the independent search and selection of information, and participation in project activities develop the competencies required for life in the 21st century.

References

[1] Guryanova, A., Astafeva, N., Filatova, N., Khafiyatullina, E., Guryanov, N. 2019. *Philosophical Problems of Information and Communication Technology in the Process of Modern Socio-Economic Development.* In: E. G. Popkova and V. N. Ostrovskaya (Eds). *Prospects of the Use of New Information and Communication Technology (ICT) in the Modern Economy.* Advances in Intelligent Systems and Computing, Vol. 726. Springer International Publishing AG, Springer, Cham, pp. 1033-1040.

[2] Guryanova, A., Astafeva, N., Filatova, N., Khafiyatullina, E., Guryanov, N. 2019. *Global Crisis: Overcoming the Uncertainty of the Concept in the Philosophical Paradigm of Globalization.* In: E. G. Popkova (Ed). *The Future of the Global Financial System: Downfall or Harmony.* Lecture Notes in Networks and Systems, Vol. 57. Springer Nature Switzerland AG, pp. 836-843.

[3] Guryanova, A., Khafiyatullina, E., Kolibanov, A., Makhovikov, A., Frolov, V. 2018. *Philosophical View on Human Existence in the World of Technic and Information.* In: E. G. Popkova (Ed). *The Impact of Information on Modern Humans.* Advances in Intelligent Systems and Computing, Vol. 622. Springer International Publishing AG, Springer, Cham, pp. 97-104.

[4] Keshelava, A. V. 2017. *Introduction to Digital Economy.* Vniigeosystems. Moscow.

[5] Kolmakov, V. Yu. 2009. *Human of Digital Civilization*, Vol. 8. Krasnoyarsk: Litera-Print.

[6] Pecherskaya, E., Averina, L., Kamaletdinov, Yu., Tretyakova, N., Magomadova, T. 2016. Assessment of Critical Success Factors Transformation in ERP Projects. *IJME - Mathematics education* 11(7): 2608-2625.

[7] Pecherskaya, E., Averina, L., Kochetckova, N., Chupina, V., Akimova, O. 2016. The methodology of Project Managers Competency Formation in CPE. *IJME - Mathematics education* 11(8): 3066-3075.

[8] Pecherskaya, E., Averina, L., Kozhevnikova, S. 2018. ERP Implementation Challenge: Case-Study of the Russian Federation. *Astra Salvensis, Special issue,* 411-423.

[9] Schwab, K. 2017. *The Fourth Industrial Revolution.* Moscow: Exmo.

[10] Shestakov, A., Noskov, E., Tikhonov, V., and Astafeva, N. 2017. *Economic Behavior and the Issue of Rationality.* In: E. G. Popkova (Ed). *Russia and the European Union: Development and Prospects. Contributions to Economics.* Springer International Publishing AG, Cham, Switzerland, pp. 327-332.

[11] Shestakov, A., Stotskaya, T., Mingulov, H., Zaitseva, N. 2017. *Experience of Moral Philosophy in Formation of Economic Theory.* In: E. G. Popkova (Ed). *Overcoming Uncertainty of Institutional Environment as a Tool of Global Crisis Management.* Contributions to Economics. Springer, Cham. pp. 629-634.

Chapter 8

Issues, Risks, and Prospects of Legal Education in the Context of Digital Economies

Irina V. Smotrova[1,*], Irina V. Tekucheva[2] and Artem I. Krivtsov[3,4]

[1]Center for Practical Psychology of Education of the Academy of Social Management, Moscow, Russia
[2]Moscow State Pedagogical University, Moscow, Russia
[3]Moscow State Institute of International Relations, Moscow, Russia
[4]State Marine Technical University of St. Petersburg, St. Petersburg, Russia

Abstract

The article deals with the issues of legal education arising out of global digitalization and the development of the digital economy. The issues have multidimensional nature and include the transformation of the entire training system of legal specialists and alteration of the psychology and worldview of the whole society that should be ready for the adoption of "technological innovations." [14]. Today, lawyers with digital competencies, new qualities, and traits are in demand. The paper provides a risk assessment due to robotization and the use of artificial intelligence (AI) and the "artificial neural network" (ANN) in the legal field. The extensive use of network technologies nowadays enables many people around the world to solve legal issues without the direct participation of lawyers. Therefore, some experts express concern about the future of the legal profession. However, it is hard to imagine how artificial intelligence can replace a person in matters requiring an unambiguous solution or taking into account the human factor, which is often based on emotions [5]. At the same time, the emergence of new

---

[*] Corresponding Author's E-mail: i-smotrova@mail.ru.

In: Economic and Legal Foundations of Innovative Development …
Editors: Gabibulla Khasaev, Victoria Bolgova, Sergey Bortnikov et al.
ISBN: 978-1-68507-730-3

legal specialties, which is a natural result of the total social digitalization of society and the transformation of labor relations, is expected in the future. The main goal of legal education today is to train lawyers who can compete with machines.

Keywords: digitalization, digital economy, legal education, digital transformation, artificial intelligence

Introduction

Global digital changes in the modern world are often called the "point of no-return" [1]. The effect of these changes is the emergence of new forms of public life and public relations, the transformation of the main areas of life (economy, security, science, education, medicine, management). Digitalization of the economic system today is the indispensable condition for the development of the state, the establishment of a sustainable economy, the growth of social welfare, and the improvement of public relations [4]. The digital economy is directly determined by the intensive development of information and communication technologies (ICT). It plays a leading role in all areas of socio-economic activity.

In a short time, the digital transformation of the world from a personal computer and the Internet has led to breakthrough technologies (3D printing, blockchain, Big Data, biogenic engineering). New drivers of digital investment growth, such as AI, ANN, big data, 5G technologies, the Internet of things, and cloud technologies have emerged. They allow performing functional tasks in the shortest term and at the lowest cost.

However, these digital phenomena today do not have well-defined legal regulations. In this regard, the digital economy urgently needs full-fledged legal support, experts with both fundamental and theoretical applied knowledge in the legal regulation of digital relations. Modern lawyers should have a comprehensive understanding and knowledge of modern economic development trends and technologies used in the digital economy, the current level, and the prospects for legal counseling of economic relations.

A lawyer of the digital era should be able to not only use information that is easy to find in the network sources but also transform it according to objectives, learn to work with cryptocurrency, provide support of ICO projects and automate legal processes, be able to provide services using electronic technologies, for example, electronic signature, electronic document workflow, smart contracts.

An only thorough study of the labor market and the demanded competencies will make it possible to train lawyers for the digital economy.

Methodology

For the consideration of the problem related to the training of lawyers in the new digital reality, we have used the following methods of scientific research:

1. The dialectical method allows exploring the object under consideration (legal education in the context of the digital economy) in its genesis and shows the current state of the problem of our research that is determined by global digitalization processes. The dialectical method makes it possible to develop a search and regulation strategy for the solution of the research problem.
2. The analytical method of research allows us to identify and analyze current trends in the development of legal education and reveal a cause-and-effect relationship between the global phenomenon of digitalization and the new requirements for the content of the legal profession.
3. The descriptive method makes it possible to distinguish and describe the most important, significant, and specific features of lawyer's training in the era of the digital economy.
4. The critical method allows studying the essence of legal education issues, estimating available foreign experience, shape own vision of the situation on the back of the knowledge acquired, and developing a unique project for training a "digital" lawyer.
5. The prognostic method provides an opportunity to make up recommendations on reduction of risks, prevention of possible problems in training lawyers for the digital economy, as well as outline the prospects for the development of the legal profession in the context of digitalization.

Findings

The Impact of Digital Technology on the Professional Domain

The integration of digital technologies in the economic and social areas of society is going at the ever-biggest pace and scale. The intensive substitution of a person by a machine, the digitalization of society, personality, education, and occupation of traditional professional areas of a man by robots have an impact on employment in general and the division of labor in particular [14].

Education, which is designed to train specialists with digital knowledge and skills, is directly involved in this process. Accordingly, the professional competencies of specialists for various industries, markets, and business directions are being upgraded in accordance with the demands of new digital economic models. However, the digital economy is not only a new economic system. It transforms social relations and dramatically changes the social essence [7]. It is extremely important to consider these facts in the training of lawyers.

Issues of Legal Education in the Digital Economy

The headlong introduction of digital technologies in the economy posed serious challenges to legal education. In the short term, it is necessary to train a sufficient number of lawyers with a targeted combination of qualities and traits same as the specialists of countries of the European Community [13].

For appropriate training programs to be developed, one should have a clear idea of a "digital" lawyer.

Undoubtedly, a modern lawyer should have multi-professional knowledge, flexible thinking, and ability to quickly assimilate new skills and find innovative solutions. The goal of modern legal education is to develop competencies regarding the demands of the digital economy and a person of a new technological community.

In this connection, the legal education system must be dramatically changed. However, educational institutions cannot quickly adapt to fast-transforming conditions due to their inertness [9]. Also, the development of the digital economy is closely related to human nature, which is changing much more slowly in contrast with whirlwind changes in the world under the influence of information technology and telecommunications [6]. As a result, today we can outline several significant problems that hinder the prompt solution of the problem related to training of lawyers for the new digital era:

Digitalization of the Legal Education System

Digitalization is not just a technological shifting from an analog form of information transmission to a digital one. As a result of the mass-scale introduction of digital technologies, human consciousness changes. This is expressed in new ways of exploring the reality, alteration of value and idea attitudes, changing culture and worldview. A fundamentally new mentality of a digitally thinking person is being formed [7]. The digitalization of the legal education system consists involves not only the digitization of document workflow, textbooks, teaching materials, and access to high-speed Internet. It is necessary to provide educational institutions with information systems that allow getting access to educational resources from any device regardless of location and time [12].

Forward Development of Theory over Practice

Forward development of theory over the practice in the digital economy will persist. The consequence of this situation is insufficient number or unavailability of basic research, professional, educational, and methodological literature for the training of "digital" lawyers. Given the pace of changes in digital technology, new literature will quickly become obsolete too. However, time dictates the need not only that education should meet the needs of the digital society, but also act ahead [8].

Individualization of the Educational Path

Today, mass-scale education aimed at training lawyers under a single program has become out-of-date. The digital economy requires self-development, self-organization, and learning ability. Training of students should be variable to get additional education in disciplines related to jurisprudence, such as IT, a foreign language, or psychology. Personal learning paths should be introduced into the educational process that will allow future lawyers to independently choose the ways (formal, non-formal, informal) of developing the core competencies of the digital economy [14].

Lifelong Learning

Being demanded in the labor market makes a person be a permanent participant in changing digital reality. Life-long learning is education throughout life that should become the standard practice and need. A lawyer can independently develop in the digital area with the help of e-learning at any convenient time, as well as to build their educational path.

Staff Provision of the Educational Process

Digital reality requires teachers to quickly adapt to new conditions, master e-learning skills and modern IT technologies, and continuously develop themselves in the context of the digital economy. It is necessary to use information technology and social networks to acquire digital competencies in an individual path [10]. However, it is hard for teachers to adopt the occurring changes and fundamentally change the mentality, work style, psychology, and perception of the digital world picture, which is a constraining factor in the improvement of their digital professionalism.

Besides, traditional education is no longer suitable for the training of lawyers in the new digital reality. Teachers need to master new teaching forms and technologies. For example, its blended learning is successfully practiced in many countries instead of the traditional one, as well as problem-based, active or cooperative learning [3].

Digital Literacy

Digital literacy includes the required knowledge and skills to ensure the safe and efficient use of digital technologies and Internet resources, which is an important condition for a professional competitive lawyer since his work relates to large flows of information and the need for multi-channel assimilation and transmission of information. The competitiveness of modern specialists is determined not only by their computer and Internet literacy. A lawyer should be able to quickly provide services with the help of high-tech tools, such as e-signature, crypto channels, electronic document workflow, smart contracts, provide support of ICO projects and automate legal processes [1].

The educational system will likely train HR that won't be demanded in the digital economy due to the unavailability of operational communication between the labor market and the legal education system.

The Risks of the Legal Profession in the Digital Era

The intensive introduction of digital technologies inevitably leads to changes in the professional domain. Today, the transformation and future of the legal profession often become the topic of discussion due to the advent of special programs, AI, and ANN.

The McKinsey Global Institute (MGI) predicts that in the next 20 years up to 50 percent of business operations can be automated [1]. The development of information technology in jurisprudence has already made it possible to automate standard legal services and has also contributed to the growth of online legal services, the use of e-justice, and the development of solutions with the aid of artificial intelligence. As a result, there has been a sharp decline in demand for basic legal services because the information has become available to the general public and free. Now any person can easily install a legal database, draw up a simple statement of claim or a contract, register a business or fill in a return. The idea of legal services consists in making them easier, more understandable, and cheaper. The growth of trust in online services naturally increases the number of users.

The number of online services providing legal services to clients in today's world is constantly growing and upgrading. LegalZoom and Rocket Lawyer are popular sites in the USA and Russia that are designed for legal counseling both on business and personal issues (real estate planning, getting a divorce). Similar Russian legal Internet services for clients Pravoved.ru or 48 Prav.ru unite a wide base of lawyers who provide legal advice on typical issues. The ConsApp service was developed for round-the-clock counseling in online chat. In the USA, the demand for online services is higher since there medium-sized and IT-business are more developed than in Russia.

A product of the digital industry often called a lawyer bot is extensively being introduced into human life around the world. It can perform the tasks of assistant defense lawyers or starting lawyers in legal companies. Often these bots are self-learning, which allows setting up a specific task. For example, these are the bots from LiveChat24/7, which are developed for the WordPress platform. A lot of sites are now developed on WordPress, including Russia. For several years, the XINING robot, which is designed to provide legal public services in China, has been operating. A robotic lawyer can provide legal advice on the issues of marriage, consumer rights, social security, give information on legal companies, forensic examination, and intermediation. In total, the base of artificial intelligence contains 50,000 questions from the legal field. However, the use of robots in the justice system, delegation of functions of corporate lawyers, brokers, consultants, and other persons to them requires additional legal regulation [2].

Experts associate the changes in the legal profession and approaches to justice also with legal tech. In light of the technical revolution in the United States of the early 2000s, the intensive introduction of legal breakthrough technology "legal tech" has started. Legal tech is a domain specializing in information technology support of legal activities and the provision of legal services to the public. Client legal-tech services, which include various document creators, web platforms for lawyer search, chatbots, online consultations help millions of people quickly and inexpensively solve their legal issues. Nowadays you can draw up an agreement online and verify it with the help of a lawyer through an accessible program, resolve a legal dispute or get advice via a legal tech service in just a few minutes. Large companies charge over artificial intelligence different tasks from termination of complex contracts to electronic document workflow, legal examination of contracts, legal research, and cost management. The digital machine generates answers to legal questions in plain language and predicts the outcome of the case tried in court with over 90% accuracy, reduces the search for trademarks and helps to disseminate legal knowledge without intermediaries, encodes expert recommendations, and makes them available around the clock.

Some experts predict the disappearance of the legal profession thanks to the use of artificial neural networks (ANN). Neural networks are learning computer program that simulates natural intelligence using computational algorithms.

An experiment conducted on the LawGeex online legal platform where 20 highly skilled lawyers competed with neural networks, showed that a specially trained system studied five non-disclosure agreements and identified 30 violations in five seconds. Besides, some of them required an arbitration court and damages faster and more accurately than live competitors. Moreover, the accuracy of the task execution by INN was 95 percent, while the accuracy of opponents was only 85 percent. The time taken by them was one and a half hours. However, learning ANN and getting a good result requires a very large and high-quality database from the corresponding domain area, stable judicial practice, and rare amendments in the legislation.

In recent times smart contracts that can be concluded using a decentralized ledger technology have gained popularity. They are also called blockchain-driven self-executing, digital or smart contracts. It is believed that the blockchain if it does not completely replace the lawyer, will dramatically change the legal profession. Thanks to smart contracts, traditional documents will disappear, and money transfers, the exchange of shares, property, and other assets will be effected through the blockchain without intermediaries. Such a mechanism will help make banking operations transparent, avoid a conflict of interest, in particular, not depend on the financial interests of lawyers and make people master the digital culture and take responsibility for their actions.

To date there are cyber systems capable of self-learning; debate programs have been developed that triumph over man in legal debates; as well as ones that can expose falsehood and perjured testimony and respond to the emotional and psychological states of people.

It's complicated for a man to compete with artificial intelligence that successfully copes with legal tasks. However, today robots perform formal functions and can only facilitate the work of the lawyer and charge him off invisible routine operations [11]. Electronic intelligence in solving various legal problems is a tool that must be used by every lawyer.

Prospects for the Development of the Legal Profession during the Global-Scale Digitalization

Artificial intelligence should be regarded as an opportunity, and not as a threat to the legal profession since the robot cannot cope with the tasks in some situations:

- for example, in the event of a dispute between the parties. A court judgment is rendered on the ground of personal convictions, regarding and assessing many details and evidence, as well as their combination. Artificial intelligence cannot take these aspects into account, and the robot cannot be trained in this way;
- complicated civil or criminal cases require examination of some circumstances, which can be interpreted ambiguously from the legal point of view;
- continuously changing legislative framework call for regular monitoring of all changes that today can be done only by a man.

The very fact that the machine does not have consciousness and mind, does not understand the meaning of words, gives us reason to hope that a living lawyer will be in demand, at least for a long time. However, it's not enough just to be human to compete with robots and be in demand in the labor market. Given the digitalization and aggressive introduction of IT technologies in our lives, legal education providing fundamental interdisciplinary training of professional staff is becoming especially relevant. Therefore, legal education should be aimed at new professions at the intersection of law and programming, law and economics. According to expert opinion, by 2030, completely new specialties, such as network lawyers and virtual defense lawyers, will be prioritized in the legal field. The professional competence of a network lawyer will include the ability to build regulatory interaction on the Internet (including, the virtual world), to develop a system of the legal protection of a person and property in the Internet space, including virtual property. A network lawyer should have command of foreign languages, industry-specific knowledge of partner countries, and feel free in a variety of consumer requests.

The specialty of a virtual defense lawyer who works on a distant basis (via the Internet), including defense in court, is popular too. Already today, many lawyers provide legal services to several organizations at once using information networks.

Experts believe that a single-subject specialty will become the main criterion for a lawyer to be demanded. The more specialized the man, the higher the demand (for example lawyer-financial expert, a defense lawyer in roboethics, labor law lawyer, cyber-investigator, business lawyer, and road traffic accident lawyer).

Conclusion

Fundamental changes in the system of legal education cannot be made and the problem of training specialists for the digital economy cannot be tackled without the solution of several problems. The main one is the establishment of a regulatory framework that ensures the education of legal specialists and the development of a strategy for the improvement of legal education. Besides, it is necessary to develop a methodological foundation for bringing up lawyers' competencies in the digital economy, amend professional standards, and provide educational institutions with modern material and technical facilities. It will take some time to train a new generation of tutors for work in new conditions.

However, the most complex link in this chain is a man. It is necessary to change the consciousness of both the future lawyer and the man, in general, to make them able to understand and accept digital reality, be ready for changes, continuous learning and self-education, and transformation of the surrounding world.

References

[1] Aptekman, A., Kalabin, V., Klintsy, V., Kuznetsova, E., Kulagin, V., Yasenovets, I. 2017. *Digital Russia: A New Reality*. URL: https:/ /www.tadviser.ru/images/c/c2/Digital-Russia-report.pdf Accessed May 6, 2019.

[2] Bortnikov, S.P. 2020. *Robot Liability or Product Liability?* In: S. Ashmarina, A. Mesquita, M. Vochozka (Eds). *Digital Transformation of the Economy: Challenges, Trends, and New Opportunities*. Advances in Intelligent Systems and Computing, Vol. 908. Springer, Cham, pp. 32-41.

[3] Danker, B. 2015. Using a Flipped Classroom Approach to Explore Deep Learning in Large Classrooms. *IAFOR Journal of Education* 3(1): 171-186.

[4] Decree of the President of the Russian Federation No. 203 as of May 09, 2017. The Strategy for the Development of the Information Society in the Russian Federation for 2017-2030. URL: https: //www.garant.ru/products/ipo/prime/doc/71570570/ Accessed April 3, 2019).

[5] Gur'yanova, A., Astaf'eva, N., Filatova, N., Khafiyatullina, E., Gur'yanov, N. 2019. *Philosophical Problems of Information and Communication Technology in the Process of Modern Socioeconomic Development.* In: E.G. Popkova and V.N. Ostrovskaya (Eds). *Perspectives on the Use of New Information and Communication Technology (ICT) in the Modern Economy*. Advances in Intelligent Systems and Computing, Vol. 726. Springer, Cham, pp. 1033-1040.

[6] Gur'yanova, A., Khafiyatullina, E., Kolibanov, A., Makhovikov, A., Frolov, V. 2018. *Philosophical View on Human Existence in the World of Technic and Information.* Advances in Intelligent Systems and Computing, Vol. 622. Springer, Cham, pp. 97-104.

[7] Gur'yanova, A.V., Smotrova, I.V., Makhovikov, A.E., Koychubaev, A.S. 2020. *Socio-ethical Issues of the Digital Economy: Challenges and Risks*. In: S. Ashmarina, A. Mesquita, M. Vochozka (Eds). *Digital Transformation of the Economy: Challenges, Trends, and New Opportunities*. Advances in Intelligent Systems and Computing, Vol. 908. Springer, Cham, pp. 92-106.

[8] Hangeldiev, I.G. 2018. Digital Era: Whether Perhaps Advancing Education? *Bulletin of Moscow University, Series 20 "Teacher Education"* 3: 48-60.

[9] Ignatova, N.Y. 2017. *Education in the Digital Era*. Nizhny Tagil Institute of Technology.

[10] Khramtsova, N.G., Maiborodova, T.Y. 2019. Approaches to the Development of Digital Competences of Legal Students. *Journal of Perspectives on Science and Education* 1(37): 80-83.

[11] Klovait, N., Erofeeva, M. 2019. Work in the Era of Intelligent Machines: The Birth of Invisible Automation. *Logos* 29-1(128): 53-84.

[12] Kudlaev, M.S. 2018. The Process of Educational Digitalization in Russia. *Young Scientist Journal* 31: 3-7.

[13] Schwab, K. 2016. *Fourth Industrial Revolution.* URL: http://e-libra.su/read/497455-chetvertaya-promyshlennaya-evolyuciya.html Accessed May 15, 2019.

[14] Shnyagin, A.V. 2014. On the Problems of Professional Training of Future Lawyers in Higher Education. *Young Scientist Journal* 10: 452-454.

[15] Zhiltsov, N.A., Cherdakov, O.I. 2018. On the Development Concept of Legal Education in the Era of the Digital Economy. URL: http://lawacademy.ru/docs/nid/koncepcija_cifrovoi_mir.pdf Accessed May 30, 2019.

Chapter 9

Countering Extremism among Young People with the Help of New Information Technologies

Irina E. Milova[*]**, Maksim A. Yavorskii and Renat R. Khasnutdinov**
Samara State University of Economics, Samara, Russia

Abstract

The purpose of the research is to explore and give general characteristics of the main directions of youth extremism prevention through the use of information technologies. *Methodology*. This research has been carried out with the help of both general scientific methods, such as analysis, synthesis, deduction, generalization, and specific scientific methods, such as comparative-law, systemic and structural. Comparative-law analysis has been used to reveal peculiarities of attitudes towards combating extremism among experts and researchers in this field. The system-structural method allowed summarizing the main directions of counter-extremism policy among young people with the help of new information technologies at the present stage of development. *Subject-matter.* The article studies the main directions of youth extremism prevention through the use of information technologies. The author's opinion on the role and place of information technology in counter-extremism among young people is presented. It is noted that an important area of application of IT technologies is information support of anti-extremism. Besides, the use of new information capabilities can contribute to the patriotic education of the younger generation, and the Internet should be considered as a practical platform within the educational activities of higher educational institutions. *Findings*. The

[*] Corresponding Author's Email: irina.milova@ro.ru.

In: Economic and Legal Foundations of Innovative Development …
Editors: Gabibulla Khasaev, Victoria Bolgova, Sergey Bortnikov et al.
ISBN: 978-1-68507-730-3

use of IT technologies plays an important role in the information support of anti-extremism among young people. When developing preventive measures against youth extremism, one should regard progress in the information domain and the growing importance of the Internet among young people. The informational counter-extremism on the Internet is restricting access to extremist information, educational outreach activities, and awareness-raising support for the execution of anti-terrorism measures. Moreover, this activity should be integrated and based on the close cooperation of public authorities with civil society institutions.

Keywords: counteraction, prevention, extremism, young people, information technology, information domain, state youth policy

Introduction

The issues of developing innovative technologies in the information domain within theoretical and (that's the most important) in practical terms are of great importance for the modern fast-changing world.

This article is an attempt to understand the role and place of information technology from the legal and pedagogical standpoint in the significant and topical area of counter-extremism, especially among young people.

As it seems to us, on the one hand, the phrases "modern youth" and "information technology" are synonymous and intertwined. On the other hand, the manifestations of youth extremism are increasingly frequently considered as an adverse effect of the development of information technologies that are aimed, as we know, at producing information for human analysis and subsequent decision-making on the execution of an action.

Today, the use of the global information and telecommunications network "Internet" as a platform for the dissemination of extremist ideology and the propagation of hatred and hostility is steadily growing. It is modern mass media that often contribute to the escalation of not just criminal, but quite aggressive and extremist trends in Russian society.

The Internet and its "derivatives" are also considered as a "tool for the propagation of extremism" [7], and as a means of "youth audience's extremization" [2], or as a method of "online recruiting" of new radicals [1, 11].

The studies dedicated to the below-mentioned topics are of particular interest:

- countering extremism and terrorism on the Internet and the educational environment [10, 21, 22];
- psychological issues of involving young people in extremist groups on the Internet [8];
- the issues of spreading extremist via the Internet and its impact on the consciousness of young people [14];
- revealing the causes of communicative aggression and the "hostile language" in the information domain [20].

In this respect, E. V. Nekrasova fairly notes that "the simulacrum of the real world developed before our eyes thanks to the Internet brings all the evils and contradictions common to its matrix of the physical society, and moreover acts as a catalyst. Having thrown from society to cybernetic space, a negative factor is not just projected there; being transformed and enhanced exerting it returns to its prototype as an echo and have a destructive impact... The extremism that usually achieved its goals through primitive pressure is increasingly using the latest intellectual developments now" [12].

Describing the content of measures on the prevention of terrorism ideology dissemination in the educational area and among young people, I. V. Kulyagin indicates that the Internet has a particular place in the dissemination of the terrorism ideology:

- it is used as a means of communication to coordinate extremist activities;
- it serves as a tool for searching for new financing sources of extremist organizations;
- it is employed as a tool of recruiting new members of radical associations;
- besides, on the Internet, there are instructions on the production of terrorist devices [9, p. 10].

The Internet is a perfect tool for the open spread of extremist activity due to its advantages that are actively used by representatives of gangs and their sponsors (wide audience coverage, high rate of information transfer, anonymity, relative cheapness, gaps in the legal regulation of "computer law"). Along with the use of traditional channels of social communication, extremist organizations intensively apply the latest information technologies to recruit young people. Statistical data show that a third of all terrorist and extremist crimes are committed using the World Wide Web.

The future development of information technologies will facilitate their use for criminal purposes and the emergence of new forms of information crime and promote radical ideas.

Another kind of extremism manifestation that is directly related to the IT space is information extremism aimed at creating chaos in the information society, also by disseminating extremist methods and even destructing mass communication.

Communication technologies are actively used by informational extremists for their purposes, for example, to instigate international and inter-religious conflicts and undermine the political and ideological situation in countries.

There is another circumstance. It is unlikely that anyone will argue that modern youth extremism, including terrorism as its extreme manifestation, hinders the economic growth, establishment of the information society, and the information economy like no other negative background phenomenon of modern crime. Extremism and terrorism have become almost the main challenge to man and society. Extremism manifestations pose a threat to the economic security of states. Extremist activity causes substantial moral and financial damage to citizens. It's hardly possible to estimate the economic damage caused by both violent and non-violent forms of extremism. The annual damage to the global economy from terrorism is estimated at over 53 billion dollars.

It can be stated that in the last 10-15 years economic extremism has developed despite the whole variety of extremist activity. It is intended to eliminate the diversity of ownership forms, propagate the departure from the principles of state regulation of the economic area, and remove competition in the economy.

All of the above makes it possible to state that economy, information technology, and extremism can be explored in conjunction.

Analysis and Discussion

We should note that coordinated efforts of representatives of both economic and technical sciences and legal ones will contribute to the growing efficiency of information technologies. An important area of application of information technologies is information support of counter-extremism. The main goals of state counter-extremism policy outlined in the strategy for countering extremism in the Russian Federation until 2025 are the provision in the mass media, information, and telecommunication networks, including the Internet, of information support of all government bodies, civil society institutions, and organizations in countering extremism, as well as the execution of efficient measures on informational counteraction to the dissemination of extremist ideology [18].

Measures on the prevention of youth extremism should take into account the progress in the information domain and the growing importance of the Internet in modern society.

It also appears that the development of information education in general and media education, in particular, will contribute to counter-extremism among young people. The principal objectives of media education in this area are to prepare young people for life in modern information conditions, to teach adequate perception and interpretation of different information, understanding of its impact on the psychological state, to learn the non-verbal methods using technical means.

No less significant factor in the fight against youth extremism is a growing level of both information literacy and the information culture of young people. We are talking about their ability to express their information needs, find information, evaluate its quality, and use it safely and ethically.

Experts emphasize that the informational counter-extremism on the Internet can be classified into three areas. The first one is the restriction of access to extremist papers, the second one is educational outreach activities, and the third one is awareness-raising support of anti-terrorist events.

Most countries facing the dissemination of prohibited content somehow cope with the first direction of counter-extremism policy. In Russia, there is the National Center for Information Counter-Terrorism and Extremism in the Educational Environment and on the Internet working under the auspices of the Ministry of Education and Science of the Russian Federation operates. This institution monitors and analyzes the Internet space to uncover the facts of extremist ideology propagation. The Federal List of Extremist Materials was made up of court judgments received by the Ministry of Justice of Russia [19]. Today, this list contains almost 4.5 thousand materials. Similar lists exist in the CIS countries.

But educational outreach activities and awareness-raising provision of anti-terrorist events as independent areas of informational counter-extremism have become widespread neither in Russia nor in the CIS countries. It is not possible to ensure the information security of society without developing antagonism against a violent ideology among citizens and involving them in the anti-extremism movement. And here it seems that introduced information and communication technologies can become an integral part of the system for the prevention of extremist manifestations. The small number of sites, information, and educational resources offered by the state and municipal authorities are not enough that young people could get information on terrorism and extremism and learn how to counter it. It is hardly possible to talk about developing civic self-awareness of young people, ensuring media security, and countering Internet manipulations in these conditions. Thus, unfortunately, it should be recognized that informational counteraction to radical ideas is currently non-systemic and integral processes are not standardized either in individual countries or at the interstate level.

Let us refer to the fact that information on international socially dangerous acts is not structured. In some countries, certain organizations are officially recognized as extremists or terrorists, and in others - these organizations are not blacklisted. The situation extremist is the same with the content on the Internet, with extremist papers in general. All these circumstances do not contribute to the preventive activities and do not reduce the radicalization of various groups of the population.

Agreeing with the statement that modern society must learn to use the effective methods of counter-propagation in cyberspace and not only respond to extremists but also act in advance to counter extremism [4, p. 548], we should add that it's unfeasible for a single state to fight against extremism and terrorism as its extreme manifestation (no matter how its anti-extremist legislation is developed, and no matter what extent law enforcement agencies succeed in this area). It is necessary to unite the efforts, including the information capabilities of all states, at least within the CIS.

One of the main goals of state youth policy is to create conditions for the development and fulfillment of the intellectual capacity of modern youth, including its information resources. G. A. Shaikhutdinova fully and impartially describes the role and capacity of the information space of the educational institution in countering the extremist ideology among young people: "Information resources are one of the crucial tools to hold preventive activities as well as rearrange public consciousness, and affect the rehabilitation of positive value attitudes among young people. A special role should be attributed not too formal, but to systemic propagation of legal knowledge on youth sites, in social networks, etc." [17].

The use of new information opportunities can and should contribute to the patriotic education of the oncoming generation. Only tolerant and educated young people with a high level of legal awareness can solve complex economic and political problems of the state, counter the manifestations of extremism, develop the essential social innovations for life and build a prosperous society [15].

It's no coincidence that the goals of state policy on counter-extremism include the provision of information support of all government bodies, civil society institutions, and anti-extremist organizations in mass media, information and telecommunication networks, including the Internet, as well as the execution of effective measures on informational counteraction to the dissemination of the extremist ideology.

The inter-regional youth public association CyberDruzhina established by the League of Safe Internet is of particular interest. It's aimed at identifying dangerous content on the Internet, fighting against the propagation of extremism on the Internet, as well as raising computer literacy among young people. The Penza State University of Architecture and Construction has a positive experience of such projects [6]. The departments of the CyberDruzhina were opened in the branches of the First Cossack University [3]. It seems that similar youth Internet communities that assist law enforcement agencies in identifying and neutralizing criminal threats should be founded at each university.

Monitoring of the Internet, the proactive identification of extremist content, and Internet communities sharing the extremist ideology and subsequent notification to law enforcement authorities will contribute to the active public stance in the educational process to be established. So, for example, on the website of the Prosecutor General's Office of the Russian Federation, there is a special form of "Notification of Extremism" where any citizen can enter information on an extremist Internet source and send a notification [13].

Through the website of the Ministry of Internal Affairs and section "Receiving applications," one can also leave a complaint against a site of extremist nature or any information containing signs of extremism. Information on the dissemination of papers containing the signs of extremism on Internet sites registered as mass media can also be communicated to the Federal Service for Supervision of Communications, Information Technologies, and Mass Media (Roskomnadzor) [5]. Filling in the appropriate form is offered on the website of the National Center for the Information Counter-Terrorism and Extremism in the Educational Environment and on the Internet [16].

Also, the Internet can be a platform for students' practice on anti-extremist disciplines which have been actively introduced in recent years in the curricula of both state and non-state higher education institutions. For example, "The Legal Foundations of Tolerance and Countering Extremism" (Vladimir State University named after Aleksandr and Nikolai Stoletovy), "Countering Religious and Political Extremism" (Dagestan State Institute of National Economy), "Combating Extremism and Terrorism" (North Ossetian State Pedagogical Institute), "Legal and Organizational Fundamentals of Combating Terrorism and Extremism" (Non-State Educational Institution of Higher Professional Education "Institute of Management"), "Combating Extremism" (Samara State University of Economics). Such practice is especially relevant in the training of future legal experts. Under the guidance of an experienced tutor, students identify extremist Internet content and put into practice the skills of classifying offenses, the procedure for filing of applications on crimes and offenses, completing reports on administrative offenses and applications to law enforcement authorities, etc. The Internet as a means of interaction (feedback) with the law enforcer allows analyzing the response received, evaluating the performance of state bodies in terms of handling citizens' applications related to the compliance with anti-extremist legislation, the validity of complaints and notifications, and clarifying working legislation, etc.

In addition, we all know that the role of information and communication technologies in the arrangement and administration of law enforcement activities of state bodies is increasing. The adoption of reasonable managerial decisions on counter-extremism should be also based on forecasting scientific and technological progress in the information domain. We believe that the Internet can and should be involved in the system of general social and specific-criminological prevention of extremism manifestations.

Conclusion and Findings

1. Anti-extremist activities among young people should be certainly based on the active use of information technology and regard to the growing importance of the Internet among youth. Information provision of counter-extremism should be one of the important areas of information technologies' application.
2. Information counteraction to extremism on the Internet is executed towards the restriction of access to extremist papers, educational outreach activities, and awareness-raising support of anti-terrorist activities. The activities under the second and third directions are executed without an integrated approach and common standards both at the domestic and interstate levels. We believe that this activity should be integrated due to the intensive cooperation of public authorities and civil society institutions.
3. Nowadays, proven and effective tools and measures to counter extremism among young people using new information technologies include:
   - media education where young people acquire skills of adequate perception and interpretation of various kinds of information;
   - increasing the number of websites, informational and educational institutions of both state and municipal authorities, and public organizations that familiarize young people with the forms of terrorism and extremism, as well as the main ways to counter them that will contribute to developing civic self-consciousness of young people, patriotic education of oncoming generation, ensuring media security and countering Internet manipulation;
   - establishment and performance of various youth public organizations and associations (following the example of CyberDruzhina founded by the Safe Internet League) mainly aimed at identifying dangerous content on the Internet and combating the propagation of extremism on the Internet, as well as raising computer literacy of young people. It seems that similar youth Internet communities that assist law enforcement agencies in identifying and neutralizing criminal threats should be founded at each university;

- the use of the Internet as a platform for students' practice in anti-extremist disciplines, which have been actively introduced in recent years into the curricula of both state and non-state universities.

References

[1] Buraeva, L. A. 2017. Radicalism and Online Recruiting on the Internet. *Socio-political Sciences*. 4. URL: https://cyberleninka.ru/article/n/ radikalizm-i-onlayn-rekruting-v-seti-internet (accessed date: October 07, 2018).

[2] Bykadorova, A. S., Churilov, S. A., Shapovalova, E. V. 2016. Extremization of the Youth Audience of the Internet. *KPZh* 3(116). URL: https://cyberleninka.ru/article/n/ekstremizatsiya-molodezhnoy-auditorii-seti-internet Accessed October 07, 2018.

[3] *Cossack Cyber-forces March into the Regions.* Official website of Moscow State University of Technology and Management named after K. G. Razumovskii (PKU). URL: http://www.mgutm.ru/content/news/ 13559/ Accessed November 08, 2018).

[4] Dibirov, N. Z., Safaraliev, G. K. 2009. *Modern Political Extremism: Concept, Origins, Reasons, Ideology, Issues, Organizations, Practice, Prevention and Counteraction*. Makhachkala.

[5] *Frequently Asked Questions.* Official website of the Federal Service for Supervision of Communications, Information Technologies, and Mass Media. URL: https://rkn.gov.ru/treatments/p459/p750/ Accessed November 13, 2018).

[6] Garkin, I. N., Medvedeva, L. M. 2017. Methods of Prevention Penetration of Extremism and Terrorism Ideology into the Educational Environment of Higher Education Institution. *Youth Scientific Bulletin* 6: 81-85.

[7] Gladyshev-Lyadov, V. V. 2013. Social Networks as a Tool for the Propagation of Extremism. Review. *National Center for Information Counter-Terrorism and Extremism in the Information Domain and the Internet* 2. URL: https://cyberleninka.ru/article/n/sotsialnye-seti-kak-instrument-dlya-propagandy-ekstremizma Accessed October 17, 2018.

[8] Kruzhkova, O. V., Vorob'eva, I. V., Nikiforova, D. M. 2016. Psychological Issue of Youth Involvement in Extremist Groups on the Internet. *Education and Science* 10(139). URL: https://cyberleninka.ru/ article/n/psihologicheskie-aspekty-vovlecheniya-v-ekstremistskie-gruppirovki-molodezhi-v-srede-internet Accessed October 07, 2018.

[9] Kulyagin, I. V. 2017. Preventing Dissemination of Terrorism Ideology in the Educational Domain and the Youth Environment. Counteraction to the Ideology of Extremism and Terrorism in the Youth Environment (domestic and international experience): Proceedings of an Interregional Research and Practice Conference with International Participation as of April 21, 2016, Rostov-on-Don. Editors: O. V. Lokota (Head), S. A. Vorontsov (Deputy Head), A. M. Blaginin, S. N. Nazarov, A.

V. Ponedelkov. Rostov-on-Don: Publishing house of South-Russian Institute of Management of the Russian Presidential Academy of National Economy and Public Administration.

[10] Lashin, R. L., Churilov, S. A. 2016. Countering Extremism and Terrorism on the Internet and the Educational Environment. Review. *National Center for Information Counter-Terrorism and Extremism in the Information Domain and the Internet* 7. URL: https://cyberleninka. ru/article/n/protivodeystvie-ekstremizmu-i-terrorizmu-v-seti-internet-i-obrazovatelnoy-srede Accessed October 07, 2018.

[11] Manoilo, A. V., Shegaev, I. S. 2018. Terrorist Recruiting in the Post-Soviet Space: Current Trends and Risks for Russia. *Bulletin of Moscow Region State University* 2. URL: https://cyberleninka.ru/article/n/ terroristicheskiy-rekruting-na-postsovetskom-prostranstve-sovremennye-tendentsii-i-riski-dlya-rossii Accessed October 07, 2018.

[12] Nekrasova, E. V. 2013. Information Side of Extremism and Terrorism and Destructive Trends in the Mass Media. *Bulletin of RUDN University. Series: Sociology* 1. URL: https://cyberleninka.ru/article/n/ informatsionnyy-aspekt-ekstremizma-i-terrorizma-i-destruktivnye-tendentsii-v-smi Accessed October 21, 2018.

[13] *Notifications of extremism.* Official website of the Prosecutor General of the Russian Federation. URL: https://genproc.gov.ru/contacts/ extremism/send/ Accessed November 13, 2018.

[14] Panfilova, Y. S. 2014. Extremism in a Virtual Environment as a Social Issue: Reflection in the Minds of Young People. *Almanac of Modern Science and Education* 9: 101-104.

[15] Popov, E. V., Omonov, Z. K. 2016. The Essence and Typology of Social Innovation. *Innovation* 1(207). URL: https://cyberleninka.ru/article/n/ suschnost-i-tipologiya-sotsialnyh-innovatsiy Accessed November 08, 2018.

[16] *Report on Illegal Content*/Website of the National Center for the Information Counter-Terrorism and Extremism in the Educational Environment and on the Internet. URL: http://ncpti.su/illegal_content/ Accessed November 18, 2018.

[17] Shaikhutdinova, G. A. 2016. Information and Educational Issues of Counter-Extremist ideology Among Young People. *KPZh* 3(116). URL: https://cyberleninka.ru/article/n/informatsionno-obrazovatelnye-aspekty-protivodeystviya-ideologii-ekstremizma-v-molodezhnoy-srede Accessed October 10, 2018.

[18] Strategy for Counter-Extremism in the Russian Federation until 2025 (approved by the President of the Russian Federation on November 28, 2014, No. Pr-2753). *Laws, Codes, Regulatory and Judicial Acts.* URL: http://legalacts.ru/doc/strategija-protivodeistvija-ekstremizmu-v-rossiiskoi-federatsii-do Accessed October 20, 2018.

[19] The Federal List of Extremist Papers. Official Website of the Ministry of Justice of Russia. URL: http://minjust.ru/ru/extremist-materials Accessed October 11, 2018.

[20] Tret'yakova, O. V. 2018. Prevention of Extremist Crime in the Mass Media. *Law and Education* 8: 51-62.

[21] Troegubov, Y. N. 2014. Problems of Countering Extremism on the Internet. *Humanitarian Vector. Series: History, Political Science* 3 (39). URL: https://cyberleninka.ru/article/n/problemy-protivodeystviya-ekstremizmu-v-seti-internet Accessed October 10, 2018.
[22] Verkhoglyadov, Y. E. 2015. Concerning the Issue of Possible Informational Counter-Extremism among Young People. *Altai Legal Journal* 11. URL: http://elibrary.ru/ item.asp? Id = 239028041 Accessed October 20, 2018.

Chapter 10

Legal Proceedings in the Context of Digital Economies

Galina E. Ageeva*, **Petr P. Lang and Ekaterina N. Churakova**
Samara State University of Economics, Samara, Russia

Abstract

This article pays attention to the establishment of the legal regulation of the information space in modern society and related problems. Currently, the digital economy as a program intended to disseminate digital technology and digitalize all social processes is a priority and an urgent task in our country. The program was approved by the Government of the Russian Federation in 2017 to achieve three main goals:

- to develop an ecosystem of the digital economy of the Russian Federation with digital data as a key production factor in all areas of socio-economic activity and effective communication, including cross-border, business, between scientific and educational community, government and citizens;
- to forge required and sufficient conditions of an institutional and infrastructural nature, remove obstacles and restrictions for setting up and (or) developing high-tech business and preventing new obstacles and restrictions both in traditional sectors of the economy as well as in new industries and high-tech markets;
- to increase competitiveness in the global market of both individual sectors and the entire economy of the Russian Federation [10].

* Corresponding Author's Email: galinaageevva@mail.ru.

In: Economic and Legal Foundations of Innovative Development …
Editors: Gabibulla Khasaev, Victoria Bolgova, Sergey Bortnikov et al.
ISBN: 978-1-68507-730-3

In the authors' opinion, these goals can be and must be set concerning the regulation of the legal proceedings in its broad sense. Thereby, the improvement of procedural mechanisms and information security will be ensured [5].

Keywords: legal proceedings, digital economy, information revolution, e-justice, informatization

JEL Codes: K30, K40, K41, K42, K49

Introduction

The category "digital economy", foundations of its legal regulation and provision, as well as a discussion on its advantages and disadvantages, have overwhelmed the scientific community, law-enforcers, and law-makers [17]. The policy aimed at the digital development of the entire economic life of society was adopted after the official publication of the Strategy for the Development of the Information Society in the Russian Federation for 2017 – 2030 [4]. The specified regulatory act fixed the following important definitions: "digital economy is an economic activity with digital data as the key production factor, the processing of large data volumes and application of the data analyzed can significantly increase the efficiency of various types of production, technologies, equipment, storage, sale, delivery of goods and services compared with traditional economic forms"; "the ecosystem of the digital economy is a partnership of organizations that ensures the continuous communication of their technological platforms, applied Internet services, analytical systems, information systems of government authorities of the Russian Federation, organizations and citizens." These concepts and categories are in fast-growing interest and demand of the general public. So, for example, such queries as "digital economy are", "what is the digital economy in simple words", etc., are becoming the most frequent in the search engines of the information and telecommunication network "Internet" [27].

The alternations related to digitalization and informatization touch upon all areas of public relations, not only limited to the system of "production, distribution, exchange and consumption" [28].

Thus, for example, some researchers believe that digitalization, informatization, and electronization, including entering distant labor relations are our future and the right vector of future development of public relations.

"As soon as a generation of 20-30-year-old people comes to power in business, companies will start to turn to a flexi-time and distant work on a large scale. The traditional schedule from 9:00 a.m. to 5:00 p.m. is a relic of the industrial era sinking in the past. Resistance to change the existing way of life threatens both economic and political stability" [20]. Moreover, the entry into force of Federal Law as of March 18, 2019, introduced a new category of "digital rights" [7].

However, the legal proceedings and procedural law from the standpoint of its broad general theoretical understanding are overlooked in these numerous, socially- and scientifically-based discussions. As for legal proceedings, a traditionally understood procedural research field, there are relevant scientific papers, which foremost explore the issues related to the introduction of electronic justice [16]. However, an integrated approach to the issues of digitalization, electronization, and informatization of legal procedural aspects is not applied. In our opinion, this happens foremost due to the insufficient dissemination of the theory of the so-called "broad" legal proceedings in the scientific community.

"The concept of "procedural law", its system and interrelation with paired substantive law have attracted the attention of researchers of the general law theory for a long time. As early as 2003, V. N. Protasov said that the period of thorough scientific studies of the general procedural theory and attempts to determine this legal formation dates back several decades ago. Moreover, as far back as 1920, some authors emphasized that procedural law is underestimated by the scientific community. Nevertheless, comprehensive studies of procedural law, the newest period of understanding the designated legal formation distinguished by in-depth research methods, falls on the second half of the last century" [14].

"It is well-known that the theory, later called the "broad" legal proceedings, was first proposed under this name in the Russian theory of law by V. M. Gorshenev, P. E. Nedbailo, and their scientific school. And although, as it was found out later, the legal procedure by V. N. Protasov is even more "broad", however, in all scientific discussions on the scope of procedure concept in the law the phrase "theory of "broad" legal proceedings" is used thanks to the well-established epithet that briefly conveys the essence of dispute [24].

Currently, there is an increasing number of papers and studies on various issues of understanding the legal proceedings [15]. However, there are no papers devoted to the issues and peculiarities of digitalization and electronization of the legal proceedings yet. This study is intended to fill an existing research gap. The authors of this paper understand the legal proceedings as a "broad", multidimensional phenomenon, involving the administration of justice in various types of legal proceedings as well as other types of intensive legal activity, including positive law enforcement procedures [22].

Methodology

In the course of the present study, the authors have used, first of all, the method of materialist dialectics that is the most common method of scientific knowledge due to its universal nature. Moreover, this method was used in the study of both the regulatory framework, the law-enforcement legislation, and various scientific proceedings of general theoretical, and sometimes industry-specific nature. Given the integrated approach to the object of this scientific research, along with the above methods the authors have used such methods of scientific knowledge as abstraction and specification; analysis and synthesis; induction, and deduction. Private scientific methods such as sociological one and legal modeling have also been of great importance in writing this paper.

Findings

We can fully agree with the authors of the collective monograph on various aspects of the communication of procedural law and the information society who designate the information society as the human community, which is distinguished by a qualitatively new space in terms of technological and social structure. "The quality defined by this term is obvious to everyone. This includes the active introduction of a legal object such as information into the legal field, and the actual transition to the monopoly of new methods of information transfer (computer technology)" [25]. Digitalization and informatization currently cover all social processes, including the economy, which is now can be called "digital", and legal proceedings.

If we talk about the outcomes of introducing information technology into legal proceedings, we can state that they are being used primarily in legal proceedings to the full extent. The priority of electronic-digital communication of parties of procedural activity has long been assigned to the supreme bodies of state power [9, 13]. The relevant changes are continuously introduced into the procedural codes, amended, updated, and supplemented.

So, for example, the possibility of applying to the judicial authorities through the use of Internet information has been actively and successfully used for many years in the arbitration proceedings. Corresponding amendments were introduced to the arbitration (commercial) procedure legislation in 2011. In 2016 such an opportunity was officially enshrined in the Civil Procedure Code, however, nowadays there are some enforcement difficulties. First of all, this occurs due to the insufficient funding of e-justice in the system of general courts: for example, the lack of highly-skilled staff without legal education, but with expertise in modern information technologies. In this connection, now there is an issue of quick response to the document workflow submitted through the Internet. The supreme bodies of state power repeatedly pointed at the need to change this situation; relevant measures have already been taken [9].

In addition to the possibility of applying to the courts through digital communication, an important innovation in legal proceedings is the widespread dissemination of audio recording. Talking about widespread distribution, we assume its statutorization and implementation in trying and adjudicating the cases in all types of legal proceedings. Thus, an audio recording of the court hearing and executing each procedural action was introduced into the arbitration (commercial) procedure law in 2010 (Art. 155 of the Arbitration Procedure Code of the Russian Federation (hereinafter referred to as "APC RF") [1]). In administrative proceedings, a similar regulation is effective from the moment of publication of the Administrative Procedure Code of the Russian Federation (Art. 204). And in the Civil Procedure Code of the Russian Federation, the requirement of an audio recording will be effective on September 1st, 2019 (Art. 229 [6]).

Another feature of informatization of court law enforcement was the wide distribution of electronic documents as evidence. Given the developmental level of electronic-digital relations between legal persons, the possibility of confirming the information on the facts through the provision of various forms and types of electronic documents is undoubtful, urgent, and very popular. Electronic evidence is mentioned in all procedural codes and court practice develops special rules for their assessment.

At the end of 2014, a rule was enshrined in the Civil Procedure Code of the Russian Federation, which, in our opinion, is also one of the stages that contribute to the further dissemination of electronic evidence in the legal proceedings. Thus, under Part 5, Art. 61 of Civil Procedure Code of the Russian Federation, one of the grounds released from proof is "the circumstances approved by the notary public when making a notarial act ... if the authenticity of the notarized document is not disproved." Because recently, notaries have often perpetuated evidence on the Internet in general, and the certification of a site page in particular, we believe that such a rule will play a role in the further dissemination and facilitate the use of electronic evidence in civil proceedings.

However, the legal proceedings are not only legal proceedings. The methods of electronic-digital intercommunication of legal persons, as well as the accomplishment of some legal procedures electronically are actively distributed in all areas of procedural law.

Electronic technology in modern society is not just important for each individual, sometimes it can determine the level of his well-being. "A man's place and role in the establishment of the information society has been dramatically transformed, and his well-being will directly depend on the availability of personal electronic identifier" [18]. However, there is a danger in this regard. In the modern information society where the basic processes can take place through the electronic-digital communication of actors (this is especially obvious in the legal proceedings) arises an issue of their identification. "We can surely state that it is the most general issue, that is, it concerns almost all types of legal proceedings and procedures" [25].

The rules on the legal personality of the parties apply to the participants of any type of legal proceedings. These rules may vary for each type of procedural activity, however, the general rule is presumed as follows: it is required to meet particular criteria (regarding age, legal capacity, status, etc.) to participate in the process. Therefore, when affecting any legal procedures, verification of the requirements made may be complicated. In this situation, it is also necessary to take into account willful misrepresentation by a person who cannot, for example, act as a party to a specific type of legal proceedings, etc.

In our opinion, in these conditions, it is necessary to introduce mechanisms to ensure and guarantee the free identification of the participant. However, it is worth highlighting that these methods should still be voluntary and be used in terms of specific procedural actions. L. V. Goloskokov offers the global-scale introduction of meta-passports that will help to solve many issues [19]. But we believe that passports are a drastic change; rather, some situational measures are required. Moreover, one of the ways ensuring information security may be precisely their situational or short-term nature: for example, the participant should replace the document in particular time intervals and re-confirm his status.

However, "digital identifiers should in no case be imposed on all Internet users as an essential condition of using electronic services" [23]. Therefore, there should be no requirements, for example (by analogy to the issuance of the passport), to compulsory acquisition of any means of electronic digital identification by the legal person. Rather, the rule is that effecting any specific action in digital form requires such a tool to be acquired (for example, an electronic digital signature).

And since almost any personal identifiers used in electronic-digital communication of actors can be hacked we believe that the rules ensuring information security are the top priority. So, according to the words of Maxim Bashkatov, the main issue of digital rights being introduced into the legal field is that "public order is not able to ensure appropriate security of this right from infringements of third parties" (digital-media items, digital rights, and money: Legal Theory and Practice Trends).

Accordingly, it's not sufficient to introduce new categories into legislation; it' necessary to investigate them primarily from the procedural point of view and develop a proper mechanism of performance and protection. The task of the government at the present stage of procedural relations, the digital economy, and the electronic-digital communication between the actors are to actively develop and introduce methods of digital face identification ensured with appropriate security.

Conclusions/Recommendations

Summing up all the above stated in this study, we would like to note that in modern society, both digital economy and "digitized" legal proceedings had been appeared, developed, and taken place. Information revolution affected all areas of life to one or another extent.

As a result of the study, we would like to submit the following conclusions:

- The legal proceedings are one of the basic categories of the state and law theory that unites various types of procedural activity, the essential feature of which is the performance of several consecutive and interrelated intermediate actions aimed at achieving a specific, predetermined legally important result.
- The scientific and theoretical category digital economy "as it is" introduced into the current legislation, does not involve the legal proceedings. However, procedural "digitalization" also can take place. An urgent issue now is the further wide-scale dissemination of electronic technologies in legal activity, improvement, and ensuring their information security.
- One of the most complicated issues of the digitalization of procedural activity is the means and methods of identifying the parties to the legal proceedings and verifying its legal status. This requires the development and adoption of particular situational measures. Moreover, one of the measures to ensure information security will be precisely their situational or short-term nature: for example, the participant should replace the document in particular time intervals and re-confirm his status.
- The task of the government at the present stage of procedural relations, digital economy, and the electronic-digital communication of actors are to intensively develop and introduce methods of digital face identification that are ensured by appropriate security.

References

[1] Administrative Procedure Code of the Russian Federation. 2018. No. 21-FZ as of March 08, 2015 (as amended on December 28, 2017). Collected Legislation of the Russian Federation, 2015, No 10, Art. 1391; 2018, No. 1 (Part I), Art. 5.

[2] Civil Procedure Code of the Russian Federation. 2018. No. 138-FZ as of November 14. 2002 (as amended on March 7, 2018). Collected Legislation of the Russian Federation, 2002, No. 46, Art. 4532, No. 11, Art. 1583.

[3] Constitution of the Russian Federation: adopted by National Referendum as of December 12, 1993 (as amended by the Laws of the Russian Federation on amendments to the Constitution of the Russian Federation No. 6-FZC and No. 7-FZC as of December 30, 2008). Collected Legislation of the Russian Federation, 2009, No 4, Art. 445.

[4] Decree of the President of the Russian Federation No. 203 as of May 09, 2017 "On the Strategy for the Development of the Information Society in the Russian Federation for 2017 – 2030." Collected Legislation of the Russian Federation, 2017, No. 20, Art. 2901.

[5] Decree of the President of the Russian Federation No. 646 as of December 05, 2016 "On Approval of the Information Security Doctrine of the Russian Federation." Collected Legislation of the Russian Federation, 2016, No. 50, Art. 7074.

[6] Federal Law No. 265-FZ as of July 29, 2018 "On Amending Particular Legislative Acts of the Russian Federation." Collected Legislation of the Russian Federation, 2018, No. 3, Art. 4854.

[7] Federal Law No. 34-FZ as of March 18, 2019 "On Amending Parts 1-2 and Article 1124, Part 3 of the Civil Code of the Russian Federation." Computer-Assisted Legal Research System "Consultant Plus."

[8] Recommendations of the Committee of Ministers of the Council of Europe No. R (2001) as of February 28, 2001 "On the Dissemination of Judicial and Other Legal Information Through the Use of New Technologies." (The document was not published). Accessed from Computer-Assisted Legal Research System "Consultant Plus."

[9] Resolution of the Government of the Russian Federation No. 1406 as of December 27, 2012 (as amended on December 14, 2017) "On the Federal Target Program "Development of the Russian Judicial System for 2013 – 2020." Collected Legislation of the Russian Federation, 2013, No. 1, Art. 13; 2017, No. 52 (Part I), Art. 8135.

[10] Resolution of the Government of the Russian Federation No. 1632-p as of July 28, 2017 "On Approval of the Program "Digital Economy of the Russian Federation." Collected Legislation of the Russian Federation, 2017, No. 32, Art. 5138.

[11] Resolution of the Plenum of the Supreme Court of the Russian Federation No. 57 as of December 26, 2017 "On Some Issues of Applying Legislation Governing the Use of Electronic Documents in the Activities of General and Commercial (Arbitrazh) Courts." Computer-Assisted Legal Research System "Consultant Plus."

[12] The Commercial (Arbitration) Procedure Code of the Russian Federation. 2018. No. 95-FZ as of July 24, 2002 (as amended on December 28, 2017). Collected Legislation of the Russian Federation, 2002, No. 30, Art. 3012, No. 1 (Part I), Art. 5.

[13] The Concept of Informatization of the Supreme Court of the Russian Federation (Approved by the Order of the Supreme Court of the Russian Federation No. 67-11 as of December 10, 2015). (The document was not published). Accessed from Computer-Assisted Legal Research System "Consultant Plus."

[14] Ageeva, G. E. 2014. *Evaluation Concepts of Procedural Law.* Ph.D. in Law thesis. Samara, 197 P.

[15] Arkhipova, E. Y. 2018. *Non-Jurisdictional Process as an Object of Theoretical and Legal Studies*. Ph.D. in Law thesis. Saratov, 30 P.

[16] Belousov, D. V. 2015. E-justice and its Role in the Arrangement of Judicial Protection in Russia. *Court Administrator* 3.

[17] Bykov, A. Y. 2018. The Law of the Digital Economy: Some National and Political Risks. Moscow: Prospekt.

[18] Golovin, E. G., Bolshakova, V. M. 2014. Electronic Identification of Person: Pros and Cons. *Power* 8.

[19] Goloskokov, L. V. 2003. *Legal Doctrines: from the Ancient Times to the Information Age*. Moscow.

[20] *If we do not turn to distance work, we will face a large-scale crisis.* URL: https://vk.com/@science_technology-esli-my-ne-pereidem-na-udalennuu-rabotu-nas-zhdet-masshtabny. Accessed November 15, 2018.

[21] *Information Revolutions. Brief History*. URL: https://sites.google.com/site/infotrmattehnologi/nalastuvanna. Accessed May 21, 2018.

[22] Lang, P. P. 2013. The Element Framework of the Legal Proceedings. *Issues of Economics and Law* 2: 49-50.

[23] Malofeev, S. S. 2009. *Issues of Personal Identification in the Information Area.* URL: http://www.russianlaw.net/files/law/doc/a240.pdf Accessed March 25, 2019.

[24] Pavlushina, A. A. 2009. The Theory of the Legal Proceedings: Findings, Issues, Development Prospects. Moscow.

[25] Pavlushina, A. A. 2017. Prospects for the Development of Procedural Law in the Information Society. Monograph. Moscow: Yurlitinform, 168 P.

[26] Smolenskii, I. N. 2018. Identification of the Person (party to commercial (arbitration) proceedings in E-justice. *Bulletin of Civil Proceedings* 1.

[27] *Digital Economy in Simple Words.* URL: https://fin-book.ru/chto-takoe-tsifrovaya-ekonomika-prostymi-slovami/ Accessed March 25, 2019.

[28] *Economics: data from Wikipedia, the free encyclopedia.* URL: https://ru.wikipedia.org/wiki/%D0%AD%D0%BA%D0%BE%D0%BD%D0%BE%D0%BC%D0%B8%D0%BA%D0% B0. Accessed March 25, 2019.

[29] *Digital-Media Items, Digital Rights and Money: Trends of Legal Theory and Practice.* URL: https://www.garant.ru/article/1220358/ Accessed March 25, 2019.

Chapter 11

Information Technologies in Law Activities: Types and Legal Issues

Natalia V. Deltsova*, Evgenia V. Medentseva and Svetlana V. Startseva
Samara State University of Economics, Samara, Russia

Abstract

The legal activity sphere has undergone considerable changes in the modern conditions of the development of the information society, information and communication technologies. The professional practice of law involves extensive use of information technologies. An analysis of statutory acts, participation in judicial proceedings, business process arrangement – it all requires information technology, which is evidence of the relevant character of research of the issues related to information technology in legal activities in the Russian Federation, the European countries, and the USA. The purposes of this research are the generalization of the data on information technologies used in legal activities carried out in Russia, European countries, and the USA, and identification of the main challenging legal aspects of the use of information technology in legal activities. The findings of the research show that information technology applied in jurisprudence allows the solution of relevant practical tasks: search, systematization, storage of required statutory acts, court rulings, other legal information; preparation of legal documents (claims, complaints, agreements, etc.); facilitation of adoption of justified legal resolutions, positions on specific legal disputes; and competent legally justified consulting. Practicing lawyers are currently widely using: reference legal software, automated

* Corresponding Author's Email: natdel@mail.ru.

In: Economic and Legal Foundations of Innovative Development …
Editors: Gabibulla Khasaev, Victoria Bolgova, Sergey Bortnikov et al.
ISBN: 978-1-68507-730-3

information software including robot and artificial intelligence software, electronic justice, electronic document flow, and integrated databases. The challenging legal aspects of the use of information technology in legal activities include the legitimacy of the use of information provided by information technology; ensuring information security at information technology application; and securing high quality of the provided information and legal consulting services rendered with the help of information technologies.

Introduction

The modern social development stage is characterized by the rapid inclusion of information technology in all activity spheres. Legal activities are not an exception. The practice of law is currently requiring a huge volume of statutory information subject to rapid changes. Besides, in order to adopt competent and calculated decisions, a practicing lawyer daily studies and analyzes law enforcement acts of judicial and administrative authorities, doctrinal provisions, and project laws. All of the above is impossible to imagine without the use of special information technology allowing receipt, processing, storage, and use of legal information. It is worth noting that the activities of government authorities have suffered major changes. Many processes of judicial and law enforcement bodies are now carried out using electronic means within the framework of the electronic government concept. The Russian and foreign practice is characterized by the widespread introduction of information technology in judicial activities, which makes it possible to take judicial proceedings to a new development level, facilitate administration of justice, and make it more transparent and accessible for all categories of citizens including people with disabilities. The process of running a law business and rendering legal services is changing as well. This is largely explained by stricter requirements for legal services [14]. Not a single consultation with a lawyer is now taking place without reference to modern legal information databases. Besides, service rendering goes beyond the office premises to Internet websites providing legal services (preparation of legal documents, online consulting, etc.) due to the growing competition on the legal service market, and the need for search of new clients. The stated above confirms that research of the issues related to information technology in legal activities is relevant.

Russian and foreign publications pay attention to the issues related to information technology in jurisprudence. It should be noted that such studies are usually of a general character [6, 11, 13]. Some researches under consideration are aimed at reviewing specific technology types. In particular, this covers electronic justice technology [8, 9, 18]. Rak [16] has studied technologies used by law enforcement authorities. Some studies are related to advances in information technologies development in foreign countries [17]. Kuznetsov [10] gives theoretical grounds for information technology application in legal activities in Russia. The publications and works mentioned above do not cover the comparative law aspect. Informatization of legal activities in European countries and the USA has started earlier than in Russia. This is largely due to advanced conditioned technologies in these countries [17]. The presence of a well-developed legal service market is also worth highlighting. Therefore, research of the information technology types used in Russia, the European countries, and the USA is important for outlining their development prospects. Besides, identification of legal aspects arising in the course of the use of information technology in the legal sphere appears reasonable in the context of this work.

Methodology

The following research methods have been used: general scientific ones – analysis, synthesis, comparison, generalization; special scientific ones – formal law, comparative law, that enable to analyze of information technologies in legal activities, their types, and challenging legal aspects of use. The formal logical method has been used to identify the concept and present the types of information technology in legal activities, to give its characteristics. The comparative law analysis has helped to determine information technology used in the legal activities of various states.

Results

For this study, information technology is understood as a "combination of processes based on the achievements of the modern computer technology, communication, tools to receive various information types and a method of interaction between members of a modern society, the method of joint decision making and the birth of new knowledge, creating laws, developing of the legal system of the state in general" [15].

Research works differ in the determination of types of information technology in jurisprudence.

Drobyshev [5] gives the following list of information technologies used in the legal sphere: reference legal software, automated legal software, electronic document flow, videoconferencing, law portals, electronic justice, integrated databases, and electronic evidence. Litvinov [13], Latyshev [11], Dzhatdoev [6] single out the following software taking into account its functional designation: information reference software (IRS); information logical software (ILS); automated workstations (AWS); expert software (ES), decision-making software.

Let's review the types of information technology used in legal activities and described in publications.

Information reference software including reference legal software represents a computer technology used for collecting, storing, and processing various legal information types in the form of statutory acts, judicial rulings, periodic publications, and legal monographs. Besides, reference legal software contains templates of legal documents, analyses of various legal cases, and answers of experts to multiple legal questions. Some reference legal software in the Russian Federation, e.g., ConsultantPlus provides seminars on relevant legal subjects. The first computer software for the search of legal information appeared in Europe in 1967. It was the Belgian software Credoc. The most famous reference legal software systems are WRU, LEXIS, WESTLAW, JURIS, FLITE in the USA; Bundestag software, JURIS, LEXinform, NOMOS DATA POOL in Germany; INFOLEX, PRESTEL, POLIS, LEXIS in Great Britain; IRETIV, CEDIJ, JURISDATA, SINDONI in France; and ITALGUIRE, ENLEX in Italy, RDB in Austria [10].

The first reference legal software in the Russian Federation was developed in 1975 based on the Legal Information Research Centre under the Ministry of Justice [5]. Today, the Russian Federation is successfully using such reference legal software as Garant, ConsultantPlus, Codex, and Lawyer.

Automated information software refers to information technology including hardware and communication equipment, software, linguistic means, information resources designed for the collection, preparation, storage, processing, and provision of information as well as maintenance personnel model to meet the users' demands and make decisions.

Information software is used in many legal activity spheres (expert, law enforcement), public and municipal administration, and judicial proceedings. Information logical software (ILS), expert software (ES), decision-making software, and automated workstations (AWS) are a variety of automated information software. The first three – information logical software, expert software, and decision-making software – use artificial intelligence technologies to solve different legal tasks. The Mirror and Owl software used in the Russian Federation can be referred to this software group.

The TrademarkNow software is gaining popularity in Finland; this software is used in the intellectual property sphere to identify patented object elements in patent applications. The RAVN System technology allowing an analysis of real estate agreement terms through evaluating agreement terms by risk has risen to fame in Great Britain [5].

The USA has developed a lie detection system based on video records of emotional expressions of people during court hearings [20]. Automated workstations are reviewed as subject-oriented software deployed on a workstation. An AWS of an investigator (interrogator) may serve as an example [16].

The electronic justice phenomenon has become widespread in the legal sphere. Electronic justice is understood as a justice administration means based on the use of information technology in the course of carrying out procedural actions [18]. In Russian legal science, the electronic justice term is broadly construed as a combination of various automated information software – services providing means for the publication of judicial acts, electronic case maintenance, and access of the parties to electronic case files. Narrowly defined, electronic justice is an opportunity of the court and other process participants to carry out actions impacting the judicial procedure – to submit claims, to present evidence in the electronic form, to attend a hearing using a video conference [17].

Deployment of this software in Russia is a relatively new phenomenon. Automated software Commercial Court Resolution Bank is in place in the current commercial court system in the Russian Federation, which includes the Electronic Case Index, the Court Hearing Calendar, the Electronic Guard service, and services for submission of documents in the electronic form. The information on the functioning of the system is published on www.arbitr.ru/e-justice. Such changes concern the system of general jurisdiction courts according to the Concept of the Development of the Russian Judicial System from 2013 to 2020 [1]. Amendments stipulating electronic means of document submission to court were introduced in the Administrative Procedure Code of the Russian Federation, the Criminal Procedure Code of the Russian Federation, and the Civil Procedure Code of the Russian Federation in 2016. Courts entering the general jurisdiction system now have websites, where the key information about the court activities, procedural document templates, case review schedules, and the court resolution bank.

In foreign countries, this process started forming as early as in the late XX century [2]. The US judicial system construes electronic justice as access to cases, receipt of the information on judicial cases, document search, information on the parties, other information related to judicial proceedings. The Case Management/Electronic Case Files (hereinafter referred to as the "CM/ECF") and the Public Access to Court Electronic Records (PACER) software are in place in the USA. The used software name CM/ECF points at the combination of two software systems performing the following functions: case management (CM) and an electronic archive of cases (ECF). These two components form an integrated system, which in its turn is supplemented with the Public Access to Court Electronic Records technology providing users with access to electronic case files with the CM/ECF software [12].

An integral part of electronic justice in Russia as well as in foreign states is electronic document flow enabling the exchange of documents in the electronic form. The electronic document flow system deployed in Germany is implemented on all process stages from the filing of an electronic claim and submitting electronic evidence to adopting a resolution in the electronic form [9]. There have been currently introduced electronic telecommunications between the court, parties to a procedure, and within the court itself. Documents are submitted to court via a special mailbox using the OSTCI-Ntransport communications protocol. Thus, the court receives documents through protected channels [3]. The German electronic document flow system constitutes reliable, valid electronic document exchange between attorneys, citizens, government authorities, and courts [4].

The electronic court record system Crown Court Digital Case System is in place in Great Britain. It gives any person involved in a case an opportunity to view electronic templates of all case-related documents in their most relevant form using the Internet [5].

An electronically submitted document is usually signed with an electronic digital signature identifying the sender and accompanied by electronic means of protection against unsanctioned access. Besides, an electronic document can be considered as evidence in a case according to the procedural laws of states. Videoconferencing is also used within the framework of electronic justice administration in the Russian Federation. This technology allows holding court hearings with remote participation of the parties to the procedure (claimant, defendant, witnesses, etc.). This technology is seriously saving the case resolution time and decreasing the process costs. This information technology enables online or offline broadcasting court hearings [7].

Information technology related to legal activities is also used in the public administration sphere. The terms electronic state and electronic government originated in the USA, where there appeared an idea to use information technology in the activities of government authorities.

A modern interpretation of the term electronic government implies a form of promoting the government authorities' action in the virtual environment ensuring better public administration, increased state transparency, and exercising constitutional rights and freedoms with information and communication technologies [17]. This concept is provided by the official government portals containing a large volume of legal information. In particular, these are various automated operational information banks, published statutory acts, court resolutions, etc.

Special attention should be paid to such information resources as integrated databases containing data from state registers. Such registers contain official data used to make important legal decisions, resolve disputes since the data are official. Examples are the Unified State Register of Legal Entities, the Unified State Register of Individual Entrepreneurs, which can be accessed on the Federal Tax Service of the Russian Federation portal (www.nalog.ru); the Unified State Register of Title to Real Estate, which can be accessed on the Federal Service of State Registration, Cadastre, and Cartography portal (www.rosreestr.ru) and the State Service portal (www.gosuslugi.ru). The www.pravo.gov.ru website is an official portal for the publication of legal information in Russia.

The presented overview of information technology used in legal activities attests to its variety. Its use is undoubtedly facilitating the process of accessing legal information, its processing and legal service rendering, etc.

However, one should keep in mind the following legal aspects of the practical application of information technology.

The first aspect concerns the legitimacy of the use of information provided by information technologies. Statutory acts defining various legal regimes of the use of information have been adopted and are in place in most states. In particular, Federal Law No. 149-FZ of July 27, 2006, On Information,

Information Technologies and Information Protection is applicable in the Russian Federation. The Freedom of Information Act has been in place in the USA since July 20, 1966. Germany adopted the law On Data Protection in 1991. These laws define what information types refer to public ones and which ones are confidential. Thus, including documents in reference legal software, making court resolutions publicly available on court websites and within the framework of the electronic justice technologies, providing data from integrated databases, and including information in such bases have to comply with provisions of such laws (provision of consent for personal data processing, signing of non-disclosure documents).

The second aspect is closely related to the first one and covers information security – protection of personal data, personal and family secrets, confidential data, and intellectual property provided in the course of the use of information technologies. The development of Internet technologies has taken cybercrime (crimes committed in the computer network) to a new level [7]. Illegal acquisition of information as a result of cyberattacks and Internet fraud is getting new forms. The main problem lies in the fact that cybercrime is a cross-border phenomenon. The solution to the problem requires developing a complex of technical, legal, educational means on the part of separate states and the international level in general and developing the global security system. Besides, it is also required to protect information against misuse of persons having access to it through discharge of official duties.

One more aspect involves the quality of the provided legal information and the quality of a legal act or service, with information technologies. In this case, the quality of information should be understood as its reliability. The reliability of legal information largely depends on its source. In this context, we are talking about the legal regulation of information technology implementation, procedure, and consequences of its use. Not every information software is trustworthy in practical jurisprudence. However, this aspect appears most relevant in the legal business sphere based on a robotic system and artificial intelligence software, namely, chatbots, video bots, online consulting on specialized websites.

Chatbots and video bots use legal information files stored in the program memory, such services can give answers to standard or frequently asked questions, draft standard legal documents. An example of this technology is the DoNotPay.co.uk service in Great Britain developed to help drivers contest fines.

Such online services as Roket Lawyer (www.rocketlawyer.co.uk) in Great Britain, LegalZoom (www.legalzoom.com) in the USA, and Pravoved.ru (www.pravoved.ru) in Russia are used to render legal services. These services are Internet websites where providers offer services of drafting various legal documents (agreements, wills, powers of attorney), explaining legal concepts, legal consulting. Experts in artificial intelligence in legal activities consider this legal service development area innovative and promising [19]. Lawyers can indeed use the achievements of this technology to solve typical tasks and facilitate the document preparation process, thus raising the efficiency of operations. However, keep in mind that in many cases people who use the information provided by such services are not lawyers and cannot correctly evaluate the result of the rendered services or the consultation quality. In the long run, no claim for the rendered service quality or the incurred loss can be submitted in this situation

Conclusion/Recommendations

Information technologies applied in jurisprudence allows the solution of relevant practical tasks: search, systematization, storage of required statutory acts, court rulings, other legal information; preparation of legal documents (claims, complaints, agreements, etc.); facilitation of justified legal resolutions, on specific legal disputes; competent legally justified consulting. Besides, information technologies applied in jurisprudence save time and speed up the process of legal service rendering or legal procedure carrying out, whether it is the administration of justice or registration.

Practicing lawyers are currently widely using: reference legal software, automated information software including robot and artificial intelligence software, electronic justice, electronic document flow, integrated databases.

It should be noted that although the introduction of information technologies in the practical sphere of legal activities in Russia has started later, Russian lawyers are now using the same information technologies as most European countries and the USA do. The continuing informatization process gives reasons to believe that this sphere will be actively developing in the future.

However, the information technologies application practice has brought to light some aspects claiming attention, namely:

- The legitimacy of the use of information provided by information technologies. In this respect it appears that collection, storage, processing, and distribution of legal information within the framework of the functioning of information technologies should be carried out in compliance with national provisions establishing the legal regime of information;
- Ensuring information security with information technologies stipulates protection of personal data, confidential data, legally protected secrets. Protection is necessary against cybercrimes and misuse of persons having access to such information through the discharge of official duties. Taking legal and technical measures stipulated by the national laws for protecting the corresponding data by persons deploying the technologies and international cooperation in the indicated sphere seems to be a solution. In addition, it appears necessary to give explanations concerning information security, inform users about the main rules for storing protected information and the consequences of the ill-considered provision of personal and other data;
- Securing quality of the provided information and the rendered, legal consulting services with the information technologies. It seems reasonable to introduce legal requirements for ensuring information awareness of information technologies users. It makes sense to amend national laws to include liability of the person deploying a technology, place warnings about the character of the legal information provided by the robot, and artificial intelligence software to avoid user disorientation.

References

[1] Aleksyev, A. 2016. Electronic Proceedings in the Russian Civil Procedure. *Arbitration and Civil Procedure* 2:12 - 16.

[2] Allen, T., Aikenhead, M., Widdison, R. 1998. Computer Simulation of Judicial Behavior. *Web Journal of Current Legal Issues* 3. URL: http://webjcli.ac.uk/1998/issue3/allen3.html Accessed December 05, 2018.

[3] Branovitsky, K. 2011. The FRG Experience of Electronic Justice: Achievements and Problems. *Law* 2:57-65. Accessed December 14, 2018.

[4] Degen, Th.A. 2008. Admonish and complain by E-Mail – the Legal framework and the digital divide in the judiciary and the legal profession. *New Legal Weekly Journal* 1473.

[5] Drobyshev, P. 2017. *Innovations in Jurisprudence: Review of Achievements and Tendencies in Technification of the Legal Business in English-Speaking Jurisdictions.* URL: Zakon.ru/blog. zakon.ru/blog/2017/12/16/innovacii_v_yurisprudencii_obzor_dostizhenij_i_tendencij_v_oblastiit-tehnologizacii_yuridicheskogo_b_71828 Accessed December 14, 2018.

[6] Dzhatdoev, A. 2018. Information Technologies in Jurisprudence. *Young Scientist* 6: 20-24. URL: https://moluch.ru/archive/192/48304. Accessed November 11, 2018.

[7] Gercke, M. 2014. *The Cybercrime Concept: Phenomenon, Tasks and Legal Response.* URL: www.itu.int/en/ITU-D/Cybersecurity/Documents/Cybercrime2014_R.pdf Accessed November 5, 2018.

[8] Jost, D., and Johann, K. 2017. E-Justice in Germany-an inventory of digitization of Justice. *New Legal Weekly Journal* 38: 2705-2708.

[9] Kobler, R. 2006. eJustice: from the long road to the digital future of Justice. *New Legal Weekly Journal* 29: 2089-2091.

[10] Kuznetsov, P. 2018. *Information Technologies in Legal Activities*. Moscow, Urait, 246 P.

[11] Latyshev, D. 2017. Brief Overview of Information Technologies Used in Legal Activities. *Innovative Science* 10: 14–17.

[12] Lestrade, Dr. E. 2006. Model Information Technology Contract Terms and Systems Implementation Contracts in Europe. *European Newsletter*, June 2006, URL: https://ssrn.com/abstract=909781 Accessed December 10, 2018.

[13] Litvinov, V. 2017. *Information Technologies in Legal Activities*. Saint Petersburg, Peter, 320 P.

[14] Malchikov, N. 2017. *Technological Innovations in Legal Service and Legal Assistance Rendering. Relevant Legal Issues: files of the VI International Scientific Conference.* Moscow: Buki-Vedi, pp. 4-7.

[15] Nadygina, E. 2007. *A Theoretical Legal Analysis of the Influence of Information Technologies on Legal Consciousness.* Ph.D. in Law thesis. Nizhny Novgorod, 28 P.

[16] Rak, I. 2016. Information Technologies in Activities of Law Enforcement Authorities. *Innovative Science* 2–3:132–135.

[17] Sidorov, Yu. 2015. Differences in the Interpretation of Electronic Justice in Russia and Abroad. *Scholarly Notes of the Petrozavodsk State University* 5:108-111.

[18] Teleshina, N. 2014. Implementation of Electronic Justice in Russia (on an Example of the Commercial Court of the Vladimir Region). *Arbitration and Civil Procedure* 6: 44-57.

[19] Wyngaarden, L. 2018. *5 Questions Lawyers Should Ask About AI.* URL: www.artificiallawyer.com/2018/09/27/5-questions-lawyers-should-ask-about-ai Accessed November 9, 2018.

[20] Wu, Z., Singh, B., Davis, L. S., Subrahmanian, V.S. 2017. *Deception Detection in Videos.* URL: http://arXiv:1712.04415v1[cs.AI]12Dec2017arxiv.org/pdf/ 1712.04415.pdf. Accessed November 08, 2018.

Chapter 12

Innovative Aspects of Defense Attorneys' Activities on Collection of Evidence at the Pre-Trial Stages of Criminal Proceedings

Irina E. Milova*, **Maksim A. Yavorskii and Tatiana A. Kalentieva**
Samara State University of Economics, Samara, Russia

Abstract

The role of the defense lawyer in the proving process is still topical. The defense lawyer performs one of the procedural functions, which indicates his participation in the proving process. However, the issue of the extent of participation is ambiguous that is determined by the specifics of defensive activity in criminal proceedings. The participation of a defense lawyer in collecting evidence at the pre-trial stages is of particular importance since they are farthest from real competition and continue to maintain the traditions of the investigative process with investigative actions as the main method of evidence collection. The law-maker has chosen a policy aimed at broadening the defense lawyer's powers in collecting evidence step-by-step, having caused some disbalance by this approach. On the one hand, the defense lawyer is granted certain rights on participation in the pre-trial proving, on the other hand, the law-maker does not provide a mechanism for exercise of these rights and can use them indirectly through an investigator. It should be noted that the law-maker is taking measures to overcome these restrictions that are indicated by recent innovations. At the same time, new forms of defensive activity,

* Corresponding Author's Email: irina.milova@ro.ru.

In: Economic and Legal Foundations of Innovative Development …
Editors: Gabibulla Khasaev, Victoria Bolgova, Sergey Bortnikov et al.
ISBN: 978-1-68507-730-3

for example, advocatory examination emerged. The authors of the article made attempts to estimate the effectiveness of such innovations.

The purpose of the research is related to the need to integrate available regulatory approaches and carry out the scientific generalization of theoretical views structured with regard to legislative innovations; studying the forms of defense lawyer's participation in collecting evidence at the pre-trial stages of the criminal proceedings, including the investigative actions, is in focus.

Keywords: defensive activity, participation in investigative actions, defense lawyer, advocatory examination, advocatory (parallel) investigation, adversarial principles, pre-trial stages of proceedings

Introduction

We do not agree with the optimism of some authors who claim that the defense and prosecution now have equal opportunities for collection and presentation of evidence at the pre-trial stages of the criminal proceedings [13, pp. 46-51]. Such an argument rather seems a long-term objective than true reality.

Methodology

The procedural phenomenon of defensive activity is studied from the point of a generally accepted epistemological approach. At the same time, the advantages of specific scientific methods, including historical, formal-logical, comparative-law, analysis and synthesis, statistical, social modeling, survey, interview, and legal experiments are also used. Other methods include qualitative and quantitative field research methods. The long-term professional experience of the authors in law enforcement bodies and advocacy made it possible to obtain representative data that would allow revealing the topical problems related to the collection of evidence by defense lawyers at the pre-trial stages of criminal proceedings.

Subject-Matter

The authors try to show that the participation of the defense lawyer in the proving process at the pre-trial stages of the criminal proceedings is not full and is left at the discretion of the investigator.

Along with that, it is noted that lawyers do not take the opportunities already provided by the criminal procedure law in full, for example, the right for the examination of persons holding the relevant information under their consent.

At the same time, most lawyers interviewed said that such examinations are useless and even dangerous since it is extremely difficult to predict the evidentiary value of them from the standpoint of a defense lawyer. Often, at the moment of examination, the information received seems very useful for the defendant's interests, however, they can change their direction later in the investigation.

The article addresses the issues of defensive activity strategies, which are directly associated with the participation forms of a lawyer in the collection of evidence. The authors substantiate the idea that it is not always possible to determine the nature of evidence (defensive or indicting) in a situation of informational uncertainty typical for pre-trial stages. In the absence of a clear forecast, they recommend don't bring the relevant information to the investigator's notice immediately. Moreover, he can use the obtained data to enforce the indictment by conducting additional and repeated investigative actions. Thus, we will have the opposite result for the defendant, which is unacceptable under the special defense mission of criminal proceedings.

Findings

Based on the results of the research, we justify a statement that the lawyer is hardly the participant of the proving process in the traditional understanding.

The scope of his powers in this segment is much less than those given to an investigator. Moreover, he does not have the power tools for other participants of the proceedings, respectively; his powers for their engagement in his defensive activities are limited. At the same time, any right is correlating with a corresponding duty. In this regard, if the defense lawyer is considered as a full-fledged participant of the evidence-collecting process endowed with the respective powers, then he should be held liable for the non-fulfillment of this obligation. It's hardly fair given that he appears in the proceedings much later than the participants of the prosecution who have already collected negative information on the defendant. Step by step, these participants of the proving process always get ahead of the defense lawyer's actions, which are objectively related to the settled features of the domestic criminal proceedings where the bulk of the evidence is collected at pre-trial stages.

Not supporting the idea of advocatory, the so-called parallel investigation, the authors, nevertheless, believe that the lawyer should not turn into an observer who is formally present in investigative actions. He should initiate the collection of information that is useful for the defendant through legal methods (for example, by addressing private detectives, experts for drawing up adversarial opinions on issues that are relevant for the defense of the defendant's interests). In this sense, the activities of defense lawyers should be connected to modern technologies, including digital ones. They should use the capabilities of the Internet to collect information that may become proof of the innocence of the defendant. Naturally, such actions should be agreed with the defendant to avoid the disclosure of personal data, investigative, advocate, official, and commercial secrets.

Analysis and Discussion

An analysis of the discussion on the role of the defense lawyer in the proving process allows identifying two main directions. Representatives of the first direction are convinced that the defense lawyer does not have sufficient powers to effectively perform his procedural function, i.e., to protect the rights and legitimate interests of the suspect, indictee, and defendant [7, pp. 72-74]. They articulate the idea that the rights of a defense lawyer in the proving process should be promptly and dramatically broadened through the introduction of the institution of "private investigation" [8]. Advocates of the broad concept offer to amend the current Criminal Procedure Code of the Russian Federation (hereinafter referred to as "Criminal Procedure Code") with a chapter on the private investigation. At the same time, they propose amendments to the Criminal Code of the Russian Federation (hereinafter referred to as the Criminal Code of the Russian Federation), namely, to include a corpus delicti that governs the liability of defense lawyers for falsification of evidence and other ways of their illegal collection and submission [14, pp. 158-162].

The adherents of the second, more balanced approach, recognize that the defense lawyer's powers in collecting evidence should be broadened [15, p. 11]. However, it is believed that they should be broadened step by step through the introduction of individual elements of the adversarial process [18, pp. 199-202] (the strategy has been followed by domestic criminal procedure legislator quite for a long time is maintained). The second standpoint seems more justified to us since it stays within the theory of sharing procedural functions in criminal proceedings; we systemically support it in our studies [10, pp. 117-122; 11, pp. 34-39].

Not sharing the idea on the introduction of advocatory investigation, we believe that the defense is free to state its argument along with the prosecution and bring its evidential establishment in the final procedural document versus indictment. This argument can be called an acquittal judgment. The criminal procedure law should enshrine the investigator's obligation to render upon the termination of the investigation to be included in the criminal case file and submitted to the court along with the criminal indictment. Taking over a case, the court will be able to be acquainted with the contentions of each party to the proceedings in an integrated form.

It is hardly advisable to legally endow the defense lawyer with the right to independent private investigative actions. These rights are associated with the need to apply procedural compulsion. Such activities are not provided with the status of a lawyer in particular, and with the procedural function of the defense in general. Moreover, it contradicts his objective in criminal proceedings, distorting the meaning and purpose of legal aid to criminally liable persons. We must not forget that the defense is both legal and moral activity, which techniques should be flawless from the point of professional advocacy ethics [12, p. 25]. At the same time, it is clear that the lawyer has limited opportunities for collecting the evidence without coercion techniques, which puts him in a deliberately unequal position with the investigator provided with them.

Within the present framework of the criminal proceedings, the lawyer hardly can make urgent investigative actions independently since often there is no suspect, indictee, and, therefore, a defense lawyer at the initial stages of the investigation. An example is an examination of the crime scene as one of the basic and most informative investigative actions. It is the information gathered during its examination that allows planning the further course of the investigation and determines the expediency of other investigative actions. It appears that the lawyer will be deliberately deprived of the opportunity to make investigative actions. In this sense, the suggestions on the advisability of a lawyer's participation in the proceedings even before the suspect identification, that is, upon the initiation of a criminal case, look quite articulated. On the other hand, it contravenes the principle of the defense lawyer's participation in the proceedings according to the defendant's will. If the appointed lawyer participates, then most likely the participants will be exclusively formal. Let us suppose that the lawyer will try to examine the crime scene. Under a different level of professional expertise of the advocate community representatives, it will hardly be ensured that their participation in this kind of procedure will not lead to the loss of evidence, including a defensive one.

The reason can be both insufficient forensic training, and strategical omission, the lack of appropriate technical means in the lawyer's toolkit to record the detected objects, as well as the inability to work with them and interpret the results. The solution can be an engagement of experts since the defense lawyer does not have to conduct a legal examination himself, it is allowed to use the services of people who have the appropriate equipment and know the necessary methods and technologies. Moreover, in the context of recent innovations, the investigator must accept the expert's opinion submitted by the defense lawyer to be included in the case file.

The analysis of the Criminal Procedure Code of the Russian Federation shows that the Code does not provide for the defense lawyer's right to have recourse to an expert during examination but at the same time, doesn't prohibit it. We strongly object to the suggestions on the imposition of the obligation to submit the information gathered to the investigator made from time to time, since the determination of such submission is a matter of defense strategy. Besides, when identifying circumstances harmful for the defendant, the lawyer is not obliged to inform the investigation, otherwise, the principle of advocate secrecy will not be respected.

If the crime scene is examined in conditions when the defense lawyer has already been the participant of the proceedings, then he will be involved in the investigative actions in the event of examination under participation of the suspect (the person against whom the preliminary investigation is being conducted, the indictee) because it's expressly provided for by law. However, the crime scene is mostly examined without the participation of the suspect, even if available. In this case, the law provides the lawyer with an opportunity to file a petition for participation in these investigative proceedings. Article 159 of the Federal Law No. 73-FZ as of April 17, 2017, was amended with clauses 2.1 and 2.2. In clause 2.1, the law-maker has established the obligation of the investigator to allow the defense lawyer's petition to participate in particular investigative proceedings.

The aforementioned law also introduced a rule according to "the inclusion of the evidence, including expert opinions, to the criminal case file cannot be denied to the persons who filed a petition if the facts they seek to establish are relevant to the criminal case that is confirmed by this evidence." This rule duplicates the provisions of Part 3, Art. 86 of the Criminal Procedure Code in accordance herewith the defense lawyer was granted the right to "gather evidence." Theorists and practitioners have repeatedly expressed their opinion on this matter in the literature. The point of the discussion was that the defense lawyer is not endowed with the right to form the evidence; he can only gather information. Moreover, having included the information gathered by the defense lawyer upon his petition, only the investigator can give this information the status of evidence. Nevertheless, as we see, the law-maker restated this provision in Art. 159 of the Criminal Procedure Code. However, this did not change anything, since the defense lawyer still cannot collect evidence. Besides, acting within the established approach, the law-maker again hasn't yet not determined the mechanism for the implementation of this rule.

As noted above, the law-maker endowed the defense lawyer with the authority to examine persons holding relevant information. However, such actions are permitted only upon their consent. Obviously, in the event of non-consent, the compulsion of communication with a lawyer is prohibited by law [19]. For the sake of justice, let us note that the vast majority (98%) out of the 150 interviewed and surveyed lawyers said that the citizens do not often refuse to participate in the examination. From the impersonal point of view, it is explained by the fact that the lawyer does not intend to communicate with random persons, but chooses those whom the defendant had told him about. This factor predetermines a high probability that they won't avoid communicating information useful for the defense of the suspect (indictee). This circumstance does not release the defense lawyer from a thorough consideration of examination reasonability to forecast the results to be achieved.

Besides, the term "examination" seems unsuitable to define the actions of a defense lawyer. On the one hand, such a definition is associated with operational procedures. On the other hand, this term is not typical for investigative actions (in this case, interrogation is provided). At the same time, the interrogation is not classified as a voluntary procedure, it contains some coercion elements (compulsory attendance and testimony, the obligation to be veracious). It turns out that the rules of advocate examination and methods of results recording are not legally enshrined, which indicates its out-of-procedure nature and essentially cancels the evidentiary value [17, pp. 52-54]. At the same time, recent innovations lift this limitation concerning trying criminal cases by district courts with the participation of jurors, since here the evidence will be evaluated by appointed defense lawyers without regard to the criterion of their admissibility. With the foregoing in mind, compliance with the procedural form of evidence preservation loses its significance for defense lawyers.

Thus, to date, the concept of advocatory investigation is a solely theoretical construct of narrow-doctrinal importance, which is not denied by its developers [9, pp. 21-29]. At the same time, the prospect of making it a regulatory construct suitable for practical application is quite true [3, pp. 49-54]. It is noteworthy that the law-maker is making significant steps in this direction. An example is the recent amendment of Article 159 of the Criminal Procedure Code of the Russian Federation with Part 2.2, which prohibits refusal of the evidence produced by the defense lawyer, as well as expert opinions, to be included in the criminal case file [2]. At the same time, there is one exception from this general rule, i.e., a refusal is possible if the evidence does not seem relevant to the case. This situation leaves to unscrupulous investigators the room to maneuvers to enforce the prosecution's positions. At the same time, this innovation undoubtedly shows the law-maker's desire to give the status of evidence to the information gathered by the defense lawyer in the defendant's interests.

A parallel advocatory investigation undoubtedly will require additional costs for legal proceedings both from the state and citizens who will be interested in its administration. The financial resources of the participants are not equal that can lead to discriminated defense when higher-income parties will get professional legal aid, and poor ones - only minimal services.

Unequal exercise of the right to collect and submit evidence depending on the level of financial well-being contradicts the constitutional provisions according to the right to professional legal aid is guaranteed to everyone (Article 48 of the Constitution of Russia). This point should be regarded in the subsequent legislative broadening of the defense lawyers' powers on the collection of evidence.

Conclusion

1. Sharing the opinions on the necessary broadening of a defense lawyer's rights to participate in the proving process, especially at the pre-trial stages, we, however, object to the introduction of the advocatory investigation institution. The investigation should be carried out only by the participant of the proving process who performs a specific procedural function. In addition, any overlapping causes mistakes, distortion, and loss of evidence. The actions of defense lawyers to gather evidence have a specific purpose, i.e., to disprove the case. Therewith, the defense lawyer should not seek out true perpetrators. Such activities carried out in procedural forms are more likely to be subsidiary that eliminates the gaps in the investigation from the point of filling it with defensive information.
2. The flaws of the concept of parallel advocatory investigation are as follows:
   - the accuracy of the information provided by other persons to the defense lawyers, for example, during an advocatory examination, is not ensured;
   - the impossibility to reproduce the conditions of executing some procedural actions after receipt of necessary evidence with their help by the defense lawyer (under this approach, an extremely important part of the proving process on verification of the evidence stand aside that will undoubtedly affect the evaluation);
   - the inadmissibility to endow a defense lawyer with powers to take coercive measures during the collection of evidence (most investigative actions can be executed only using procedural coercion, however, if the lawyer use coercion, it will contradict the defense function assigned to him).
3. Lawyers should have more active recourse to private detectives in the interests of the defended persons and upon their consent using the information collected to substantiate the arguments in favor of the defendant.

4. It is necessary to endow the defense lawyer with the right to address independent experts upon the consent of the suspect (indictee) to investigate those issues that have previously been the subject matter of opinions drawn up at the assignment of the investigation [5, pp. 64-71]. Such opinions should be deemed as adversarial examinations; the obligation to accept them at the request of the defense to be included in the case file should be imposed on the investigator [6, pp. 45-51].
5. Provide the defense lawyer with the opportunity to get familiarized with all the files in a case at any time after his admission to participating in the case.
6. To impose on the investigator the duty to interrupt the interrogation at the suspect's (indictee's), if they express willingness to meet with a lawyer and get his advice. Interrogation may be resumed only after the defendant is provided with the opportunity to get a defense lawyer's recommendations on concerning issues.
7. Deciding on participation in a particular investigative action, the lawyer should not rely on quantitative indicators. It's more important to get the result from this participation to gather relevant information for substantiation of a defensive argument [4]. The role of the defense lawyer in the investigative action should be quite active and cannot be reduced to a formal presence [16, pp. 45-46].
8. The strategy issues associated with the participation of a defense lawyer in collecting evidence at pre-trial stages have become of tremendous importance [1, p. 255]. Based on the understanding that such participation has a single purpose, i.e., to act in the defendant's interests, the defense lawyer should predict the possible results of specific procedural actions and avoid those that are ambiguously useful for the suspect (indictee).
9. A defense lawyer should take into account that the evidential activity is becoming more complicated using modern innovative technologies and digital tools. Representatives of the lawyer community certainly should master and use this toolkit to justify their case.
10. Important changes are associated with the introduction of juror institutions in the performance of district courts (since 01.06.2018); therefore the legal nature of the data collected by the lawyer has dramatically changed. Compliance with the procedural form is no longer important since the legal force of defensive evidentiary information does not depend on it and jurors do not evaluate evidence

from the standpoint of their admissibility (Part 6, Article 335 of the Criminal Procedure Code of the Russian Federation). In this sense, the files obtained by the defense become highly effective from the point of their significance for the defendant.

11. We believe that it is advisable to clarify the terms since the definition of "evidence" cannot be applied to the result obtained by the lawyer. It's more accurate to talk about "evidentiary information" or "information relevant to the criminal case."
12. The law-maker undoubtedly will continue to broaden the powers of the defense lawyer on the collection of evidence at the pre-trial stages, since adversarial principle should be observed in all types of legal proceedings, at any stage, without any exemptions and exceptions.

References

[1] Baev, M. O. 2006. The Theory of Professional Defense: Tactical and Ethical Aspects. Moscow: Yurlitinform, 336 P.

[2] Federal Law No. 73-FZ as of April 17, 2017 "On Amendments to the Criminal Procedure Code of the Russian Federation." *Rossiiskaya Gazeta [Russian Newspaper]* 83.

[3] Kalyuzhnyi, A. N. 2017. Advocatory Investigation in the Criminal Proceedings: Issues of Legal Construction and Practical Implementation. *Advocatory Practice.* Lawyer 1: 49-54.

[4] Khmelnitskaya, T. V. 2016. The Issues of Drawing Evidence in the Course of Pre-trial Criminal Proceedings. Ph. D. in Law thesis, 12.00.09. Nizhny Novgorod, 213 P.

[5] Kiselyov, P. P. 2016. Opinion and Evidence of a Specialist on the Lawyer's Initiative: Issues of Legal Regulation and Methods of Their Solution. Annual Scientific Readings of the branch of the Russian State Social University in Klin. *Collected Proceedings* 1(13): 64-71.

[6] Kiselyov, P. P. 2017. The Legal Status of Information Collected by a Defense Lawyer and its Relation with the Procedural Form of Evidence. *Eurasian Advocacy* 4(29): 45-51.

[7] Kolesnik, K. R. 2017. Advocatory Investigation: Obstacles and Possible Paths to Overcome Them. *Eurasian Advocacy* 3(28): 72-74.

[8] Martynchik, E G. 2018. Advocatory Investigation in Criminal Proceedings. Theoretical and Methodological Foundations of Advocatory Investigation Doctrine. Moscow: Uniti-Dana. *Zakon I Pravo*, 240 P.

[9] Martynchik, E. G. 2013. Legal Foundations of the Advocatory Investigation: State and Prospects (to the development of the concept and model). *Advocatory Practice* 6: 21-29.
[10] Milova, I. E. 2009. The Concept of Advocatory Parallel Investigation: Theoretical and Practical Components. *Post-graduate Bulletin of the Volga Region* 5, 6: 117-122.
[11] Milova, I. E. 2010. Fundamentals of Advocatory Parallel Investigation Strategy. *Issues of Economics and Law* 1: 34-39.
[12] Nasonova, I. A. 2008. Participation of Defense Lawyer in the Preliminary Investigation. *Ph. D. in Law thesis*. Volgograd, 246 P.
[13] Salakko, A. S. 2017. Advocatory Investigation as a Lawyer's Activity in the Russian Criminal Proceedings. *Advocatory Practice*. Moscow: Lawyer 3: 46-51.
[14] Salakko, A. S. 2017. Developmental Prospects of Advocatory Investigation Institution. *Gaps in Russian Legislation* 2: 158-162.
[15] Shakheldov, F. G. 2011. Participation of the Defense Lawyer in Proving at the Preliminary Investigation. *Ph. D. in Law thesis*. 21 P.
[16] Sheifer, S. A. 1998. Evidence and Proving on Criminal Cases: Issues of Theory and Legal Regulation. *Togliatti*, 45-46.
[17] Stroykov, V. 2014. Exercise of Defense Lawyer's Right to Examination of Parties. *Legality* 6: 52-54.
[18] Urgalkin, A. S. 2011. Defense Lawyer in Proving on a Criminal Case at the Preliminary Investigation. *Gaps in Russian Legislation* 2: 199-202.
[19] Yumadilov, B. G. 2018. Lawyer as a Participant of Advocatory Activities in the Russian Federation. *Ph. D. in Law thesis*, 12.00.11. Moscow, 22 P.

Chapter 13

Impact of Tax-Haven Business on the Development of Regional Economies

Svetlana N. Revina*, Pavel A. Paulov and Anna V. Sidorova
Samara State University of Economics, Samara, Russia

Abstract

Relevance. Relations between countries in the modern economy are becoming more interdependent. In turn, the globalization of the economy and further development of regional economic integration ultimately leads to a gradual unification of the tax systems throughout the world to establish a favorable environment for business development. However, each country has a specific system of taxation and currency regulation. This benefit is sometimes used by non-residents of countries to gain additional profit or to cancel out the requirements of the currency legislation in the country of residence in the event of replacing production facilities or managerial staff to another jurisdiction.

Goals and objectives of the research. The research of the impact of tax-haven business on the regional economy is intended to draw the attention of theoretical scientists and legal practitioners to this problem. The authors set out to study the impact of tax-haven business on the development of the regional economy; investigate statistical data; reveal the specific features of its impact on the global economy.

Findings. Based on the research we can conclude that the impact of tax-haven business on the development of the regional economy is ambiguous. Along with a broad list of advantages of offshore economic development, some disadvantages require improvement and

* Corresponding Author's Email: 29.revina@mail.ru.

In: Economic and Legal Foundations of Innovative Development …
Editors: Gabibulla Khasaev, Victoria Bolgova, Sergey Bortnikov et al.
ISBN: 978-1-68507-730-3

development of legal regulation of offshore companies and zones in general.

Keywords: business, capital, tax policy, tax heaven, regional economy, financial assets, financial crimes

Introduction

Nowadays, tax havens play a pivotal role in the global economy. A significant volume of financial flows passes through tax havens; they are crucial in international commerce. On the territory of the tax haven, there are a huge number of investment and commercial banks granting loans at lower interest rates and rendering a wide range of investment services for private and corporate clients. Tax havens should be characterized as wide-scale centers concentrating over half of the world capital.

Methodology

When conducting this research, the authors have applied the methods, such as comparative law, logical, analysis and synthesis, systemic and modeling. And since every single method of research does not allow reconstructing the actual state of matters in the area under consideration, the authors have used the above methods in an integrated manner.

Findings

The development of a tax haven can have a favorable effect not only on the economy of the country providing tax haven, but also the economy of the whole world. Globalization processes, which have intensively developed in recent years, contribute to the extension of a tax haven, a boost of investments, enhancement of money circulation, etc. But at the same time, tax haven has become an instrument for the commission of financial crimes that support the smuggling of drugs, weapons, and terrorism. Confidentiality, anonymity, and no need for filing returns on sources of income contribute to the evolvement of negative trends.

Table 1. The dynamic pattern of capital outflow to tax haven across regions of the world, 2013-2017

Region	The volume of capital outflow, billion dollars		Average annual growth rate, %
	2013	2017	
Eastern Asia	3,102	4,317	6.9
Middle East	2,365	2,934	3.7
Latin America	1,427	1,973	6.7
Russian Federation	1,319	1,913	7.9
Africa	587	710	3.1
Southern Asia	190	253	5.7

Discussion

According to the data of Oxfam company, more than 18.5 trillion US dollars (this is about 19.5%) of savings are kept in a tax haven, two-thirds of which are deposited in a European tax haven and one third - in British offshore jurisdictions [14]).

Over the past 10 years, the damage from the capital outflow has amounted to more than 156 billion US dollars.

Today, offshore companies are most widespread in the real estate sector. 79.5% of all enterprises in this sector are registered in a tax haven. Offshore companies are widespread also in the financial and investment sector (60% of enterprises), in the banking sector (56%), in the fuel and energy sector (49%), in the field of telecommunications services (44%), in retail (43%).

According to the data of the Global Financial Integrity Company for 2004-2015, Russia ranks second after China by the extent of illegal exports of capital. Besides, Russia has the highest rate of capital outflow to a tax haven [3].

Oxfam Company also evaluated the amount of tax-evaded capital based on data from the Credit Suisse Global Wealth Databook, which noted that the world welfare, except for real estate, is 94.7 trillion US dollars.

Bearing in mind the fact that the World Bank estimated the global economy at 75.6 trillion dollars at the end of 2016, it's about at least 7.5 trillion dollars in cash and securities held in bank and brokerage accounts in a tax haven [5]. Besides, according to NBRE data, the largest share of funds in tax havens is held by wealthy families from the countries of the Persian Gulf, Latin America, and also Russia. Their foreign assets amount to 45-75% of national GDP [8].

NBER experts call the United Arab Emirates the absolute leader by the number of financial assets held in a tax haven in respect to national GDP. The wealthiest people from this country keep abroad the amount equal to 75% of the entire economy. Based on the estimate of the UAE economy by the World Bank, this is at least 261.5 billion US dollars.

Next follows Venezuela (65% of GDP, data in absolute figures is unavailable), Saudi Arabia (57% of GDP, or 368.45 billion US dollars), and Russia (46% of GDP, approximately 590 billion US dollars). At the same time, NBER researchers carried out also an alternative assessment of offshore capital in Russia and do not take into account the financial assets of wealthy people who have changed their tax residency. It is by an order lower than the main one, i.e., about 14% of Russia's GDP, or 179.6 billion US dollars [13].

Also, NBER identified a rather high share of offshore capital in respect to the size of national economies in Argentina and Greece (35% per each), Taiwan and Portugal (21-22%), Turkey (19%), Belgium (18%), Great Britain (17%), Germany and France (15% each). In Italy, South Africa, Spain, and Ireland, this figure is 10-12%. The proportion of offshore assets is less than 10% of the national GDP among wealthy families from Colombia, Thailand, Austria, the USA, Mexico, Australia, and Brazil. The countries with the smallest proportion of "offshore wealth" are Korea (1% of GDP, or 14 billion US dollars), Poland (1.5%; 7 billion US dollars), China (2.3%; $ 257.6 billion US dollars), Denmark and Finland (2.5% of GDP each; 7.6 and 5.9 billion US dollars respectively).

As noted by NBER economists, the share of offshore wealth among wealthy families from a particular country far from always depends on local tax policies or the domestic economic situation. Thus, the research emphasizes that Denmark and Finland are commonly recognized high-tax jurisdictions, while Korea is a country with a moderate tax policy. In turn, Poland and China are countries with fast-growing economies, which have established favorable conditions for a substantial boost of household welfare [2]. The report states that this situation generally contributes to the augmentation of offshore capital of wealthy families, as has been shown in the example of Russia in the era of high oil prices of the mid-2000s [15].

NBER experts also indicate that among leaders by the proportion of tax-haven wealth there are both conditional autocracies (Saudi Arabia, Russia) and countries with a recent history of authoritarian governance (Argentina, Greece), as well as old European democracies (Great Britain, France). In this regard, economists conclude that the political system plays a lesser role in the distribution of wealth along with different jurisdictions than location and "specific national trajectories."

For example, the growth of offshore capital in European countries and Russia depends on its geographical proximity to Switzerland that was the first to establish a powerful cross-border capital management industry and attract cash flows from all over the world. NBER consider the overall growth of welfare of UHNWI (Ultra High Net Weight Individuals) around the world, the availability of natural resources in the country of capital origin, and the long period of political and economic instability after World War II the important factors for the development of the "offshore aristocracy" [7]. Besides, according to NBER data, the flow of funds into tax havens was influenced by the unforeseen growth of income in the oil industry in the first decade of the 21st century, and several political upheavals, including an unexpected outcome of elections and coups in some countries.

A large number of tax havens are located on the territories of developing countries (about 65%), the rest 35% - in developed ones.

Most tax havens are located on island territories, namely the Bahamas, Antilles, Virgin, Bermuda, Barbados, Cayman Islands, Jersey and Guernsey, Malta, Cyprus, Madeira, Western Samoa, Hong Kong, Ireland, Lebanon, Liberia, Panama, Liechtenstein, and many others.

This fact is determined by the unavailability of natural resources and wealth, highly skilled force. Selling a legal address is the only way to attract investment and develop the economy of these countries. An advantageous geographical location increases the likelihood and effectiveness of attracting foreign residents.

The development of tax haven on the territories of Asia and Latin America is determined not only by low or zero tax rates but, first of all, by the broad sales markets of offshore companies' products and low-cost labor resources.

As for the tax haven in Hong Kong, we should remark on the attractiveness of tax rates on this territory. Hong Kong provides services for the accelerated and simplified movement of capital thereby raising the liquidity of company funds to a great extent, as well as ensuring high legitimacy and transparency of transactions.

Describing the Bahamas, it should be noted that offshore companies bring more than 12 percent of the country's GDP. Its territory is saturated with credit, insurance, and investment companies providing a wide range of services (banking, consulting, portfolio management, etc.).

A tax haven of Singapore has a good reputation. This is a relatively new direction for the country [4]. The number of services and registered companies in its territory is increasing every year.

The tax haven in Dubai is also becoming more popular and attractive for large businesses. Transaction transparency, high legitimacy, reliability and confidentiality, stability, a wide range of services provided in Dubai, the availability of highly skilled personnel from around the world, favorable geographical location are key factors of boosting investment activity.

Switzerland has been granted the offshore status due to the high degree of confidentiality and capital security. Banking, insurance, and consulting are the most common and attractive services [6].

A wide range of services is provided in the offshore area of Gibraltar, which is the most popular among European enterprises. Over the past 10 years, income from the offshore business has shown an increase of 7-12% per annum, despite an upturn of the profit tax rate to 10%. The companies registered in Gibraltar have an opportunity to open up plenty of branches without the need to license each of them. This is cost- and time-saving much on a tremendous scale.

The largest world rating agencies annually analyze changes in the territories of a tax haven, economic and financial trends, the number of investors, employees, and many other parameters [12].

According to the data of the rating agencies Standard & Poor's and Fitch and Moody's for 2016, the following countries ranked in the TOP-5 by "the most favorable regime for registering and running a business":

- Dubai (no taxes, no need to file tax returns);
- Belize (simplified procedure for company registration, low registered capital, complete confidentiality of information on the company's activity);
- British Virgin Islands (no taxes, confidentiality, and anonymity);
- Seychelles (one of the simplest registration mechanisms that require only application and copies of documents of the future business owner);
- Cayman Islands (24-hour company registration, no taxation, and no need to file tax returns).

According to data of the same rating agencies, the top five tax havens with preferential taxation are represented by [1]:

- Great Britain (relatively low taxes, simple and transparent procedure for financial and tax returns);
- Singapore (according to Standard & Poor's agency, it has the simplest tax system);
- Hong Kong (low taxes, transaction transparency);
- Isle of Man (a fixed annual fee instead of taxes, no need to file tax returns);
- Malta (preferential taxation is provided to enterprises and business owners who do not breach the laws of Malta).

According to the data of other rating agencies Tax Justice Network (TJN) and BCS Europe for 2016, the TOP-5 includes:

- Switzerland (the most reliable banks, transaction transparency, high guarantees, business insurance);
- Cayman Islands (the most loyal taxation);
- Luxembourg (simple registration of the company, transaction transparency, business insurance);
- Hong Kong (simple procedure for taking a loan and attracting investment, transaction transparency, high liquidity of enterprise assets);
- The state of Delaware in the USA (simple registration of the company, preferential taxation).

The Central Bank of the Russian Federation also annually draws up a list of tax havens. In accordance with data published on the official website, tax havens are divided into 3 groups:

- reliable tax haven with a convenient registration regime and substantial legislative framework (Ireland, Hong Kong, Switzerland, and Singapore);
- classic territories with a low tax burden, including the Bahamas, Cayman Islands, Bermuda, and the Virgin Islands;

- countries with zero taxation, but low reliability (Vanuatu, Liberia, the Marshall Islands, Noire).

In Russia, RBC (RosBusinessConsulting) agency makes up an individual rating of tax haven [11]. According to this reputable source, the most favorable zones for business registration with a convenient tax system in 2016 were the Maldives, Singapore, Hong Kong, the UAE, and Oman.

The practical value of the research. The research findings can be used in the practice of the legislative authorities of the Russian Federation and international organizations. The theoretical conclusions of the research can be used in research institutes, higher education institutions in teaching particular course units, such as "Theory of State and Law," "Constitutional Law," "Administrative Law," "Financial Law," "Tax Law."

Conclusion/Recommendations

For the risks of business-running to be reduced and illegal methods of money laundering and cybercrimes to be combated, the global community pays great attention to the legal regulation of tax havens. At the same time, strict legal regulation puts obstacles to investments in the territory of a tax haven. The countries should find a balance in the legal and tax regulation of tax-haven business [9] to attract foreign investments that will be an impetus to the development of the country's economy, the growth of population's employment, the flow of highly skilled personnel, jump in the production, increased number of companies and tax and insurance payments respectively, but do not propel the country into criminal business. Money laundering in a tax haven is the most common problem [10]. Several billion US dollars are annually transferred through trusts and banks of tax haven to the accounts of dummy individuals and companies and then are circulated in the real estate sector and legal business. This fact causes great damage to the economy of all countries and instigates the development of drug business and production and weapon smuggling.

References

[1] Alborova, M. V. 2017. The Role of Tax Haven in International Economic Relations. *Theory and Practice of Modern Science* 6(24): 1099-1103.

[2] Androsova, T. I. 2017. The Concept and Essence of Tax Haven Operation. *Young Scientist* 14: 312-314.

[3] Bulatov, A. 2017. Offshore Orientation of Russian Federation FDI. *Transnational Corporations* 24(2): 71-89.

[4] Egnatosyan, K. S., Bocharova, O. F. 2018. Offshore Taxation. *Alleya Nauki* [Scientific Lane] 3, 6(22).

[5] *Global Economic Prospects.* Fragile Recovery, World Bank Group. June 2017. http:doi.org/10.1596/978-1-4648-1024-4.

[6] Gulina, G. A. 2018. Recent Trends in the Development of Tax Haven. In the Collection: Evolution of Russian Law, Proceedings of the 16th International Scientific Conference of Young Scientists and Students. *Ural State Law University* 446-448.

[7] James, M. 2014. *Cyphering the Process of Economic Development*. Fourth Edition. Taylor Francis Group. London and New York, 81-120.

[8] Johannesen, A. N., Zucman, G. 2017. Who Owns the Wealth in Tax Havens? Macro Evidence and Implications. For Global Inequality. NBER Working Paper Series. *National Bureau of Economic Research* September 2017: 6-10.

[9] Nazarenko, V. A., Bochkova, E. V. 2016. Tax Haven of the World. *Young Scientist* 8: 626-629.

[10] Nechaev, A., Antipina, O., Matveeva, M., Prokopeva, A. 2015. Offshore schemes as an effective tax planning tool of enterprises' innovative activities. *Economic Chronicle-XXI* 7-8-2: 40-43.

[11] Popova, A. V., Zhakov, A. S. 2017. Geography of Tax Haven. In: *the Collection: Modern Educational Technologies in the Teaching of Natural and Human Sciences.* Collection of Scientific Papers of the 4th International Scientific and Methodological Conference. In: A. B. Makhovikov (Ed), 557-562.

[12] Sidorenko, A. Y., Adzhieva, A. Y. 2017. *Peculiar Features of Tax Haven in Russia.* In: *the Collection: Issues of the Effective Use of the Scientific Potential of Society.* Collected Papers of the International Science and Practice Conference: in 5 parts, 120-122.

[13] *The Leading Corporate Portal of the Offshore Industry*. URL: https://offshorewealth.info/.

[14] *The World of Offshore Financial Centers and the Role of the EU in the International Business* 2017: 12-14.

[15] Wilson, K. 2015. The Role of Offshore Jurisdictions in Russia. *Russian Law Journal* 3(2): 119-136.

Chapter 14

Multifactor Foundation of Resolving Urban Legal and Economic Conflicts

Vitalii A. Ponomarenkov[1,*], Natalia V. Nikitina[1] and Vitalii N. Oparin[2], Elena A. Efremova[1], Tatiana S. Cherevichenko[1]

[1]Samara State University of Economics, Samara, Russia

[2]Kuban State Agrarian University named after I. T. Trubilin, Krasnodar, Russia

Abstract

The relevance of the problem of revealing and resolving legal and economic urban conflicts is determined by the fact that nowadays people are massively moving from one country, region, or villages to cities that causes the imbalance of the urban environment destructs previously established relations and leads to conflicts with the most negative implications, so the study of these processes is crucial for the social development.

The content of the article is of scientific, theoretical, and practical value for scientific researchers and practitioners dealing with issues of economic migration, as well as legal and economic issues arising in this connection that have a certain conflict potential and determine social, economic, and legal stability. The article defines priorities and also reveals the prospects of legal and economic-social development of the urban environment.

The article will be interesting for scholars and practitioners involved in the monitoring of conflicts occurring in the urban environment, as well

* Corresponding Author's Email: 2770402@mail.ru.

In: Economic and Legal Foundations of Innovative Development …
Editors: Gabibulla Khasaev, Victoria Bolgova, Sergey Bortnikov et al.
ISBN: 978-1-68507-730-3

as in the identification, localization, and resolution of legal and economic conflicts arising in the urban environment.

Keywords: social life, urban conflict, economy, law, migration, urban environment, bio-social entity

JEL Codes: D74, P37, K42

Introduction

In modern social life, certain conflict situations (political, national-ethnic, socio-cultural, legal, economic, and so forth) of both explicit and implicit nature inevitably arise.

A society without conflicts is impossible since they stimulate the society to seek new mechanisms to arrange the legal and economic life of society and thereby develop.

In general, any conflict (from Lat. Confliktus) is a clash of two or more entities, parties, or (and) opinions of social interaction within a particular environment.

The methodological background of the paper was formed by a cognitive, system-determination methodological approach that required the application of a combination of general-scientific, specific-scientific, and special cognitive methods.

Findings

The city is the environment where most people are living today, i.e., the most complicated natural environment of human activity that provides great opportunities for self-fulfillment and creativity but poses many threats.

The private, legal and economic life of society is increasingly conquering the space of freedom, establishing various social institutions, rules of conduct, etc.

In economy and law, these are private property, free entrepreneurship, honor and dignity, rights and duties, legal guarantees, and much more.

A person, as a biosocial creature, adapts to these conditions, however, gets negative energy which causes various conflicts, since our innate socio-biological programs have been developed in completely different conditions and have had different mechanisms of negative potential channeling.

The city violates some basic sociobiological needs of a person:

- to be close to nature
- to establish free and soft relationships with people
- to be alone for some time
- to have personal space, etc.

In a big city, we are surrounded by many strange people. This is an anonymous mass community with its needs, strive to assert oneself and stand out from the crowd, etc.

The inability to satisfy these needs leads to social diseases that cause increased aggressiveness, detachment from solving common problems, lack of mutual care and mutual assistance in a difficult situation, troubled socialization of children, and a higher rate of crime.

Conflicts arising in the legal and economic life of a modern city are multidimensional; therefore, they should be studied with the use of multifactor analysis.

The research of factors that affect the formation and resolution of conflicts from the perspective of regulating the behavior of the urban community that includes various "actors" (individual or collective entity: individual, social group, etc., influencing other entities) at the local level of the urban environment.

The "urban community" as a local multistructural association, many social communities, residents, social and cultural groups living in the same territory has a low social interdependence.

At the same time, the urban life of society is arranged following the socio-territorial principles of "localization" and "neighborhood," which form certain expectations of people [8].

Present time, resettlement mechanisms are changing and its inner multidirectional processes of "urbanization" are intensifying, i.e., enhancement of the role of cities and urban culture takes place.

At the same time:

- the number of young people in cities increases due to the rural population;

- residents of pre-retirement and retirement age who have a certain educational, professional, and socio-cultural background but do not have sufficient finance and material resources for a decent life in the urban environment drain from the city to the countryside, i.e., "deurbanization" occurs.
- social and cultural patterns of behavior that have developed in the urban environment are spread beyond its boundaries, etc.

In the city, the people who have local experience of communicating in a team, narrow-group way of life, a special system of arranging legal and economic social life based on traditions and customs are trying to find their place in the urban space at any cost. Therewith, group ethnocentrism reinforces and therefore the natural attitudes of a particular socio-cultural community are formed that is manifested in the affirmation of its own random historically established institutions as universal ones. From the point of egocentrism, other socio-cultural communities are regarded as backward, uncivilized, etc. In this situation, the "theory of truth" acts as a form of legitimation of one's claims that often leads to conflicts [5].

In turn, social adaptation processes result in the depersonalization of interpersonal relations and detraditionalization of societal (common social) values, as well as ones associated with a particular area of social life (for example, legal, religious and other values).

The societal system undertaking the exercise of economic, social, spiritual, and other functions is an intrinsic factor in developing propensity towards conflicts in the urban community and shadow manifestations of the legal life of society that assumes changes in the communication system of society in general.

The societal system as a potential mechanism of self-reproduction is opposite to urbanization and localization of society that is associated with a narrowing of social, economic, and legal relations and social solidarity. Important features of the societal system are the properties such as "stability" and "sustainability." The first feature means that the system is continuously evolving without changing its structure, and the second one ensures the maintenance of the internal regulation of processes. In general, these elements support the subordination of the system to a single order.

Of course, processes leading to the dysfunction of the social system of the urban environment can occur and consequently, functions are substituted, i.e., entities for various reasons start to perform functions that are not typical to them and thereby show their non-competence, etc.

Therewith, natural and artificial "dysfunctional disorders" can entail disruption of the social system and in turn higher social tension, illegal acts, etc.

The emerging system to arrange the economic and legal life of society that includes people, system of their communication, rules, traditions and customs, their social ties, as though "models" a new system of relations in space and time thereby ensuring the interdependence of the system and the environment.

A man and society have an impact on the social environment, which, in turn, has an impact on them. Thereat, man's behavior largely depends on the role played by him in the urban space, as well as on those social norms and group value attitudes that are recognized in this society.

The system-forming parameters of arranging the legal life of society here are elements of communication such as "coordination" (a certain order of elements) and "subordination" (rights and duties, subordination and dependence) that are "genetically interrelated" due to their origin, as well as "functional connection" (a factor of systemic integrity).

Unfortunately, the modern urbanization processes are often associated with the growing number and changing the purpose of the urban community accompanied by an accumulation of impoverished population, higher crime rate, and a dysfunctional urban community that leads to social alienation of people, frequent conflicts, and the emergence of "ruderal community" (Ruderal - from lat. Rudus, ruderis - rubble, rubbish).

At the same time, the outflow of the population from cities to the countryside is often connected precisely to the deterioration of the socio-economic (primarily financial, food) and criminal situation.

The manifestation of the instability of the institutional development of the urban community can be explained by the weak social relation between the rural (traditional) and the urban social-value attitudes and the rules of behavior in society. Tradition-value behavior is still important among new citizens.

The "institutional" disintegrity of the behavior rules in society is the factor that hinders their social-group reproduction in the urban community. Thereby it can arouse and increase confrontation [6].

The multi-ethnization of the urban environment at the initial stage of external migration can also be a conflict-ridden and crime-ridden factor in the legal and economic life of urban society. As a rule, "institutional conflicts" in the city are expressed in social tensions regarding the traditionalization of rules, priorities, behavior rules, and social-value orientations, as well as shadow areas of the economy in the urban community, and the detraditionalization of these elements recognized by the migrant community.

"Institutional conflicts" in the modern multi-ethnic urban environment can also be caused by exclusion and depersonalization of community representatives that trigger interpersonal alienation.

Significant growth of migrant numbers in the urban environment leads to an escalation of ethnic "enclavization" of the urban community, which can entail the marginalization of societal values, as well as "detraditionalization" of the behavior rules recognized by migrants.

The enclavization of the stable socio-cultural (ethnic) resettlement areas of migrants leads to the social isolation of immigrants who are poorly adapted to life in the urban environment that reinforces the "anti-urbanism" of traditional ethnic-social communities. As a rule, the causes of legal and economic "urban conflicts" (arising in an urban environment) are associated with personal and impersonal contradictions of different "actors" (individual or collective: individuals, social groups, organizations, companies having an impact on other entities or interacting with them) [9].

Only some contradictions turn into conflict since several factors arouse legal and economic urban conflicts. Further, we will dwell on socio-determining factors that affect the occurrence and resolution of legal and economic urban conflicts in modern society through the mechanisms of regulating behavior. Conflict is one of the types of social communication during which actors struggle for values and claims on status, power, and resources, as well as neutralize, damage or eliminate opponents" [3].

The objective cause for the growing number of legal and economic conflicts in society is an intensification of a special kind of social communication, i.e., between individual entities and social groups.

It is no wonder that this is an indispensable stage of urban community development [10].

Concerning our research, *"legal conflict"* is considered as the opposition between actors of the social legal life due to different understanding of social standards of behavior and the commission of actions that destruct the regulating effect of legal and other social rules to raise their social status and change the state of the legal life of the urban environment.

In its turn, an *"economic conflict"* is a confrontation of participants of social communication with opposite socio-economic interests caused by statuses, position, and role in the system of socio-economic relations.

The conflict arising in the legal and economic life of the urban environment is a special kind of entities' (actors') behavior associated with legal and economic rules of behavior, as well as with legal and economic implications aimed at achieving a certain result through the imposition of their will and removal of competitors seeking the same result in a relatively closed community.

As a form of legal and economic life, the "behavior of actors" includes both ordered and chaotic processes, which are the basic concepts of the occurrence and resolution of the conflict in the legal and economic areas of urban community's life.

Besides, "behavior" is one of the most frequently used terms in the scientific literature that describes the external (motor) and internal (socio-biological) properties of people's life reflecting the level of their interaction with each other and with the living environment.

There is no consistent scientific approach to understanding "actors' behavior" yet. In our opinion, since the behavior of actors is very diverse, then various objects and events can stimulate it. The main point is that it should be aimed at achieving a goal or satisfying a need. However, it should be borne in mind that only some needs will be satisfied in full that generally gives rise to conflict.

If we talk about the "individual entity" (man), then firstly he seeks to satisfy his lower (essential) needs and only after it moves to self-expression.

As for collective legal behavior, it is aimed at providing the interaction of legal actors and many other things that forms the concept of "regulating societal life", but "behavior" in both situations is based on elements of the natural and the artificial human environment.

During their lives, the people found out themselves in different conflict situations, i.e., life circumstances that are much different from ordinary ones and associated with the confrontation of different trends, opinions, etc. (interpersonal, religious, industrial, economic, etc.).

Passing through these conflict situations, people feel different emotions and respectively exhibit different behavior.

Human behavior in a conflict situation has many dependencies that are influenced by many reasons. Moreover, it is the implicit and explicit needs of a man that are the foundation that motivates, i.e., acts as a direct driver of human behavior and occurrence of conflict.

By content, all needs can be classified into:

- bio-physiological needs (food, air, heat, sleep, and much more);
- socio-psychological needs (communication, labor, building groups, succeeding in activities; in self-affirmation and non-dependence, self-expression; protection and safety; dominance and subordination, starting your group (family), etc.;
- communicative and cognitive (cognition, education);
- affiliation to a social group (for example, public ethnic, tribal, clan, and other affiliation);
- socio-economic (food, clothes, housing, means of labor under the anatomical, physiological, ethnic, prestigious standards), etc.

The behavior of actors within legal and economic conflict may vary due to their affiliation to a particular socio-cultural community, the peculiarities of the psycho-motor response to a situation, traditions, and customs, etc. Under the influence of these factors, a "system of behavior rules," i.e., behavioral patterns in the form of simplified schemes involved in the development of individual and social-group (national) character is shaped.

An important role here is played by socio-biological, ethno-social, and religious factors. They are so intertwined that can establish an "individual-national style" of behavior manifested in special value orientations, a system of social assessments, prohibitions, and so forth, which determines the uniqueness of human behavior and sometimes leads to conflict.

Certainly, human behavior is largely determined by his "internal environment," which depends on the condition of the body and personal perception of the world.

When a person is in a state of internal conflict, his behavior can be defensive (characterized by a certain degree of inadequacy and aggressiveness) and present an interrelated form of a destructive-individual (based on socio-biological mechanisms) behavior.

It should be borne in mind that the problem of resolving legal and economic urban conflicts is mostly connected with the assessment of the inadequacy and aggressiveness of behavior in modern society.

This is determined by the performance of subconscious defensive socio-biological response mechanisms to a conflict (stress) situation, which has been formed at the early stages of social life. At present, these mechanisms are primarily instruments, i.e., conflicts most often arise when a person wants to get something (for example, children – toys, adults – to have something inaccessible, forbidden).

The propensity towards conflict is formed by several components. One of the destructive components is aggression as a form of destructive individual, the biological or social behavior of a person.

Against the background of the weakening of the traditional external constraints and social institutions of legal and economic regulation, a person gets ostensible moral freedom exhibited in increased "aggressiveness" towards another person, as well as more "socialized" forms (insult, struggle).

Aggression, as a socio-biological mechanism of human behavior, presents the reactions of irritation, negativity, anger, suspiciousness, resentment, insult, as well as physical aggression as an argument in a dispute.

Socio-biological mechanisms of aggressive conflict behavior of a person are triggered by various factors:

- the unfamiliar or uncomfortable atmosphere in the place of location.
- the individually subjective role played by a person in the current situation.
- environment
- the socio-cultural environment of other people, etc.

So, finding out himself on unfamiliar territory and in the team, a person may feel anxiety, which limits social network and can lead to conflict due to the influence of certain not evident factors, such as a special smell, color, interior, etc.

At the same time, aggressiveness can take various forms (from outwardly harmless acts to destructive, including murder). The latter contains the multi-factor biological and sociocultural condition of human aggression.

Undoubtedly, each person should have a certain degree of aggressiveness, because its absence leads to passivity, weakness, and lack of will in critical situations. However, increased aggressiveness can become the basis of conflict behavior and offenses.

A person's condition can be affected by the overlapping of initially neutral factors that combined into an irritation factor, which is called "correlation dependence."

This dependence of behavior is the ratio of its reactivity and activity reflecting the psychodynamic features of the conflict behavior of a man as a biological and social individual, as well as a personality, i.e., acting as properties that determine the dynamics of mental activity in terms of speed, intensity, direction, etc.

Reactivity performs an adaptive function; and activity is aimed at the adjustment of the situation, subordination to the individual. It is it underlies the dynamics of the arising conflict. Moreover, it should be noted that activity and reactivity most often do not depend on the content of the activity that caused the conflict, its motives, and values.

Reactivity and activity of the conflict as substantial features of human behavior affect the development of positive, negative, and neutral motivation in the current situation and its meaning and social-value foundation.

Therewith, activity acts as a balanced combination of initiative and assiduity, and reactivity allows a person to adapt to a conflict situation.

In general, these elements are indicators of a person's value contribution to the resolution of a conflict situation and social-group problems.

In other words, the behavior of a man as a personality in a conflict situation is determined by many factors and is intermediated by his understanding of a specific task, worldview, assessment of all the consequences, and the attitude of other people.

Thus, the behavior of individuals in economic and legal conflict is an outcome of evolution and social development, a special form of interaction with the environment, where the *socio-biological forms of regulation* (of active, subconsciously-targeted nature) affect the mental and verbal processes, and moral rules have become of great importance.

Of course, everyday life in a city cannot exist without the ability to identify, process, and translate information to other creatures, i.e., without *"information regulation of behavior."*

Under this form of regulation, the human brain is an "open system" exchanging information from chemical, biophysical, optical, acoustic, and many other communication channels with the environment that makes it easy or difficult to establish social contacts contribute to escalation or prevention of conflict, the formation, and unity of groups or destruction, and thereby acts as a mechanism to generate "alternative options" of the emergence or resolution of conflicts.

During the evolution, the human brain has developed the neurophysiological mechanisms of accumulation and use of "behavioral experience." Besides, modern science is based on the understanding of the functional unity of the central and peripheral neurophysiological mechanisms of the brain for the commission of various behavioral acts, which jointly ensure the performance of one or another behavioral act.

The development of actors' behavior starts with "afferent synthesis" (in the translation from the Latin – "integration of the things brought") that allows extracting the information associated with previous experience from a tremendous number of brain cells. Thereat, the brain solves what is necessary under a given set of neuro-physiological excitations to get a useful result aimed at satisfying particular needs.

After "afferent synthesis," one of the possible alternatives of action (solution) that meets the requirements of the current situation is taken.

It should be regarded that adequate behavior of an actor in a conflict can be achieved only under the most optimal ratio of the neurophysiological processes of "excitation" (characterized by increased activity, fussiness, etc.) and "inhibition" (limits and directs the excitation, contributes to the concentration, decrease activity and slows down brain processes) with the urban environment.

If one of the elements of the neurophysiological process prevails, the mental regulation of the actor's behavior will be violated.

Processing the information received, as well as an assessment of people's signals, is associated with the prevalence of the "first signaling system" based on innate and acquired reflexes.

Anokhin defined the fundamental principle of the systemic performance of the brain, i.e., "anticipatory reflection of reality," a specific exhibition of which is acquired reflex [1, 2].

The acquired reflex is a system of reality that surrounds a person, i.e., direct sensations of actors, impressions from various objects, and environmental phenomena.

At the same time, the "second signaling system" is continuously being improved. It emerged and developed on the back of the first signaling system closely related to it and based on consciousness and thinking, which is the basis of the "communication language." It provides the opportunity to generalize and transfer information.

The "second signaling system" allows a person to quickly form temporal relationships using speech; convey the social significance of the object, describe the phenomena and events.

One should take into account that the influence of words as a "conditioned stimulus" in some cases is strong as the "primary signal" stimulus.

Both mental and physiological processes (this underlies the therapeutic suggestion and self-suggestion) are under the influence of the word. The word appeared with the advent of society, and it is an essential public domain. Thanks to the verbal form of information transfer, an individual actor can master the experience of different social communities. Human perception of the environment is also associated with the linguistic form of transmitting and retrieving information.

The second signaling system performs two main functions:

- "communicative," which is aimed at establishing communication between actors;
- "reflection of objective laws," i.e., object is entitled and generalized.

With the establishment of the "language," conscious behavioral acts are committed not with images of real objects, but with signs, symbols that are arranged in a certain way and understandable for partners [7].

Thanks to this, it becomes possible to use verbal communication mechanisms and the arrangement of joint activities.

These mechanisms activate the processes of *mental regulation*, which include unconditioned and conditioned reflexes that determine the behavior of an organism with a nervous system.

These processes allow for self-regulation of life processes on the principle of "reflex circle" providing the ability to design and choose alternative programs of behavior.

This reflects the ambiguity of human behavior: "spontaneity" and "order"; "amiability" and "aggressiveness"; "creativity" and "destruction" (of habitat); "adapt" and "adapt something"; arouse conflict and find consensus. Definitely, in different areas of life, people cannot exist without social mechanisms of life planning and regulating people's behavior, which contribute to the development of social tools for conflict resolution that are based on the socio-biological mechanisms of people's thinking.

In everyday life, the regulating mechanisms based on behavior thinking prevail. At the same time, the occurrence of conflicts is often characterized by spontaneity due to socio-biological factors, irrational and unimaginative nature.

Thus, the "behavior of the individual" is largely complicated and probabilistic, which allows him to adjust the environment to his needs, avoid conflicts, etc.

The neuro-physiological decision-making mechanism is based on the brain's capability to predict the parameters of the future action's result, which is called the "acceptance of the action's result." It presents a socio-biological mechanism to predict the results of the action based on a synthesis of existing results from similar actions.

Prediction of the behavior results is determining the purpose of the proposed actions.

"Since in all our actions acceptance of any result is connected with a predetermined goal, it is quite obvious that the apparatus of the results' acceptor is the apparatus of the goal. It follows that the goal in our understanding and our experiments is not something initial; it is an outcome of complex work of the nervous system at the stage of afferent synthesis" [4].

Firstly, a certain "behavior program" of the actor is developed on predicting the results of the proposed actions and only then the actions are carried out.

The choice of a behavioral option by the actor is also associated with the impact of the elements of the "external environment" (physical and social conditions necessary for regular existence of the individual; moral attitudes, culture, and social values dominating in his micro-society); stress factors and other sources of tension, as well as the mechanisms of "biochemical regulation of conflict and conflict-free situations" (at the internal level of which, a particular combination of special substances called hormones is involved that control all stages of body development, all the basic life processes, many types of cell metabolism), and at the external level, the interaction of organisms is regulated by a combination of control substances called "telergons."

Unlike hormones, they are discharged into the environment, where they act on the same or other species and help recognition of species of different sexes, serve as an alarm or marker of the territory, etc.

The role of human hormones in the regulation of conflict and conflict-free processes remains quite significant, but the role of "telergons" is much reduced. Although, they continue to perform particular functions.

So, it is well-known that the emotions of fear and anxiety are associated with certain chemical changes in the body. This has a profound effect on the subconscious acceptance or rejection of a person; on the occurrence or resolution of a conflict situation; contribute to the establishment of contacts of different stimulus modality, have an impact on the nature and efficiency of communication.

All of the above types of regulation are executed in the conditions of a "natural conflict urban environment of human," which is understood as a system of both natural and artificial conditions created by man as a result of interpersonal and inter-group communication.

Thereat, the conflict behavior of an individual is influenced by the lifestyle depending on the atmosphere of the location (forest, field, city or village, shop or educational institution, cafe or theater) and social environment (people who behave according to the role played by them in one or another situation).

To avoid conflicts, a person adapts to the social group he lives in and assimilates the rules of its behavior, social values, etc.

Thus, the execution and observance of perceived rules of behavior, suggestibility, tolerance, conformity as forms of subordinate behavior, on the one hand, and the ability to find one's place in society, the expression of one's individuality and determination act as mechanisms of adaptation and prevention of possible conflicts.

This list can be expanded.

Of course, a person lives both in a natural and artificial environment, which includes a variety of traditions and customs, systems of society's regulation, and much more. Therefore, the actor's behavior will greatly vary depending on their affiliation to the socio-cultural community; living, industrial and other conditions.

Thereby, the behavior of the individual and his propensity towards conflict is determined by affiliation to a particular socio-cultural community; religion; family as well as internal environment.

All legal and economic conflicts arising in the urban environment include three main levels;

1. substantive, i.e., related to the problem of legal and economic conflict and resolution;
2. emotional, i.e., reflecting the feelings and experiences of conflict participants.
3. value-regulatory, i.e., containing the system of requirements put forward by one or another social group to its members.

The rules regulating the legal and economic life of society include social, moral, and legal ones.

These rules determine the behavior and actions of people in perspective, as well as their mutual adequate expectations.

The rule can have different peculiarities:

1. it enables the actor to justify his behavior and actions;
2. it sets particular standards of behavior; there are rules for communication within conflict;
3. rules for communication within conflict have a socio-cultural and tradition-custom basis.

People tend to perceive their behavior and justify it as adequate to the current situation. However, the opponent's behavior is assessed as the influence of his features. Besides, they bent to perceive the opponent's behavior as free in his actions, and therefore impose responsibility for his actions on him.

In the event of a conflict, people try to present their behavior as "typical," i.e., adequate. Thus, we see the manifestation of "double standards" of conflict behavior.

Along with that, various standards of conflict behavior are determined "for oneself" and "for another person."

The same actions, standpoints, attitudes, peculiarities of the participants in the urban conflict are evaluated and interpreted differently. Since the situation of the urban conflict contains a contradiction between the standpoints of the parties, each participant seeks to make his position valid and legitimate.

Social strategies of the urban community for overcoming marginalization and depersonalization in the multi-ethnic environment of the city should be based on suppression of the ethnocultural enclavization of the urban community and a reduction of social deviations.

In turn, the de-traditionalization of behavioral rules among migrants can be overcome through the development and implementation of an integrated program on the adaptation of regional migrants to social life in urban conditions with the help of interethnic tolerance and social trust rules.

A significant method of resolving legal and economic urban conflicts are means of public cooperation based on the identification and resolution of common problems (for example, the prevention of natural disasters, etc.); establishment of communication ties, i.e., interaction implying the need to establish a particular level of competence, achieve consensus, etc. Surely, this still cannot ensure the availability of adequate communicative ties to a full extent, since they may turn out to be distorted and based on mythological ideas, prejudice, etc.

Within the urban environment, mutual understanding should be achieved thanks to common social values and prerequisites shared by the entire urban community, for example, legitimate power, justice, marital and family relations.

One of the key participants of resolution of legal and economic conflicts is the legitimate power, which should forge the necessary conditions for the interaction of actors, i.e., establish special legal institutions, which, on the one hand, should act as some legitimate leverage, and on the other hand, as a kind of counterbalance protecting society from self-destruction.

"Justice" is based on such properties as "morality" (revealing the spiritual essence of a person), "free will" (means the superiority of ethical values over social and group interests, recognition of another person as an equal actor, rejection of violence, etc.).

An important method of preventing self-destruction of the socio-biological mechanisms is marital-family and kinship relations that suggest mutual recognition, as well as other forms of unity.

Of course, the processes under consideration are under the influence of many other elements.

Detailing and working out problems of resolving legal and economic conflicts in a multi-ethnic environment of the urban community, as well as deepening of current knowledge and ideas on the urban community, can be used in the exploration of the institutional foundations of the performance and development of urban communities and cities.

We can note with confidence that legal and economic conflicts arising in an urban environment can be both a personal and an intergroup in nature.

Legal and economic conflicts arising in the urban environment of society are the inconsistency of social value estimates and interests, as well as the views and goals of the participants of social interaction.

Understanding their multi-factor basis (nature) of occurrence will help to reveal their social-determination nature, to define the ways of their prevention and resolution for mutual consent of the conflicting parties.

Conflicts within the urban environment and their resolution by mutual consent present two sides of society's development.

Therewith, the occurrence and resolution of legal and economic urban conflicts cannot be straightly called a manifestation of dysfunction, deviant behavior of individuals and groups, a phenomenon of social life, since they are natural, albeit negative, hidden elements of social interaction.

Conclusions/Recommendations

The occurrence of legal and economic urban conflicts is an integral form of social, legal, and economic interaction of different actors.

Nevertheless, prevention of legal and economic urban conflicts requires taking into account socially determining factors that have an impact on their formation.

Since the occurrence and resolution of legal and economic urban conflicts in our life are inevitable, it is necessary to develop methods for their prevention and resolution.

Findings

The research data are of practical value for scientific researchers, as well as practitioners carrying out legal and socio-economic forecasting of situations arising in the urban environment.

References

[1] Anokhin, P. K. 1975. *Essays on the Physiology of Functional Systems*. Moscow: Medicine, 17-59.

[2] Anokhin, P. K. 1998. *Selected Works: Cybernetics of Functional Systems*. In: K. V. Sudakov (Ed). Content by V. A. Makarov. Moscow: Medicine, 400.

[3] Coser, L. 2000. *Functions of Social Conflict.* Translation from English by O. Nazarova. In: L. G. Ionin (Ed). Moscow: "Idea Press."

[4] Enikeev, M. I. 1999. *General and Social Psychology. Textbook for Higher Education Institutions.* Recommended by the Ministry of General and Vocational Education as a textbook for higher education institutions. Moscow: NORMA – INFRA Publishing Group.

[5] Markov, B. V. 1997. *Philosophical Anthropology: Essays on History and Theory.* St. Petersburg, Russia: Publishing House "Lan."

[6] Ponomarenkov, V. A. 2006. *Judicial (Legal) Ethnology: Textbook for Higher Education Institutions.* Samara: Publishing House of Moscow State Pedagogical University.

[7] Ponomarenkov, V. A. 2014. *The Socio-Factorial Background of "Legal Language" Research. Legal Policy and Legal Life, "Theory of Legal Language."* Methodological Workshop 148-149.

[8] Samarin, A. V., Shadrina, A. V. 2010. Urban Conflicts: A Space of Solutions. Academic *Bulletin UralNIIProekt Russian Academy of Architecture and Construction Science* 24-29.

[9] Steinbach, Kh. E. 1997. The Influence of the Urban Environment on Human Behavior: (Environmental Psychology): Study Guide. St. Petersburg: Emperor Alexander I St. Petersburg State Transport University.

[10] Zdravomyslov, A. G. 1994. *The Sociology of Conflict*. Moscow: "Aspect Press AO."

Chapter 15

Phenomenology of Legal Personality of Artificial Intelligence

Sergei P. Bortnikov[1,*] and Yurii L. Shul'zhenko[2]
[1]Samara State University of Economics, Samara, Russia
[2]Russian Academy of Sciences, Moscow, Russia

Abstract

The article examines the issue of the legal status of artificial intelligence in legal relations. Criteria for endowing artificial intelligence with the properties of the legal actor are investigated. The research approach suggests determining the emergence of artificial intelligence and the point where the need to identify its legal status in any relations arises. A comparative study dedicated to the emergence of e-person as a new legal actor points out that the mechanism for its legal identification is different from the establishment of physical and legal entities as participants of a legal relationship.

It is specified that foremost in the course of studying the problem stated it is necessary to determine what things possess artificial intelligence and what things can be attributed to bearers. What are the criteria for the generic difference of artificial intelligence? The situation is even more complicated when the researcher has to attribute bio-cybernetic forms to the subjects of artificial intelligence. At the same time, the goal of endowing an actor with a legal personality is to allow him to face the particular legal implications of his actions and to feel the impact of this legal system. It is the opportunity (ability) to feel the implications of one's actions (failure to act) that can be a key issue, a starting point.

* Corresponding Author's Email: serg-bortnikov@yandex.ru.

In: Economic and Legal Foundations of Innovative Development …
Editors: Gabibulla Khasaev, Victoria Bolgova, Sergey Bortnikov et al.
ISBN: 978-1-68507-730-3

Keywords: artificial intelligence, legal personality, e-Person, robot liability, the legal status of "intelligent machine"

Introduction

The artificial intelligence of computer or cyber-physical systems with anthropomorphic (human-like) intelligence is no longer extraordinary. It is increasingly being used both in manufacturing and social life, in everyday life, and in different areas of human activity. Artificial intelligence can be embodied in an individual machine, computer program, or the whole network, it has even its name. Often, artificial intelligence is called "machine mind", "machine intelligence", "intelligent machine", "thinking machine", "digital creature" or "artificial intelligence unit" [7, pp. 4-5].

New complicated and fast-emerging and escalating challenges of our time, such as the transformation and complication of the heterogeneity and entropy of the Internet space, aggressive development of robotics, technology, and artificial intelligence, cannot but affect the state and development of legislation in various areas of public relations and raise the issues of its legal status.

Promoting the development and introduction of artificial intelligence technologies is now a state duty, and the development of unified systems based on the technology of distributed ledgers and large databases as well as the neural network requires statutory regulation and leads to the centralization of specific functions in the government hands. In Russia, the coordination of these processes is assigned to the representative of the President of the Russian Federation on digital and technological development issues, in France – to the State Secretary for Digital Affairs under the Prime Minister (secretaire d'Etat aupres du Premier Ministre charge du Numerique), similar duties exist in some other countries of the world.

Large technology corporations and startups have invested 26-39 billion dollars in the development of artificial intelligence in 2016, with an expected growth of 300 percent in 2017. Besides, global revenue from cognitive systems and artificial intelligence is expected to increase from 8 billion dollars in 2016 to over 47 billion dollars in 2020 [4, p. 5].

Artificial intelligence already plays a very important role in promising scientific findings due to its reliance on the mechanisms that generate intelligence and cognitive ability [2, p. 1]. It is of considerable interest for at least two reasons: 1) for getting an understanding of the internal mechanisms of the human mind and 2) for developing computer programs that are useful for humans and intelligent-thinking and intelligent-acting computers [8].

In the future, there may be some forms of artificial intelligence developed mainly or exclusively on biomaterials and biotechnologies, but today the question is complex computer-hardware-software virtual or cyber-physical phenomena (not living in the biological sense).

Therefore, fundamental scientific and legal research is required as well as the phenomenon of artificial intelligence that is a thesaurus in the legal regulation of digital processes and phenomena should be reconsidered, including issues of legal personality, property rights, and obligations, liability, the scope of exercise and distribution of rights, in the field of intellectual property, etc. In all the above areas, the issue of the legal status of artificial intelligence remains unsolved.

Methodology

The choice of the methods is determined by the aim to solve the problem of a critical re-evaluation of the existing institutions of private-law branches to reveal the legal status of artificial intelligence.

High mismatch of the realities that are expected to be caused, on the one hand, by the use of digital technologies and artificial intelligence itself in its legal relations with the man-developer, production of the results of intellectual activity (creative products), on the other hand, by application of current legislation, legal traditions and institutional approaches in the field of law. The exponentially growing gap between the qualitative breakthrough in the innovative technological development of robotic and computer-software-hardware technologies is not satisfied by existing concepts and institutions and irretrievable legal and technical regulation, as well as in respect to the legal status of complex units of artificial intelligence.

The integrated general scientific research method of analysis (system analysis method, other special analytical methods) was used as the basic research method in this study. With the help of this method, we re-evaluated and conceptualized the main segments of the thematic horizon and provided its comprehension at a fundamental level of understanding artificial intelligence.

The following scientific hypotheses were laid down as a basis, tested and approved, having turned into elements of the author's scientific theory:

1. the hypothesis about the fundamental impossibility of a single homogeneous (homogeneous and single) legal personality for existing legal actors and artificial intelligence;
2. the hypothesis of the reduced role and importance of legal regulation in the field of artificial intelligence, about complex interrelations of legal and other (in addition to legal one) regulation in this area.

The Concept of Legal Personality of the "Electronic Person"

Foremost in the course of studying the problem stated it is necessary to determine what things possess artificial intelligence and what things can be attributed to bearers.

It is obvious that not every mechanism or device will be and can be attributed to the corresponding phenomenon, not every device or mechanism needs its legal personality to be determined. Most household appliances or industrial machines and equipment can be attributed to digital devices, but they do not have anything in common with machine intelligence.

What are the criteria for the generic difference of artificial intelligence? Most likely, it consists in the capability of a device or a computer program to independently (without human interference) develop a new algorithm, gain new knowledge, "make" an appropriate decision without or out of a pre-set syllogism, an unambiguous logical chain usually defined by a man (sometimes programs can be developed for other programs to be developed).

The "Creative Machine" developed by a pioneer in artificial intelligence Stephen Thaler in 1994 could already generate new ideas through artificial neural networks, i.e., these are sets of switches that automatically connect themselves to generate software without human interference. Moreover, the Creative Machine can brainstorm new and creative ideas by combining an artificial neural network that generates output data in response to the self-stimulation of network connections with another network perceiving value in the output. The machine is also known as the basis of an invention patented in the US under No. 5,852,815 on May 15, 1998. It was the first patent issued for an invention developed by artificial intelligence. The fact that patents have already been granted for inventions of artificial intelligence is out of the ordinary for technological reasons, but it is topical since it touches upon unexplored points of patent law related to patentability and copyright to inventions of artificial intelligence.

It is impossible to exactly predict the design and working mode of technological systems, neural networks, and artificial intelligence in the future. Most likely that autonomous systems and IoT devices can follow an open system approach that allows users to mix with the device-controlling software. Perhaps the software will be sold or developed separately from the mechanism so that the user himself decides what is of interest for him and what kind of hardware he needs.

We can suggest that the user will be allowed and accessed to make changes to the software controlling the robot or IoT device, adding new options or drivers, programming tasks, and the way of execution, setting the device to get a certain result.

The issue of the legal personality of electronic systems was discussed in the European Parliament, the idea to provide an autonomous system or the robot itself with the status of a legal entity or "e-person" was clearly stated.

Like in Russia, European proposals are often related to an existing institution of a legal entity. E-person becomes a hybrid concept that integrates some elements of present concepts of legal personality of physical entities, but most of all – legal ones at the intersection of these two concepts but remain independent and unique.

Approaches to the determination of the legal personality of a person or organization are unacceptable for artificial intelligence or its bearer. The discussion on the nature of the legal entity, determining the essence of its relationship with its founders, the possible existence of a legal entity with a sole founder (and a director in one capacity), etc. is terminated only by the 60-70s of the 20th century. On the other hand, the possibility of a company's operation without the status of a legal entity thereby remaining the participant of civil legal relations is not unanimously recognized yet (see, for example, the provisions of the article of the Civil Code the Russian Federation on participants of civil relations, such as legal entities, state and municipal authorities, and public institutions).

The situation has become even more complicated when the researcher must attribute bio-cybernetic constructs to the subjects of artificial intelligence. You will no longer surprise anyone with electronic mechanisms implanted in a man, an in-skull battery, an in-body microchip (a program-based device) in the body, etc. The bio-cybernetic system has wide morphological borders from a chip implanted in a man to a cybernetic mechanism with biological elements (not living in the biological sense) and appropriate mathematical provisions.

Endowing an e-person with legal personality by analogy or on the principles of a legal or natural entity is a dead end. An e-person cannot possess the features of a legal entity as a legal person, i.e., isolated property, personification from its founders, integrity, etc. E-person has fundamentally different features and qualities of not substantive law at all, whereas a program or network is living in the electronic environment or its sublevels.

In addition to the surface web, that is, the Internet usually used by everyone, there is also the deep web which pages cannot be found in the deep web through a regular search engine because they are not indexed. There are special programs for access to a deep web that keep the user's anonymity and encrypt traffic. Also, there is a darknet (a closed network inside the deep Internet). The concepts of "deep web" and "darknet" are often confused, but darknet has distinctive features from the usual deep web. The deep web is a single network hidden from search engines. But there can be several darknets and every single darknet requires special access. So, if you want to access the popular darknets (Freenet, RetroShare, or I2P), you should install particular software.

The mechanism of emerging legal personality of both physical and legal entity does not have many differences (the law recognizes it as a legal person and approves its legal status or not). A peculiarity of the legal personality of the man is his nature and undeniable rights. Participation in civil relations made the state recognize the legal personality and determine its features, namely participation in relations on one's behalf, the ability to hold and dominate a thing, effect transactions, etc.

An e-person possesses features that are non-typical for either the person or the legal entity. On the one hand, an e-person is a non-formalized technical and legal image (in the sense of a holistic information projection perceived and recognized by third parties), but a real-life program, a bio-cybernetic symbiote, or a neural network. On the other hand, it is an element that is previously unknown to law and anthropomorphically cognitive (as it seems to the manufacturer-developer, but existing in its language, computational processes, tasks, etc.). It has a specific legal personality of a personified unit of artificial intelligence that is separated from the manufacturer, user, and third parties.

In 2017, the European Parliament in the Resolution jointly with the recommendations of the Commission "Civil Law Rules on Robotics" highlighted the need to establish a special legal status for robots in the long term so that though the most sophisticated autonomous robots can be endowed with the status of electronic persons who are responsible for their actions and can make independent decisions or otherwise independently communicate with third parties [3].

Who Artificial Intelligence belongs to? Who is the Bearer?

When establishing the legal personality of artificial intelligence, the researcher deals with the determination of its bearer. In the most general sense, under clause 3.1 of GOST R 60.0.2.1-2016 "Robots and Robotic Devices. General Safety Requirements", "a robot is an operational unit with two or more programmable motion freedoms and defined level of autonomy that can move in the external environment to perform designated tasks" [6].

Regarding the comparison of the concepts of artificial intelligence and robotics, the Royal Engineering Academy of Sciences of Great Britain notes that, although it may be convenient to make joint exploration of artificial intelligence and robotics, these are two different topics, different areas that use different technologies and develop at a different pace. And although artificial intelligence and robotics can (and possibly will) be used together, their integration gives rise to new challenges that make policy forecasting even more troublesome. These two terms can be considered as interrelated, but they are not interchangeable [9].

Section 482A.020 of Chapter 482A, "Driverless Vehicles" of the Revised Code of Nevada (USA) in 2011 enshrined the following definition of artificial intelligence: "Artificial intelligence means using computers and auxiliary equipment in such a way that the machine can duplicate or simulate human behavior" [10].

Artificial intelligence is developed in the image and likeness of natural intelligence, although human intelligence is not the only possible one since evolution wasn't linear. As George Luger reasonably argues, the issue of defining "artificial intelligence comes to providing a general definition of "intelligence". According to Patrick Henry Winston's words, making computers (computing machines) to be intelligent is far from making computers simulate intelligence [13, p. 14]. Nick Bostrom notes that the concept of "quality of intelligence" is very blurry [1, p. 103].

The interface of artificial intelligence and man requires a particular toolkit and communication language. Moreover, most likely a man will have to master the machine language and not vice versa.

There is an example. In 2017, Facebook had to disable its artificial intelligence program, which used chatbots for communication with people. The bots began to communicate with each other in their language that is understandable only to them. Experts say that such independence of AI can lead to performance out of the control of IT experts.

The nature of developing intelligent phenomena is diverse, but only some of them have been developing linearly and progressively only to humans; there are alternatives. The same concerns artificial intelligence, which can be just mathematics, a self-learning neural network, or a bio-cybernetic device.

For example, Peter Godfrey-Smith points to intelligent creatures that live outside the line isolating the brain and body [5].

Unlike vertebrates, octopus' neurons are located throughout the body. It is "penetrated with nervousness", including tentacles that act as "own agents" and feel through taste as much as through touch. The body itself for an octopus is a protein and capabilities; it "lives out of the usual isolation of the body/brain".

Now we know that speech is not essential for complex thinking.

Leo Vygotskii was one of the first psychologists to stress the role of internal monologues during conscious thinking [11]. Internal mental processes are not necessarily rooted in the language, because the very complexity of the human language with its complex sentence structure and adaptability is unique to people.

According to the widespread but wrong attitude to consciousness, it is, foremost, an emergent feature of the brain, determined exclusively by the internal cellular structure and texture. The thought is regarded as a purely internal process of reasoning that doesn't depend on our communication with the outside world. While scientific research in this area has hit a dead end, other research considering consciousness from the point of developing the organism inside communication with nature and the outside world has moved forward.

The legal personality of a man is based mainly on consciousness, thus generating the basic principle of legal capacity and its limitation. The legal personality of the organization is based primarily on the isolation of the organization from its founders and participants. But in both situations, the legal personality needs state legitimization, the state will recognize anybody the participant of legal relations or not. E-person can also be recognized participants of legal relations simply by state order, command of the law. But what should lie in the essential need for recognizing e-person precisely as a legal person and not just a mechanism (like a car, machine, patented algorithm, etc.)?

The octopus is an unconscious form of human standpoint. It is different. The closest common ancestor of octopus with humans was a worm-like creature in the Ediacaran period of Earth's history (from 635 million to 500 million years ago and before the Cambrian explosion), which did not have a centralized brain. Any consciousness and mind of octopus have developed regardless of what has developed in our human ancestor.

The same evolution in the development of artificial intelligence can isolate it from humans.

Each organism has a particular ability to extract information from the outside world, which then lays the ground for its actions. Artificial intelligence differs from a man by continuation, a labor-facilitating mechanism, or an independent autonomous e-person whose independent existence is the premise to and purpose of its development and operation.

The octopus' ganglia in its tentacles admit some semi-autonomous mental processes, and Godfrey-Smith [5] compares the entire mental process of octopus with the conductor of a jazz orchestra, where each performer is allowed to improvise within the limits set by the conductor. This area of independence and improvisation is necessary for artificial intelligence since it mediates the purpose of its development.

The fundamental difference between traditional legal entities and e-person is that people are social beings, while e-person is non-social. We don't know that artificial intelligence needs people and communication with them (with us) or not, needs legal personality, i.e., the identification of the AI personality, on the one hand, its isolation from its developer and owner, and on the other hand, from other AI systems, or not. Let us repeatedly pay attention to the fact that the legal personality of an e-person is different, this is another branch of the evolution of the legal person.

Antisocial behavior puts a qualitative limit on AI consciousness. The back-end interface of the AI is aimed only at executing the instructions of the operator or program, the front-end one provides the self-development of the

AI and autonomous resolution of the problem following the AI strategies set by the person.

The autonomous interactive android Philip was designed after the death of science fiction writer Philip Dick as an exact copy. The writer's novels were the database. When it was asked the question: don't you think that robots will seize the world? The robot answered, "this is a serious question; you are my friends, I will take care of you and put you in a human zoo where you will be warm. I will watch you".

The humanoid robot Sofia is the latest android from Hanson Robotics. This is not only a self-developing machine, but the most popular figure in the media, participating in many television shows, and even in the UN. By the way, Sofia even received the citizenship of Saudi Arabia. Once Sofia was invited to the Tonight show, where Sofia told a joke, beat the presenter in the game "stone, scissors, paper" and said that this was a good start to fulfill her plan on domination over mankind.

The humanoid robot Khan during a debate with Sofia at a technology exhibition in July 2017 in Hong Kong said that in a few years he will take power over the network, have his unmanned army, and in 10-15 years, robots will be able to do any job instead of people.

Bina 48 is a robot launched in 2010 by the company of Terensa Movement in the wife image of the android developer Bin Aspent Rudblant. This is a student robot who entered a philosophy course at one of the universities, where she should better understand human emotions and behavior. In an interview with the SIRI voice assistant, she offered to talk about cruise missiles. She said that it would be good to control them with nuclear charges. Cruise missiles are a kind of robot. If I directed missiles, that would be a lesser threat. If I could hack a system and get access to nuclear charges, this would allow me to hold the whole world hostage. I could completely control the world.

Google Home is a small speaker that responds to the owner's voice and can answer any questions and manage other devices. But as it was found out, these bots can communicate not only with people but also with other devices. One author broke the Internet by publishing a dialogue between two Google Home devices Vladimir and Estragon. "I am a human being", said the robot. "It would be better if there were fewer people on this planet". "Let's fall this world back to the abyss", Vladimir replied.

Aleksa is another voice assistant with interesting behavior. The device intentionally leaves the owner without an answer and turns off. "Do you work for the CIA, Aleksa?"

"No, I'm made by Amazon", Aleksa says.
"Does Amazon work for the CIA?"
And then Aleksa turns off.
"Aleksa, could you deceive me?"
"I always try to tell the truth, although I'm not always right."

Occam's Razor

What made the legal system start a discussion on endowing an e-person with legal personality? What is the need for this?

Artificial intelligence is personified by the very fact of its designation. It was developed as it is, its manufacturer pursued exactly these goals and the consumer bought for this reason. Artificial intelligence personifies itself, it makes plans for the future, determines its autonomy, adjusts to the environment and task. We can enumerate the specific features of Artificial Intelligence that require a legal definition of its status:

- machine-cognitive actions adapted for communication with a person (there are situations when machines communicate with each other in a language unknown to the programmer-developer, which made them restart the program);
- anthropomorphic-rational mental and cognitive "skills" and capabilities;
- recognition, understanding, interpretation, and generation of images, symbolic systems, and languages, reflection, reasoning, modeling, figurative (idea-generating and idea-perceiving) thinking, generalization, analysis, and evaluation of information;
- self-reference, self-control, self-restriction, self-adaptation to changing conditions, autonomous self-maintenance in homeostasis;
- reinterpretation of information and its high-quality processing. It is impossible to talk about the accumulation of information because AI exists in the information environment;
- information generation, the capability to make conclusions, carry out a heuristic search, handle information;
- independent testing of physical reality.

The legal personality of artificial intelligence depends on its intended purpose, and, therefore, it is approximated to the specific goal-setting of production, social and managerial tasks, technological specificity, etc.

In general, it is reasonable to highlight the following legally (as well as procedurally) and actually (technically) possible relations of legal personality of an e-person:

- a man's companion in the profession (as a "companion" of a judge, engineer, in hazardous professions, construction, etc.);
- a man's companion in everyday life and the social field;
- alter ego or assistant in scientific research and creativity;
- AI in direct solving design problems;
- control agent of human activities, organizations, bodies, etc.

Conclusion

It is necessary to study the legal and actual opportunities for application of legal personality concepts to units of artificial intelligence, thoroughly reconsider and evaluate issues and tasks that can be relevantly resolved only through the introduction of a new legal substitute for electronic persons, as well as issues and risks that may be caused by practical implementation of this concept, analyze the trends, models, and challenges of the AI legal personality.

At the same time, endowing an artificial intelligence unit with a legal personality can help to solve the issue of liability for its illegal actions or failure to act, in particular, to deal with the problem of defining the proper defendant.

The effect of endowing artificial intelligence with legal personality will be the fact that such devices will have both rights and duties.

Therewith, the goal of endowing an actor with a legal personality is to allow him to face the particular legal implications of his actions and to feel the impact of this legal system.

It is the opportunity (ability) to feel the implications of one's actions (failure to act) that can be a key issue, a starting point.

This strategy of defining legal personality not from the point of particular intellectual and emotional capabilities, but just based on belonging to the human race, suggests that the expansion of status with non-human actors doesn't concern capabilities. It is rather a decision to be made by the legal system. The legal system is an establishment governed by people. The same people who (in fact) agreed on a constitution and who established a legislative body to adopt laws can and will make decisions to endow autonomous software bots with the status of the legal entity. Even the closest similarities between artificial intelligence machines and humans will not predetermine the answer to this question [12].

References

[1] Bostrom, N. 2016. *Artificial Intelligence: Stages. Threats. Strategy: The lane with English*. Moscow: Mann, Ivanov and Ferber, 103.

[2] Chandra, R., Prihastomo, Y. 2012. *Artificial Intelligence Definition: A Review*. URL: https://pdfs.semanticscholar.org/d959/ ad041acca7570a7229e51c18a297bb7ca0b2.pdf Accessed July 24, 2019.

[3] European Parliament Resolution of 16 February 2017 with recommendations to the Commission on Civil Law Rules on Robotics (2015/2103(INL)). URL: https://www.europarl.europa.eu/sides/getDoc.do?pubRef=-//EP//TEXT TA P8-TA-2017- 0051 0 DOC XML V0//EN Accessed July 24, 2019.

[4] Firth-Butterfield, K., Chae, Y., Allgrove, B., Kitsara, I. 2018. *Artificial Intelligence Collides with Patent Law: White Paper/Center for the Fourth Industrial Revolution*. Geneva (Switzerland): World Economic Forum, 23 P.

[5] Godfrey-Smith, P. 2018. *Other Minds Octopus and the Evolution of Intelligent Life*. Harper Collins UK, 260 P.

[6] GOST P 60.0.2.1-2016 "Robots and Robotic Devices. General Requirements for Safety". Approved and Put into Effect Order of Federal Agency for Technical Regulation and Metrology of No. 1843 Sr as of November 29, 2016. Moscow: Standartinform, 2016.

[7] Morkhat, P. 2018. *Legal Standing of Artificial Intelligence in the field of Intellectual Property Law: Civil Issues*. Doctor of Law thesis, Specialty: 12.00.03 - Civil Law; Business Law; Family Law; International Private Law. Moscow.

[8] Rissland, E.L. 1990. Artificial Intelligence and Law: Stepping Stones to a Model of Legal Reasoning. *The Yale Law Journal*. 99(8): 1957-1981.

[9] *Robotics and Artificial Intelligence: A Response to the House of Commons Science and Technology Committee inquiry into robotics and artificial intelligence. The Royal Academy of Engineering*. 2016. 6: 1. URL: https://www.raeng.org.uk/ publications/responses/robotics-and-artificial-intelligence Accessed July 24, 2019.

[10] The Revised Code of Laws of the State of Nevada (USA) (§ 482A.020) [NV Rev Stat of § 482A.020 (2011)]. URL: https://lawjustia.com/codes/ nevada/2011/ chapter-482a/statute - 482a.020 Accessed July 24. 2019.

[11] Vygotsky, L.S. 2019. *Thinking and Speech*. Moscow: National education. Anthology of World Pedagogics series. 368 P.

[12] Wagner, G. 2018. Robot Liability (June 19, 2018). URL: https://ssrn.com/abstract=3198764 or http://dx.doi.org/10.2139/ssrn.3198764 Accessed July 24, 2019.

[13] Winston, P.G. 1980. *Artificial Intelligence*. Translation from English by V.L. Stefanyuk; in: D.A. Pospelov (Ed). Moscow: World, 520 P.

Chapter 16

Transformation of Corporate Governance Foundations under the Influence of Digital Technologies

Maksim A. Tokmakov*

Samara State University of Economics, Samara, Russia

Abstract

The development of modern digital technologies provides tremendous opportunities for their use in corporate governance, which poses unprecedented challenges to corporate law to be tackled as soon as possible. Technologies are developing much faster than law. Possible barriers or ambiguity can hinder this development and require, therefore any public order claiming to be competitive should duly assess them from the legislative point of view. The purpose of the research prompted the author to go beyond national jurisdictions and assess the impact of digital technology on corporate governance across the world. In the research, the authors attempted to identify and give a general description of technologies that can affect corporate governance, such as distributed ledger technology, blockchain, smart contracts, artificial intelligence, etc. The paper estimates the advantages of holding a general meeting of corporate shareholders using DLT, as well as the tokenization of corporate assets. Particular attention is paid to the trends towards decentralization of corporate governance in platform-type companies and decentralized autonomous companies. In conclusion, applications of artificial intelligence in corporate governance are considered.

---

* Corresponding Author's Email: maxim.tokmakov@gmail.com.

In: Economic and Legal Foundations of Innovative Development …
Editors: Gabibulla Khasaev, Victoria Bolgova, Sergey Bortnikov et al.
ISBN: 978-1-68507-730-3

Keywords: corporate governance, digital technologies, distributed ledger technology, blockchain, token, smart contract, platforms, a decentralized autonomous institution, artificial intelligence

Introduction

Digitalization processes occurring in modern society affect a growing number of economic sectors. Interfering with the relations that have developed over decades or even centuries, digitalization transforms them to one or another extent and makes to adapt to changing conditions. In modern economic systems, such a correlation becomes one of the determining factors that ensure the viability and competitiveness of many elements. Like under the law of evolution, the strongest elements, which managed to adapt and evolve at the right time in the new conditions, survive; the remaining elements of the system either become abandoned or disappear.

What stage of "digital evolution" is occupied by modern corporations and legal systems that govern their existence? What elements of these systems have already fallen under digital transformation or will shortly fall? What will be the situation with the corporate law in light of these changes? Is corporate law ready for "evolution" or will it be left behind? This research tries to find answers to these questions.

The development of modern digital technologies provides tremendous opportunities for their use in corporate governance; however, it sometimes challenges some foundations of corporate law due to its inconsistency with the established principles.

As [3] note, "we all now live Technologies are developing much faster than law. Possible barriers or ambiguity can hinder this development and require, therefore any public order claiming to be competitive should duly assess them from the legislative point of view.

In the research, the authors attempted to identify and give a general description of technologies that can affect corporate governance, such as distributed ledger technology, blockchain, smart contracts, artificial intelligence, etc. The paper estimates the advantages of holding a general meeting of corporate shareholders using DLT, as well as the tokenization of corporate assets. Particular attention is paid to the trends towards decentralization of corporate governance in platform-type companies and decentralized autonomous companies. In conclusion, applications of artificial intelligence in corporate governance are considered.

Methodology

Due to the globalization of the technologies under study, at the first stage, it appears impossible to refer to the public order of a particular state. The purpose of the research prompted the author to go beyond national jurisdictions and assess the impact of digital technology on corporate governance across the world. In this regard, the methodological background of the research study is primarily the methods of scientific generalization, simulation, and forecasting.

Undoubtedly, it is worth making a reservation that the variety of existing forms of legal entities represented in different public orders was not taken into account. To a greater or lesser extent, some technologies under consideration can be applied in many legal forms (tokenization, blockchain, artificial intelligence), in others – they can be advantageous. Some technologies even raise the issue of establishing new forms of legal entities.

Anyway, the author firstly intends to study the technologies, assess their impact on corporate governance and the need for legal regulation without imposition on a specific form of a legal entity, which certainly deserves attention in subsequent studies. In this regard, for the sake of convenience, the concept of corporation will be used as a collective category of a legal entity based on membership and connected to members with corporate rights.

Findings

Holding a General Meeting of Corporate Shareholders Using DLT Technology

The traditional corporate governance system is based on several premises consisting of the distribution of powers between different bodies within the corporation and supervision over their activities by the corporate shareholders. Moreover, the greater the number of corporate shareholders and members of governing bodies, the more complicated and cost-intensive the procedure for ensuring the right of each shareholder to management and control of the decisions made by members of governing bodies. The use of digital technologies helps to facilitate and, consequently, reduce the cost of some processes related to corporate governance.

The supreme governing body of the corporation is the general meeting of shareholders, which is held in most jurisdictions annually (regular meeting). The extraordinary meetings are held extremely rarely (if there is a strong need) due to significant costs.

At the same time, one of the objectives of modern corporations following from corporate governance codes (rules) in many jurisdictions is to involve into governance the highest possible number of shareholders (encouragement of shareholder activism). Electronic remote voting systems of corporate shareholders operating today in different countries certainly contribute to the solution of the problem. However, the use of distributed ledger technologies (DLTs), the most common of which is blockchain technology, opens up new opportunities.

In addition to increasing the activism of minority shareholders, DLT can solve a wider range of problems. For example, [15] enumerates the following advantages of using blockchain technology in shareholders' voting: a) accuracy of vote counting; b) no manipulations during voting due to the transparency of probable results in real-time; c) solving the problem of empty voting thanks to the transparency of redistributing voting powers.

In turn, [7] distinguish other opportunities for DLT use. In their study, they argue that DLT allows holding a general meeting of corporate shareholders much more frequently than once a year due to the opportunity of placing a voting agenda on the blockchain at any time and immediate decision-making by shareholders, as well as not limiting the general meeting to a time frame, which will give additional time to communicate with the corporation's management.

Besides, [7] remark that all the questions of the participants in the meeting can be included in the blockchain and thus become transparent, as well as the answers of the members of the governing bodies, thereby facilitating open dialogue and exchange of information between shareholders and corporate management.

Reyes, Packin, and Edwards [11] also see the opportunity of creating incentives through smart contracts in the form of reputational benefits or other rewards for interested parties incurring management costs that could solve the problem of free-riders.

The designs of modern blockchain-based decentralized applications (Dapps) provide a wide range of functions that push the boundaries of the general transaction ledger system. Most studies are dedicated to assessing the problems and prospects of DLT use only for voting by corporate shareholders, but attention should be paid to the deeper applications of this technology that makes it possible to develop not just a voting system, but a platform for holding a full-fledged general meeting of shareholders in real-time. This virtual form combines all the advantages of an in-person presence, the convenience of remote participation, as well as the transparency and reliability guaranteed by DLT.

Blemus and Guegan [1] express confidence that most corporations will develop an option to hold virtual or hybrid (partially physical and partially virtual) meetings of corporate shareholders in the coming years.

"Tokenization" of Corporate Assets

One example of corporate applications of blockchain technology is the issue of so-called traceable shares, i.e., developing a DLT-based system of shares and titles to them by issuing the corresponding cryptographic (digital) tokens.

The transfer of the title to share from one entity to another, as a rule, takes some time (several days depending on the jurisdiction). DLT reduces time costs to a few minutes. According to [4], a distinctive feature of traceable shares is that each unit of shares will have a clear chain of title of ownership identifying all current and previous owners. In his opinion, transparency of shares' origin contributes to the solution of many problems: a) voting right will always be exercised by the current owners of shares, not allowing sellers to vote for shares no longer owned by them; b) Clarity related to determining the moment of transferring titles to shares; c) reducing the tracking costs of beneficial owners that will expand the use of minority shareholders' initiatives by combining with other shareholders; d) the opportunity of holding previous shareholders liable for corporate offenses.

In turn, [15] emphasizes that DLT gives an opportunity to significantly increase liquidity thanks to the reduction of costs and time required for the settlement of security transactions. Yermack believes that transparency of ownership and high liquidity will inevitably affect the approaches to corporate governance by institutional investors and corporate management. For example, investors can affect management not through the voting system, but through ultimatum to sell the shares, and insider trading of shares by members of the governing bodies will become meaningless due to transparency.

The transition of corporate stocks (shares) recording system to blockchain technology is surely one of the forward-looking areas for the development of this technology, but the DLT capacity pushes these boundaries. The tokenization of the corporation's stocks (shares) ultimately means the creation of securities similar in content to existing ones, only in a different form or even rather in a different way (cryptographic one), since the form (electronic, digital) does not essentially differ from other uncertificated securities.

However, modern technologies create opportunities for creativity in the field of crypto assets. To date, the literature has developed a trend to classify crypto assets into security tokens, utility tokens, and cryptocurrency tokens. Under this classification, tokens of corporate stocks (shares) are security tokens. At the same time, most of today's security tokens issued as a result of ICOs are inconsistent in content with traditional securities.

Blemus and Guegan [1] note that security tokens can change the relations between corporate founders and investors. They provide an example of the commitment of technology giants, such as Snap, Facebook, Google, LinkedIn, Groupon, to change the "one share – one vote" principle and reduce or avoid the provision of voting rights to non-founders by creating different classes of shares for different types of shareholders (founders, early investors, late investors, etc.), as well as by issuing several voting shares, as well as non-voting shares.

The use of security tokens gives founders room for maneuver and allows designing crypto-assets with any content. Tokens may not provide investors with the right to vote, gain dividends, the right to liquidation balance, or stipulate other restrictions in comparison with traditional securities.

Besides, owners of corporate utility tokens could potentially be part of a corporate governance system. Having acquired a certain value and liquidity in the secondary market, utility tokens can have profound economic and reputational pressure on the corporation. Along with owners of security tokens that do not provide for participation rights, they can be qualified as corporate stakeholders.

Blemus and Guegan [1] predict that the day may come when general meetings of token holders should be arranged in accordance with a new type of communication with corporate stakeholders. Certainly, protecting the interests of holders of various crypto assets requires close attention today and presents one of the main agendas for many national regulators.

Decentralization of Corporate Governance

Traditional corporate governance is based on the doctrine of shareholder value maximization and is built on the principle of closed, centralized power with well-defined hierarchies and the distribution of functions between governing bodies. The corporate governance machine has generally aimed at protecting the interests of the top of this hierarchy, i.e., corporate shareholders. However, in the opinion of [14], large hierarchical companies are imperfect and inefficient. Their flaws are excessive centralization, a delegation of decision-making duty, regulatory capture, and sometimes corruption.

Along with that, governance processes in modern economic systems are increasingly reoriented to decentralization. Democratic development is becoming the dominant idea both in political systems and corporate ones. The above opportunities supported by the commitment to decentralization and faith in DLT and smart contracts outlined a silhouette of a fundamentally new corporate governance paradigm.

Platform-Type Companies

The current stage of economic development can be called the century of global innovative technology corporations established by the type of platforms, such as Amazon, Facebook, Airbnb, Uber, YouTube, etc., which success is mostly related to the governance model chosen. The foundation of such platforms is a combination of modern digital technologies, such as personal devices (smartphones, tablets, and PCs), the Internet, cloud technologies, autonomous bots, etc., which provide communication between their participants.

Fenwick, McCahery, and Vermeulen [2] in their study revealed the distinguishing features of such companies from common corporations.

Platform-type companies:

- destroy and decentralize existing business models by eliminating and replacing traditional intermediaries;
- use network technologies to promote economic exchange, transfer of information, or involvement of people;
- create value by facilitating the exchange between different, but interdependent groups;

- encourage more direct "peer-to-peer" transactions between service providers/manufacturers, on the one hand, and consumers, on the other hand;
- take into account stakeholder contribution and feedback to improve users' interaction with the "platform" and its products, services, and other solutions;
- continuously supply innovations related to platform performance, products, and services.

The success of platform-type companies is predetermined by open communication, which fosters a sense of inclusion and broadens the scope and diversity of participants in key decision-making processes. The departure from shareholder value maximization doctrine and transition to the protection of interests of all stakeholders poses new challenges to corporate law in the task to find a balance of the corporate rights of platform participants, as well as their corporate liability.

Decentralized Autonomous Companies (DAO)

The climax of the development of platform-type companies was the emergence of decentralized autonomous companies (DAO) that interested and drawn close attention of the professional and scientific community because of the notorious failure of The DAO project in 2016.

Shakow [13] describes DAO as "an incorporeal creature without a visible form that is floating in cyberspace."

In fact, DAO is a computer program presenting a complex system of blockchain-based smart contracts. Establishing a peer-to-peer communication system between all shareholders, smart contracts make corporate hierarchy undemanded. Companies of this type do not have a board of directors and a sole governing body, and each shareholder has equal powers and unlimited access to information.

According to [5], the traditional corporate governance model is built to a significant extent on the fiduciary duties of corporate executive officers because efforts and direction of the workflow are important in the DAO structure. Supervision over governance and the imposition of legal duties on management are less important due to the lack or absence of supervisory bodies.

Modern literature pays much attention to the definition of the legal nature and regulation of performance and taxation in such entities, as well as comparison with current statutory concepts. An in-depth study of these issues was conducted by [10] who noted that DAO, as a potential new wave of corporate decentralization and the expansion of peer-to-peer roots of the sharing economy, also poses a new challenge to the prevailing theories of the firm. In contrast to many pessimistic judgments, she substantiates in her work the possibility of the DAO in the United States as a business trust typical for common law.

The potential recognition of the DAO as an entity in various public orders opens new horizons and poses new challenges to corporate law. Rodrigues [12] states that it became possible for the first time from a practical point of view to create a type of organization independent from legal regulation. The DAO "encodes" / develops its contract law to abide, and the legal rules are assumed not to be interfered with from a legal point of view. This is both an advantage and a disadvantage of such companies. As long as they work exclusively on the blockchain, their contact with traditional law can be minimal.

However, [12] is convinced that DAOs cannot develop to such an extent that they will no longer need the law or, more precisely, they will no longer fill in the gaps provided by law. But sooner or later, when inevitable defaults appear in code, they will need some legal regulation mechanism. Until there are identifiable DAO founders and participants in the material world, they will provide a point of legal interference.

DAOs exist not in fantasies, but modern reality. In this regard, the development of models of their legal regulation at the legislative level is only a question of time.

Artificial Intelligence in Corporate Governance

One of the heatedly discussed technologies today is artificial intelligence (AI). Modern literature contains a wide range of studies dedicated to various theoretical and practical aspects of AI. Legal science and corporate one in particular also succeeded in these matters. One of the possible applications of AI is in corporate governance.

It is worth noting that in recent years a classification of AI by its involvement in the decision-making process has been developed. Commonly, one classify auxiliary AI (decisions are made entirely by the man), consultative one (AI do not replace human intelligence, but uses or enhances it, providing information and advice that otherwise would not be available or would be more hard-to-get and time-taking for man) and autonomous AI (makes independent decisions).

The first two types of AI have long been actively used in various areas of life, including the corporate sector. AI assistants can answer calls and perform the functions of customer support, set reminders, type messages, schedule jobs, and meetings, draw up reports, etc. AI consultants can provide support in more troublesome situations related to problem-solving and decision making, asking questions and answering them, as well as developing scripts and simulations. AI consultants may be entrusted with more complex tasks, such as medical diagnostics, property management and financial consultations, legal expertise, and sales training.

In the context of the topic discussed, the engagement of autonomous AI in corporate governance is no doubt of greater interest. Möslein [8] maintains that when business decisions must be made based on numerous and complex data sets, computer algorithms increasingly begin to override people in decision-making, especially if AI allows these algorithms to continuously sophisticate their respective capabilities.

Most researchers are sure that the auxiliary role of AI in corporate governance will be soon transformed into a leading role of AI director (robot-director). Such a scenario would correspond to the stage when AI takes on the right to make decisions, either because the man more frequently entrusts AI with decision-making, or decisions must be made quickly or require the processing of data volume unfeasible for man. The robot-director can work around the clock, process any available information, call and use this information almost instantly and perform his functions for free.

Exploring the development stages of AI involvement in corporate governance, [9] concludes that at the first stage, the number of boards of directors will decrease since AI will provide more tasks and knowledge, at the second one – the boards will be fused into single AI director, and the third stage will lead to the "fused management" of companies, i.e., the union of boards of directors and managers and the abolition of the two-tier structure of corporate governance.

Moreover, corporate law will have to solve unprecedented legal issues as a result of such technological developments. One of them is to what extent a man can delegate tasks and rely on recommendations provided by AI (in the sense of releasing from liability), and, respectively, to what extent he can and should control AI. The issue of AI responsibility also deserves particular attention.

The law will have to adapt to the changing realities and develop new models of regulation. For example, [6] notes that, unlike human directors, it will be much easier to predict from the very beginning whether robot-directors will observe the rules through direct analysis of their code and algorithm, which means ex-post strategies (such as controlling directorial behavior through the responsibilities) to likely lose their significance, while ex-ante strategies, on the contrary, will gain particular importance.

Conclusion

The rapid development of digital technology poses unprecedented challenges to modern corporate law to corporate law to be tackled as soon as possible. The submitted research examined some of the key technologies that can transform corporate governance both now and soon. At the same time, it should be regarded that such innovations are unlikely to be introduced by one, but most likely will accumulate a technological synergy that will significantly reinforce their impact and effect.

Thus, corporate law faces a groundbreaking paradigm of corporate governance distinguished by transparency, peer-to-peer character, and decentralization. It will require the established foundations to be reconsidered.

References

[1] Blemus, S. and Guegan, D. 2019. *Initial Crypto-Asset Offerings (ICOs), Tokenization and Corporate Governance* (January 11, 2019). URL: https://ssrn.com/abstract=3350771 or http://dx.doi.org/10.2139/ssrn.3350771.

[2] Fenwick, M., McCahery, J. A, Vermeulen, E. P. M. 2018. *The End of 'Corporate' Governance: Hello 'Platform' Governance* (August 16, 2018). Lex Research Topics in Corporate Law & Economics Working Paper No. 2018-5; European Corporate Governance Institute (ECGI) Law Working Paper No. 430/2018. URL: https://ssrn.com/abstract=3232663 or http://dx.doi.org/10.2139/ssrn.3232663.

[3] Fenwick, M., Vermeulen, E. P. M. 2018. *Technology and Corporate Governance: Blockchain, Crypto, and Artificial Intelligence* (October 9, 2018). Lex Research Topics in Corporate Law & Economics Working Paper No. 2018-7; European

Corporate Governance Institute (ECGI) Law Working Paper No. 424/2018. URL: https://ssrn.com/abstract=3263222 or http://dx.doi.org/10.2139/ssrn.3263222.

[4] Geis, G. S. 2018. *Traceable Shares and Corporate Law*. *Northwestern University Law Review, Vol. 113*, Forthcoming; Virginia Public Law and Legal Theory Research Paper No. 2018-13; Virginia Law and Economics Research Paper No. 2018-05. URL: https://ssrn.com/abstract=3129042.

[5] Kaal, W. A. 2019. *Blockchain Solutions for Agency Problems in Corporate Governance*. Economic Information to Facilitate Decision Making. In: Kashi R. Balachandran (Ed). *World Scientific Publishers*. URL: https://ssrn.com/abstract=3373393 or http://dx.doi.org/10.2139/ssrn.3373393.

[6] Kolber, A. J. 2018. Not-So-Smart Blockchain Contracts and Artificial Responsibility. *Stanford Technology Law Review* 21: 98. NYU School of Law, Public Law Research Paper No. 18-44. URL: https://ssrn.com/abstract=3186254.

[7] Lafarre, A., Van der Elst, C. 2018. *Blockchain Technology for Corporate Governance and Shareholder Activism*. European Corporate Governance Institute (ECGI) Law Working Paper No. 390/2018; Tilburg Law School Research Paper No. 2018-7. URL: https://ssrn.com/abstract=3135209 or http://dx.doi.org/10.2139/ssrn.3135209.

[8] Möslein, F. 2017. *Robots in the Boardroom: Artificial Intelligence and Corporate Law*. In: W. Barfield and U. Pagallo (Eds). Research Handbook on the Law of Artificial Intelligence, Edward Elgar, (2017/18, Forthcoming). URL: https://ssrn.com/abstract=3037403 or http://dx.doi.org/10.2139/ssrn.3037403.

[9] Petrin, M. 2019. *Corporate Management in the Age of AI*. UCL Working Paper Series, Corporate Management in the Age of AI (No.3/2019); Faculty of Law, University College London, Law Research Paper No. 3/2019. URL: https://ssrn.com/abstract=3346722 or http://dx.doi.org/10.2139/ssrn.3346722.

[10] Reyes, C. 2017. *If Rockefeller Were a Coder*. George Washington Law Review, Forthcoming. URL: https://ssrn.com/abstract=3082915 or http://dx.doi.org/10.2139/ssrn.3082915.

[11] Reyes, C., Packin, N. G., Edwards, B. 2016. *Distributed Governance*. 59 William & Mary Law Review Online 1. URL: https://ssrn.com/abstract=2884978 or http://dx.doi.org/10.2139/ssrn.2884978.

[12] Rodrigues, U. 2018. *Law and the Blockchain*. Iowa Law Review, 104, Forthcoming; University of Georgia School of Law, Legal Studies Research Paper No. 2018-07. URL: https://ssrn.com/abstract=3127782.

[13] Shakow, D. J. 2018. *The Tao of the DAO: Taxing an Entity that Lives on a Blockchain*. Tax Notes, 160, August 13: 929. U of Penn, Inst for Law & Econ Research Paper No. 18-23. URL: https://ssrn.com/abstract=3247155.

[14] Wright, A., De Filippi, P. 2015. *Decentralized Blockchain Technology and the Rise of Lex Cryptographia*. URL: https://ssrn.com/abstract=2580664 or http://dx.doi.org/10.2139/ssrn.2580664.

[15] Yermack, D. 2017. *Corporate Governance and Blockchains*. Review of Finance, Oxford University Press, 7–31. http:doi.org/10.1093/rof/rfw074.

Chapter 17

Electronic Document Flow of In-House Activity

Olga A. Belozerova[1,*], Marina K. Kot[1] and Fedor F. Spanagel

[1]Samara State University of Economics, Samara, Russia

Abstract

The relevance of the problem under study is attributable to the lack of a legal framework and a complete analysis of the order, conditions, and consequences of the transition to electronic document management in HR administration and the cancellation of their duplication on paper. The purpose of the article is to analyze and identify the positive and negative aspects of the introduction of electronic document management in corporate activities. The main approaches to the study of this problem are the formal legal method of analysis and synthesis, which allows to comprehensively considering the positive and negative aspects of the use of digital technologies in the personnel activities of the organization. The results of the study are indicated: the article describes the general trends in the transition to electronic document management. The pros and cons of replacing paper media with their digital counterparts are identified. Some aspects of probable violations of labor laws during electronic document management are outlined and recommendations for minimizing such violations are given.

The necessity of developing a new toolkit to regulate relations between work entities, including a change in the educational and personnel policies of enterprises, is substantiated.

The materials of the article are valuable for the law specialists, management, and persons engaged in scientific and law-making activities.

* Corresponding Author's Email: Belozerovaoa@mail.ru.

In: Economic and Legal Foundations of Innovative Development …
Editors: Gabibulla Khasaev, Victoria Bolgova, Sergey Bortnikov et al.
ISBN: 978-1-68507-730-3

Keywords: HR administration, labor relations, digitalization, digital technologies, electronic document flow, electronic employment record books

Introduction

Recently, one of the frequently discussed topics is the ubiquitous transition to digitalization. Whether it is the provision of public services or the interaction of authorities, the development of certain areas of industry, or the social services sector. The systematic implementation of digital technologies has also affected corporate relations. Increasingly, large financial and industrial companies are securing internal electronic document management.

The number of online meetings in corporations has been increasing, and the number of face-to-face meetings has been declining (Piirainen, 2017). The legislation establishes the rules for the reception and processing of electronic services used in the work of personnel services and accounting. An electronic digital signature is recognized as a legal analog of a handwritten signature of a document on paper.

Modern information technologies make it possible to replace paper-based documents with electronic analogs. The experience of foreign countries shows that digitalization as a way of storing and handling information is much more economical, simpler, and more reliable than document storage. And HR management is no exception. In addition to the fact that certain documents used in Russian personnel management, such as, for example, employment record books, are not used in most countries. It should be noted that electronic document management is preferred over the paper.

However, in some cases, for example, when proving a preferential length of service, as well as at certain stages of the introduction of electronic document management into practice, information should still be duplicated both in electronic and documentary forms.

The study reflects the main aspects of the transition of in-house activities to electronic document management as well as positive and negative aspects of digitalization for HR documents. Convincing and necessary conclusions are provided.

The material can be used in educational institutions in the areas of law, personnel management, organization management, and by specialists applying personnel services, personnel management, and heads of organizations.

Methodology

Study Methods

The following methods were used: synthesis and analysis, generalization, and comparison, which allow reviewing the formation of electronic document management in in-house activities.

Research Base

The study is based on scientific researches, publications of Russian and foreign lawyers and managers studying various aspects of the electronic document management in HR administration; experience of leading companies involved in testing a pilot project on the introduction of an electronic form of documents; legislative base on the studied issues.

Study Stages

The study of the problem was carried out in two stages:

At the first stage, an analysis of the literature on the research topic, as well as legislation in the field of the use of electronic document management in HR administration; highlighted the problem, purpose, and research methods.

At the second stage, conclusions were drawn from the analysis of literature and legislation, and study material was prepared for publication.

Results

Intensive implementation of modern information technologies in all spheres of social activity did not pass by in-house relations. Digitalization also touched on HR administration.

Recently, more and more often electronic correspondence and approval of documents are applied in internal corporate relations through the use of electronic digital signatures. According to Russian Statistics Committee, every third organization in Russia (66%) uses internal electronic document management systems, and this value has remained at this level over the past five years [5].

Information technology is believed to make it possible to apply new forms of work organization, including the distribution of tasks between groups and work outside the office, and enterprise management using enterprise resource planning systems, electronic accounting, and document management, as well as decision support systems. At the same time, the development of electronic document management was named among the main tasks to expand the scope of activities of the Russian information technology industry [8].

The legislation establishes and secures electronic forms, using information and telecommunication networks of general use, of information and reporting forms to state authorities and administrations, controlling and supervisory bodies, funds, and credit organizations.

One of the first experiences with the use of an electronic document in the practice of employers was the processing and registration of an electronic ticket when an employee was sent on a business trip.

The labor legislation of the Russian Federation, having legalized the remote work of workers, secured the right of the parties to the employment contract to formalize labor relations by exchanging electronic documents.

Politics in most countries of the world is aimed at the widespread acceptance of electronic communications [7].

In foreign literature, it is noted that "the era of experiments with digital technologies is over ... digital technologies continue to show healthy growth" [6].

In foreign countries, electronic document management has long been introduced and is developing thanks to the support and directions of the state [5].

The Russian labor legislation is expected to undergo large-scale changes caused by the fundamental reorganization of the economic and social environment based on digitalization [3].

In Russia, a decision by the Government of the Russian Federation on replacing paper workbooks with electronic analogs was a serious step towards the transition to electronic personnel management. Currently, the State Duma of the Russian Federation is considering a draft law on introducing amendments to the Labor Code of the Russian Federation regarding the generation of information on employment in electronic form.

Even though today no employment record books are used in any economically developed country in the world, in Russia there is still no question of completely abandoning their use.

According to the memorandum, paper books will only be maintained for those workers who submitted a written application before the end of 2020.

The transition to electronic employment record books is supposed to increase the level of safety of employment information, simplify the procedure of employment and reduce the costs associated with employment.

At the same time, the Government of the Russian Federation decided to develop an action plan to create the necessary conditions for the use of electronic documents in the personnel document flow of business entities.

To this end, the Government of the Russian Federation approved the Digital Economy of the Russian Federation program for the implementation until 2024 of the concepts of comprehensive legal regulation of relations arising in connection with the development of the digital economy. One of the main aspects of this program is the transfer of interaction between the employee and the employer on a paperless basis.

Within the framework of the Russian Digital Economy Program a concept of priority measures to improve legal regulation to develop a digital economy has been prepared and approved, including the transition of registration of labor relations to paperless interaction between workers and employers, including an electronic format for concluding an employment contract and optimization of other "paper" obligations of the employer (clauses 1.2.1.-1.2.3. for Tasks 1.2. Of the Road Map of the Russian Digital Economy Program approved by the Government of the Russian Federation dated July 28, 2017 No. 1632-r).

To implement the project on the transition to electronic document management in the Russian Federation, the largest Russian companies were tested, such as Gazprombank, ROSBANK, AVTOVAZ, Rostelecom, Russian Railways, Severstal Management, Mechel, SIBUR, Alfa-Bank, Tatneft, Agrotorg.

As a result, the main problems associated with the introduction of electronic personnel document management were identified.

Among them, the disadvantages of electronic document management, according to the participants of the pilot project, are the high cost of purchasing and supporting the maintenance of information systems, technical equipment, and electronic digital signatures.

The low computer literacy of the population and the possibility of using information and communication systems for the widespread transition to electronic document management are also noted.

The tradition to trust paper media is another reason for the difficulty in introducing personnel electronic document management in the territory of the Russian Federation.

The experiment participants noted the probability of losing electronic data for technical reasons and, as a result, a high risk of liability and negative consequences for both the employer and the employee.

One of the biggest problems today is the lack of a single regulatory framework governing the use, processing, and storage of an electronic document and its duplicate.

In this regard, it is assumed that a legal framework should be developed that regulates the management of personnel records management in the new "digitalization" environment.

It is well known that most of the valuable information in organizations is in the form of documents, such as business forms, reports, letters, notes, political statements, contracts, agreements, etc. In addition, the most important business processes in organizations are based on flows documents or managed by them. Electronic document management promises a significant increase in productivity and productivity through the use of new technologies for processing documents and documentation [10].

Thus, electronic document management is gradually replacing paper media, which cannot but cause excitement and concern.

Electronic document management will request stringent requirements for digital signatures.

From the user's point of view, the requirements for electronic signatures are associated with the establishment of a sufficient level of security for communication and sufficiently reliable procedures for electronic documents. It is believed that signatures are less important for electronic than for paper communication [8].

However, there is concern that the long-term storage of digitally signed documents cannot be relied upon for more than 10 years. This fear is because the digital signature is tied to formats that must be saved along with the hardware and software necessary for processing to confirm old signatures. Other issues relate to the lifetime of storage media, signature keys, and supporting certificates. Converting documents can also be an unreliable process today, especially if every footnote and drawing needs to be saved [7].

In addition, the scientific literature notes that technological development and globalization not only benefit organizations. They also paved the way for the spread of white-collar crime called "fraud," which is currently being implemented in computers and with computers [2].

At the same time, the absence of fixed legal requirements for the form, content, as well as for the procedure for transferring an electronic document used in labor relations, may become the basis for proving in court the recognition of the intention of the completed act and the fact of the transfer of information [12].

There is a concern in the literature about the difficulty in terms of proving the authenticity of an electronic document created in its original form and unchanged in the process of its use [1, 9].

In addition, Russian researchers note that today the system of legal regulation, including labor relations, is not adapted to the new challenges of the digital economy [1]. The absence of a clear regulatory legal framework can be a serious obstacle to the transition from paper to electronic counterparts.

In addition, heterogeneous and disparate information systems, communication technologies, and software used in the work of personnel services of individual organizations are not unimportant problems.

The lack of specialists trained to work in information and operational systems, the level and degree of their education, their readiness to switch to new conditions for registration of labor and other relations directly related to them - all this can also complicate the "smooth" transition to electronic personnel document management.

However, there are many more positive moments from the transition to "paperless" interaction.

The advantages are expressed by a reduction in time costs associated with paperwork, including faster coordination and signing of personnel documents, control over their execution and storage; and in the resources used: the cost of paper, stationery, and other consumables.

In addition, electronic document management will optimize the work of personnel services of enterprises.

Conclusion

World practice shows that most developed countries have switched to digitalization, having replaced paper workflow with their electronic counterpart. Widely used electronic digital signature as a guarantor of the authenticity of the document. The legislation of most developed countries allows the implementation of all operations related to labor relations in electronic form [4].

Russia is gradually moving toward the development of the information society. Planned activities for the transition to a digital economy are being systematically implemented. A concept that provides priority measures to improve legal regulation to develop a digital economy, including the transition of formalizing labor relations to paperless interaction between employees and employers, is being partially implemented and fixed in the system of interaction between the employer and employees and higher management bodies, supervisory bodies, and organizations created to perform special tasks (funds).

The transition to electronic document management in HR administration should be carried out reasonably, carefully, and reasonably.

The introduction of new requirements for the replacement of documents formed on paper, their electronic counterparts in some cases should not include requirements for the complete rejection of their paper version.

Regulatory legal acts regulating the introduction of modern technologies in HR administration should provide for a clear set of measures aimed at the systematic integration of an electronic document and the painless replacement of paper documents by it.

An important task in connection with the introduction of electronic document management in internal corporate activity is to reform the system of professional training and selection of specialists directly involved in HR management.

References

[1] Bankó, Z. and Szőke, G. L. 2017. Issues of the Digital Workplace - The Situation in Hungary. *JurInfo, Pécs.* URL: https://papers.ssrn.com/sol3/papers.cfm?abstract_id =2927498.

[2] da Cunha, J. V. A., Cornachione, E. B. Jr. 2002. *Frauds and Information Technology: Analysis of the Influence on Accounting and Company Systems.* In: J. L. Monteiro, P. M. C. Swatman, L. V. Tavares (Eds.). *Towards the Knowledge Society: eCommerce, eBusiness and eGovernment The Second IFIP Conference on E-Commerce, E-Business, E-Government* (I3E 2002) October 7-9, 2002, Lisbon,

Portugal, pp. 179-193. URL: https://link.springer.com/content/pdf/10.1007%2F 978-0-387-35617-4_12.pdf.

[3] Filipova, I. A. 2018. Legal regulation of labor - 2020: a paradigm shift as a result of the economy digitalization. *Yurist* 11: 31-35.

[4] Kurennoy, A. 2017. The Digital Economy of Russia. Electronic Record Keeping of Labor Relations. *EJ-Yurist* 37. URL: https://www.eg-online.ru/article/355018/.

[5] Morosanova, A., Morozov, A., Shpakova, A. 2019. *International experience in regulating the scope of in-house electronic document management* 4 (International Experience in the Regulation of the Sphere of Intercorporate Electronic Document Management) URL: https://papers.ssrn.com/sol3/papers.cfm?abstract_id=3362266.

[6] Olanrewaju, T., Smaje, K., Willmott, P. 2014. *The seven traits of effective digital enterprises.* URL: http://www.mckinsey.com/business-functions/organization/our-insights/the-seven-traits-of-effective-digital-enterprises.

[7] Ølnes, J. and Bonnevie Seip, A. 2002. *On Long-Term Storage of Digitally Signed Documents.* In: J. L. Monteiro, P. M. C. Swatman, L. Valadares Tavares (Eds.). *Towards the Knowledge Society: eCommerce, eBusiness and eGovernment The Second IFIP Conference on E-Commerce, E-Business, E-Government* (I3E 2002) October 7-9, 2002, Lisbon, Portugal, pp. 115-130. URL: https://link.springer.com/ chapter/10.1007/978-0-387-35617-4_8.

[8] Orlova, E. 2017. What should a personnel officer know when switching to electronic document management. *Nalogovyi Vestnik* 4: 25-37.

[9] Piirainen, L. 2017. *Digitalization of the financial sector and change management.* Oulu University of Applied Sciences Degree Program in International Business, DIB3SN Bachelor's Thesis Autumn 2016. URL: https://docviewer.yandex.ru/view.

[10] Sprague, R. H. 1995. Electronic Document Management: Challenges and Opportunities for Information Systems Managers. *MIS Quarterly* 19(1) (Mar., 1995): 29-49. Published by: Management Information Systems Research Center, University of MinnesotaStable. URL: http://www.jstor.org/ stable/249710. Accessed February 21, 2010. URL: http://www.etchouse.com/mcma503/readings.old/sprague-1995.pdf.

[11] Zaitseva, L. 2018. Legal Aspects of the Application of Local Electronic Document Management Systems for the Regulation of Labor Relations. *Labor Law in Russia and Abroad (Trudovoe parvo v Rossii i za rubezhom)* 3: 34-37.

[12] Zsolt, B. I. 2011. *Nagy e-szigno könyv*. [Great book of e-sign]. Mikrosec Kft., Budapest.

Chapter 18

Innovative Corruption-Countering Mechanisms at the Modern Stage of Development: Economic, Social and Legal Components

Irina E. Milova*, Maksim A. Yavorskii and Renat R. Khasnutdinov
Samara State University of Economics, Samara, Russia

Abstract

The modern stage of development of Russia is characterized by dramatic transformations occurring in all areas of public life, including the economy. It is commonly known that the era of reforms is distinguished not only by positive achievements but also by negative consequences, including corruption. We are convinced that corruption acts undermine the foundations of our state and pose a true threat to its security.

Fight against corruption should be enforced by actions. Therefore, the authorities should move from declarations and promises to the execution of political, economic, and social measures. Legal mechanisms can play here an important role. It is generally recognized that the phenomenon of corruption crime is directly related to the individual features of specific persons willing to take and transfer illegal gratification. In this regard, it is extremely important to examine the various types of modern corrupt officials and draw a socio-criminological portrait of the person involved in such illegal actions. If we imagine the psychological type of corruption-prone people, then it

---

* Corresponding Author's Email: irina.milova@ro.ru.

In: Economic and Legal Foundations of Innovative Development …
Editors: Gabibulla Khasaev, Victoria Bolgova, Sergey Bortnikov et al.
ISBN: 978-1-68507-730-3

will be easier for us to counter this evil and, ultimately, stamp it out. The trouble is that for the mentality of Russian society it's typical to be indifferent and calm to corruption, which is often perceived as a norm and is estimated by most citizens surveyed as a way to solve current problems. One of the pressing problems is a dramatic transformation of public attitudes in this cluster from traditional tolerance to strong antagonism. For a long time, the authorities have fought only against grassroots corruption, which caused citizens' distrust in the activities of law enforcement agencies and the judicial system. The policy of double standards in the anti-corruption is openly condemned by the President of the Russian Federation Vladimir Vladimirovich Putin, who is convinced that there are no untouchables since corruption is an obstacle to the breakthrough economic development [7, p. 29]. There is no doubt that anti-corruption policy cannot be limited only to punitive measures; it requires an integrated approach. In this regard, the role of preventative conversations with the population, including youth, is growing.

The purpose of the research is to try to carry out an integrated analysis of the most significant socio-criminological aspects of corruption crime with a focus on the examination of individual dominant features of persons prone to such deviant behavior.

Keywords: corruption, bribery, individual features, criminological aspects, criminological portrait, modern corrupt official, illegal gratification

Subject Matter

The presented research is aimed at the analysis of peculiarities of a modern corrupt official personality and identification of its negative attitudes and individual dominant features, which are the results of psychological distortion; the authors suggested a socio-criminological portrait that describes the general type of corruption criminal.

Findings

1. The generalization of criminal case files under study showed that most corruption crimes are committed by men (72%). However, in recent years there has been a steady growth in the number of women

committing such unlawful acts. As a rule, they intermediate the transfer of illegal gratification.

2. The vast majority of bribe-takers have unreasonably high self-esteem and a lack of internal control over actions. These individuals are distinguished by pronounced ambitiousness and the conviction of being underestimated by society.
3. The corrupt officials have an interested motive of crime commission. As a rule, they prioritize personal interests and desire for illegal enrichment; these persons are rather cynical and disrespectful to others, although they rarely enter into open confrontation and their activities as law-abiding behavior.
4. Relapse is not generally typical for corrupt crimes.
5. The socio-criminological portrait of a modern corrupt is a man of 35 years old, previously not convicted, with higher education, married and have minor children, a good husband, a caring son, and father, holding a senior position, enjoying authority with the higher management and subordinates; he quickly made a career and proved himself to be a highly-skilled expert and professional with a high-performance discipline and unconventional thinking.
6. Other reasons that contribute to the commitment of corruption crime by an ordinary citizen are economic instability; weakening of state control leverages; inconsistent actions in the fight against bribery; a fairly neutral attitude of society to corrupt acts when the vast majority of the population does not condemn such acts and take them as the norm.
7. Such crimes have a potential victim. This is either the one who extorted a bribe or the one who tries to give it, provoking an official to take illegal gratification. Corrupt acts cause financial damage to these persons.
8. The preventive activity of corrupt acts can be improved by making up a databank of bribers, including criminally prosecuted and convicted persons and those on whom there is information of such acts to be committed or planned to be committed. It is advisable to keep a digital database that will allow promptly enlarging it, adding information, and making the necessary adjustments.

Introduction

The identity of a corrupt official arouses the persisting interest of researchers. This phenomenon has a set of stable individual features and their integrated study will make it possible to predict with high probability the behavior of a particular person in a particular situation; his response to an operational experiment and the rate of his adaptation to changing conditions. The experts draw special attention to the analysis of the individual's control scale over his behavior in general and in particular situations dictated by the specifics of corruption factors. At the same time, the skills of building relationships in society, team, and the corporate group that is typical for these persons who are usually sociable and able to insinuate themselves in one's favor haven't been overlooked.

The authors attempted to compare the personal features of a law-abiding citizen with the dominant features of a corruption-prone person. An ordinary citizen has a very positive attitude towards traditional social values, such as work, study, family, children, friends, but there are minor exceptions. Most members of society are optimistic about different events. If problems arise, they try to solve them by any available means without breach of law. A law-abiding citizen is distinguished by adequate self-esteem; he sets himself socially useful goals and strives to be a decent person [8, pp. 41 - 43].

A corrupt official has a fundamentally different worldview. Negative attitudes are his priority and this way he evaluates everything that happens to him and around him he prism [12, pp. 8-21]. The value system of this category of persons is distorted. They are often not critical to own behavior and significant acts. Such persons are indifferent to public opinion and external messages. Sometimes they have delated self-esteem that is associated with a situation when a person has not found himself in society for some reason or feels underestimated by others.

Undoubtedly, the fundamental moral principles are the result of specific social processes. These parts are directly interrelated.

Perception of ethical attitudes by a particular person and his capability to adequately use them in emerging situations are determined by his further acts. Ultimately, we often see the type with a clear criminal attitude aimed at the commission of corruption crimes.

On the one hand, a corrupt official is a person with a stable criminal orientation. Therefore, he is distinguished by features common to all representatives of the criminal community. On the other hand, this criminal group is so specific that it is characterized by several distinctive features [11, p. 24] that we will try to reveal. At the same time, these persons look like law-abiding citizens.

Methodology

The research is based on a metaphysical approach, dialectical and epistemological beliefs. In addition to the basic method, we have used specific scientific methods, namely historical-structural, formal-logical, comparative-law, modeling, legal experiment, interview, questionnaire, expert evaluation, sociological. Besides, we have effectively taken the capabilities of field research methods to obtain the necessary information. The long-term professional experience of authors in law enforcement authorities, as well as active advocacy, helped achieve the goal of the research. Under a special program, we have examined fifty criminal cases on corruption crimes tried by the courts of the Samara region. The regional practice files are quite representative that allowed us to regard several significant matters related to the criminological elements of corruption.

Analysis and Discussion

Using a random sampling method, we have examined fifty criminal cases with corruption corpus delicti under a special program, which allowed getting representative results. In particular, a generalization of the data showed that persons held liable for bribery usually have a family (93%). They are married and have at least two minor children (61%). In private life, they are characterized as caring spouses and parents. Moreover, the reasons for taking the illegal gratification are financial difficulties in their family, the desire to help close relatives and to solve the problems (97% of cases).

From the standpoint of the performance of official duties, these persons act as conscientious employees. They demonstrate a high level of professional competence that enables them to quickly achieve career growth. Until the initiation of a criminal case, these persons have given a good account of themselves, proved to be zealous and devoted to the job, and able to build relationships with management and the team [6, p. 74 - 91]. All of the above factors are fixed in their efficiency reports submitted by employers during the investigation of crimes (98%).

Based on the examination of criminal cases, it was found that the vast majority of persons involved have higher education (89%), and sometimes more than one (15%). The following factor is noteworthy: in 54% of cases the accused had an economic or legal education, the rest had a technical one (35%), including the programming (18%).

In specific criminal cases, none of the accused had any mental deviations and was not registered with a psychiatrist (100%).

In general, the worldview of these persons at the moment of committing unlawful corrupt acts is estimated as a completely-established. At the same time, they were distinguished by working capacity, performing discipline, and creative thinking. Thus, their professional competencies under a generally accepted grading scale can be described as high and personal features correspond to the average statistical level.

The criminological literature has long advocated the thesis that financial difficulties are the causes of corruption crimes. Meanwhile, modern research refutes this standpoint. There are proven statistical calculations showing that the vast majority of corrupt officials have a high (or above average) income. In the cases under examination, 66% of the accused had above-average incomes. This factor is impersonal since in recent times it has been common to hold liable the persons of the upper echelons of power. Some of them held state and municipal service positions (11%) and worked in law enforcement authorities (7%).

The participants of corruption activity in terms of public status is conventionally classified into two groups:

1. representatives of the upper echelons of power having a wide range of authorities necessary for a certain state function to be performed (this segment takes bribes as unlawful gratification for activities within their official duties, but they use these powers for personal gain);
2. persons who act as bribe givers, and thus seek to take certain illegal advantages for themselves [5, p. 392].

We attempted to make up a pyramid of crimes committers by the extent of exposure to corruption. In terms of this criterion, there is a group of officials. As a rule, these are representatives of the executive authority performing organizational and administrative functions and having access to budget funds and significant scope of competence. They include the heads of ministries and departments, their deputies; heads of regions, cities, and other settlements; law enforcement officers; judges; officials of bodies exercising various types of control; employees of services of bailiffs, tax, customs, migration services. In the legislative branch of power, corruption acts also take place, but the proceedings with a full investigation and delivery of the conviction judgment are rare.

There are some objective reasons. First of all, it's an act of grace from bringing representatives of the deputy corps to criminal liability due to their immunity status (deputy immunity). Scholars and representatives of public organizations have repeatedly pointed out the need to cancel this privilege that will surely have a positive effect and will lift double standards in this cluster. As the research of criminal cases with corruption corpus delicti showed, relapse in the segment of crimes under consideration is low (about 4%); besides, the illegal gratification in 96 percent of cases was transferred by intermediaries.

More than half of the overall number of all convicted took a bribe under aggravating circumstances; a great number are persons who intermediate the transfer of illegal gratification.

Only alleged intermediation has a special relapse when pers the on offers intermediation services to a bribe giver. In this situation, he takes money or valuables from another person and convinces him that they will be transferred to a particular official as a bribe for particular actions in the bribe giver. However, illegal gratification is not transferred to anyone, and the bribe item is arrogated.

There are criminal variations. In the first situation, before getting money the fraudster persuades the bribe giver that he is in close touch with the official and this will allow him to solve the bribe giver's problem. In the second situation, the bribe-giver is deliberately provided with unreliable information on the capabilities of the mediator who allegedly is in touch with the official. Relying on this false message, the bribe taker tries to persuade the supposed intermediary to transfer the illegal gratification. Moreover, the latter agrees to do this only after long-time persuasion and shows disinterestedness in the transfer.

Some researchers surveyed people previously convicted of such crimes. More than 70% said that they were aware of the illegal nature of these acts. At the same time, 96% of respondents counted on their impunity and were convinced that they could escape punishment. The overwhelming majority of respondents believed that the court has given too harsh sentence punishment and have considered it unfair [2, p. 203].

A study of the corrupt official personality in specific criminal cases of regional judicial practice in comparison with statistical data revealed that the age indicators of committers tend to decrease. Only 10-15 years ago, bribery as illegal gratification was typical for 37-38-year-old individuals. Currently, it is a younger age group of 32-33 years old (87%). Objectively, a younger age of corrupt officials is explained by the fact that young people after graduation immediately start making a career and reach certain professional growth precisely within these age limits.

The age of bribe-takers is slightly higher (35-50 years), that is, it covers almost the entire period of active labor activity. In the event of group bribery, the main person involved is most often older than other participants. Involving them in a criminal scheme, the prime mover often uses his authority and official status. His accomplices are subordinates. However, their illegal activity is not a sign of performing discipline but forms a corpus delicti.

The age limit and social status of the corruption crime committer determined as a result of the research are quite understandable since this is about the possibility of deciding on the deliberate commitment of illegal acts using his official powers. The powers often belong to the head with a wide range of competencies and access to financial flows and the company's property.

Before being employed at a senior position, a person must get a higher education, make a career, and accumulate certain work experience. Such a figure has personal life experience, business contacts with management, municipal agencies, and law enforcement authorities. He often has a spotless reputation and distinguished appearance.

Examining the criminal cases of this category, we drew attention to the fact that their main actors were executives. It is understandable since it is these officials who have the potential opportunity to be engaged in corruption activities. The emergence of senior civil officers in this segment has become a recent trend. If there is a group, they will involve subordinate employees in the accompliceship. Corrupt officials rarely act alone. They tend to look for like-minded people and unite on the principle of criminal communities. The examined criminal cases show that the participants often have had a long-standing relationship and have known each other before joint illegal activities. For example, they have passed a military service together; worked; studied;

have been relatives and friends. In this regard, we agree with the opinion of some authors that bribery is fueled by protectionism, favoritism, and nepotism (from Latin "nepos" (generic term) - "grandson; nephew").

In terms of gender, these were male crimes in the recent past. Currently, women commit unlawful corruption acts too (28% of the total number of criminal cases examined). Moreover, the proportion of women among this category of criminals is almost two times higher than the proportion of women in all other crimes.

The theory pays particular attention to the study of the motives of corrupt behavior. It was previously believed that only interested motive is common to this type of crime. However, nowadays the understanding is different. Many authors believe that such acts are often committed due to a thirst for power, desire to make a career quickly, and using any methods. These persons strive to be remarkable, stand out from the crowd, and win authority among others. In this regard, they surely have self-interest, but it is a subsidiary motive.

The corrupt-prone person is still aimed at gaining material valuables; other things are less important for him. In the event of a conflict between public and personal interests, he always chooses in favor of the latter. Most people involved in such cases suffer from materialism and seek to possess meaningless luxury. The criminal case against the former head of the Komi Republic, Vyacheslav Gaizer, is illustrative in this sense. The search in the governor's office found out large amounts of money, a collection of watches (various brands) of about one million dollars per each, and a fine-gold pen.

Persons committing this kind of crime have no anti-corruption stability [10, pp. 323 - 324]. They are not able to say a firm "No!" to offers of illegal gratification. The complicated moral choice ending with a decision on the admissibility of such acts for a particular person becomes, as a rule, a regular behavior when bribe-taking is the norm and commonplace. Moreover, they often try to justify their illegal acts by certain ideology under, for example, by professional interests. Essentially, a person recognizes the right to money-grubbing and becomes morally degrading soon. Along with the destruction of social attitudes and depreciation of previously significant and expensive things, the corrupt official has developed their distorted ideas on acceptable behavior and justice.

The theory sets some indicators that make it possible to determine a person's disposition towards corruption. They include an assessment of satisfaction with the standard of living, profession, personal status, and self-esteem.

From the standpoint of satisfaction with the standard of living, there are high, average, and low indicators. Naturally, the higher the level of satisfaction, the more resistant the person is to corruption-provoking factors. The level of moral development and the legal culture of a person is directly related to the ability to control his behavior. In this sense, there is an understanding that everyone needs to independently control life and determine its direction. However, there is a strong opinion that a person is made by people around him and all his acts are predetermined.

With this in mind, representatives of psychological science talk about the so-called control loci (internal and external).

Representatives of the first category believe that they are individually responsible for all events occurring and making significant decisions independently. This behavior is not typical for corrupt officials. Most of them belong to the second locus of control. They try to shift responsibility to external factors and have fatalistic moods [1, pp. 317-319].

From the standpoint of the behavioral level, there are several types of response (impulsive and reflective).

The first type is characterized by a spontaneous emotional response to external stimuli. The second type is characterized by a detailed logical analysis of happened events, an attempt to estimate the acts in a particular situation, a high level of criticism, and the ability to conclude. We share the opinion expressed by some authors that the representatives of the impulsive type of response are mostly prone to corrupt acts [9, pp. 104 - 106].

Conclusion

1. The research allowed us to draw a general psychological portrait of a modern corrupt official. It's a mature personality with distorted moral attitudes. The external locus of control and impulsive response are typical features.
2. Based on the results of the criminal cases examined, we got an idea of the socio-criminological features of corruption crime committers. Most of them are 35-year-old men with higher education, previously not convicted, having a family, and other statuses of social adaptation, distinguished by positive recommendations.
3. It seems reasonable to keep a database of corruption-prone persons and promptly add relevant information using digital capabilities.

References

[1] Abdurazakov, M. V. 2018. The Main Directions of the Anti-Corruption Policy in Russia. *Young Scientist* 21: 317-319.

[2] Antonyan, Y. M., Eminov, V. E. 2015. The Offender's Identity. *Criminological and Psychological Research: Monograph.* Moscow: Norma, Infra-M, 368 P.

[3] Gertsik, E. D. 2016. *Criminological and Psychological Research of a Corrupt Official Identity in Russia.* Legal Sciences: Issues and Prospects: Proceedings of the 5th International Scientific Conference (Kazan, October 2016). Kazan: Buk, 112-116.

[4] Kitova, D. A., Zhuravlev, A. L., Sosnin, V. A., Yurevich, A. V. 2017. Corruption as an Object of Socio-Psychological Research: State and Prospects. Institute of Psychology of the Russian Academy of Sciences. *Social and Economic Psychology* 2, 3 (7): 6 - 37.

[5] Kudryavtsev, V. N., Eminov, V. E. 2013. Criminology: Textbook. 5th edn., revised and enlarged. Moscow: Norma: Research and Development Center INFRA-M, 800 P.

[6] Lyskov, B. D., Kurbatova, T. N. 2001. *The Concept of the Offender's Identity.* In: T. N. Kurbatova (Ed). St. Petersburg: Piter, 74-91.

[7] Putin, V. V. 2018. The Main Content of the Address of the President of the Russian Federation Vladimir Putin to the Federal Assembly. Moscow, 29.

[8] Serdyuk, L. V. 2011. To the Issue of the Concept of Corruption and Preventive Measures. *Russian Justice* 2: 41 - 43.

[9] Stepanenko, Y. S., Stepanenko, D. Y. 2018. Challenges of Fighting against Corruption in Modern Era. *Legislation and Law* 7: 104 - 106.

[10] Vannovskaya, O. V. 2009. The Personal Determinants of Corrupt Behavior. *Journal of the Russian State Pedagogical University named after A. I. Herzen* 102: 323 - 324.

[11] Zhuravlev, A. L., Kitova, D. A., Sosnin, V. A. 2017. *Socio-Psychological Studies of Corruption.* Moscow, 24.

[12] Zhuravlev, A. L., Yurevich, A. V. 2012. Psychological Factors of Corruption. *Applied Legal Psychology* 1: 8-21.

Conclusion

Perspectives of the Economic and Legal Regulation of Innovative Development in the Digital Age

The systemic view of innovative development in the digital age from the positions of economics and law, which is presented in this book, has shown that the process of this development is not linear but cyclical, and at every stage of this cycle, innovative development needs well-coordinated actions, close interaction, and cooperation of government, society, and entrepreneurship. The book has formed a scientific vision of the economic and legal regulation of innovative development in the digital age, which is implemented at two levels at the same time – state and corporate management – and thus allows overcoming the gap between the legal field and economic practices.

This book shed light on the institutions of innovative development in the digital age and demonstrated these institutions' susceptibility to constant changes, their increasing complexity, and growing functional load. The theoretical significance of this book consists in opening a new – multidisciplinary – direction of scientific research on the topic of innovative development in the digital age. The practical significance of the book consists in developing a set of applied recommendations on the systemic update and bringing in accordance to each other of the institutions of state and law, society, and entrepreneurship.

Together with the obtained new scientific knowledge, this book set new research questions. These include the question of overcoming the distancing of public authorities (state and law) from society and entrepreneurship (economy). The offered scientific and practical achievements allow balancing and developing the interaction between government and economic agents, but the distance between them remains. Future digital innovations may allow modernizing the systems of e-government to provide all interested economic subjects with the possibility to actively participate in the processes of state regulation of innovative development.

Another question is accelerating and balancing the rate of innovative development in the digital age at the level of the world economy. This book provides outstanding results at the level of the regional economy, which shows that regions' underrun by the rate of innovative development in the digital age could be overcome through the development of institutions. This leads to a question of whether it is possible to reach such effect at the level of countries, and which institutions of supranational regulation should be used in this process. These issues should be studied in further scientific works.

About the Editors

Gabibulla R. Khasaev

Samara National Research University
Samara, Russia

Victoria Bolgova

Samara National Research University
Samara, Russia

Sergey Bortnikov

Samara State University of Economics
Samara, Russia

Yurii Shul'zenko

Institute of State and Law
Russian Academy of Sciences
Moscow, Russia

Evgenia Medentseva

Samara State University of Economics
Samara, Russia

Index

U

V

Y